James Taylor

The cardinal facts of Canadian history

James Taylor

The cardinal facts of Canadian history

ISBN/EAN: 9783337207663

Printed in Europe, USA, Canada, Australia, Japan

Cover: Foto ©ninafisch / pixelio.de

More available books at **www.hansebooks.com**

THE CARDINAL FACTS

OF

CANADIAN HISTORY.

CAREFULLY GATHERED FROM THE MOST
TRUSTWORTHY SOURCES.

BY

JAMES P. TAYLOR.

TORONTO:
THE HUNTER, ROSE CO., LIMITED, PRINTERS.
1899.

Entered according to Act of Parliament of Canada, in the year one thousand eight hundred and ninety-nine, by JAS. P. TAYLOR, in the Office of the Minister of Agriculture.

WORKS CONSULTED.

*Adams's "History of United States."
*Appleton's "American Biography."
*Bancroft's "History of United States."
Bouchette's "British Dominions in North America."
Bourinot's "Cape Breton."
Bourinot's "Constitutional History of Canada."
Bryce's "History of Canadian People."
Campbell's "History of Nova Scotia."
Campbell's "History of Prince Edward Island."
Caniff's "Settlement of Upper Canada."
Charlevoix's "History of New France." Shea's trans.
Christie's "History of Lower Canada."
Coffin's "Chronicle of War of 1812."
Correspondence.
Dent's "Last Forty Years."
Dodsley's "Annual Register."
"Dominion Year Book."
*Fiske's "Discovery of America."
Garnean's "History of Canada."
Gavin's "Irishmen in Canada."
*Gay's "Life of Madison."
Harris's, Dean, "Cath. Church in Niagara Peninsula."
*Headley's "Second War with England."
"Jesuit Relations," in English.
*Johnson's, Rossiter, "War of 1812."

*Johnston's "American Politics."
*Jones's "Campaign for Conquest of Canada."
Kingsford's "History of Canada."
Lindsey's "Life of Wm. L. Mackenzie."
Mackenzie's "Life of George Brown."
*Marshall's, O. H., "Early History of West."
Morgan's "Dominion Annual."
*Parkman's Works.
Poole's "History of Peterboro'."
*Poor's "Manual of Railroads."
Raffrey's "Scot in Canada."
*Ridpath's "History of United States."
Roberts's "History of Canada."
*Roosevelt's "Naval War of 1812."
Ryerson's "Loyalists."
Scadding's "Toronto of Old."
*Schouler's "History of United States."
Stewart's "Lord Dufferin in Canada."
Todd's "Life of Sir John A. Macdonald."
Todd's "Parliamentary Government in the British Provinces."
* " "Treaties and Conventions," Washington, 1889.
Tupper's "Life of Gen. Brock."
Warburton's "Conquest of Canada."
*Winsor's "Cartier to Frontenac."
*Winsor's "Narrative and Critical History of America."
Withrow's "History of Canada."

*American.

PREFACE.

THIS book contains the principal facts of Canadian History, given in the real order, the order of time. It is a *vade-mecum* for every Canadian that takes any interest whatever in his country's history; and, as respects quantity of information,—whether political, military, ecclesiastical, social, or commercial,—it is the very fullest History of Canada extant. It contains not only all the cream of all the published histories, but a good deal of valuable information obtained by correspondence; and, during the War of 1812, American writers are drawn on largely to show, that, on the admissions of Americans themselves, the Canadians came out of that trying struggle, honourably and triumphantly. In a work of this kind absolute accuracy will be naturally expected, and, if unusual labour in testing and re-testing will ensure it, the book is not blemished with many errors. In a word, the greatest pains have been taken to make it trustworthy in every particular.

J. P. T.

THE CARDINAL FACTS

OF

CANADIAN HISTORY.

1492, Oct. 12, Christopher Columbus landed on one of the Bahama Islands.
1497, June 24, John Cabot, in the service of Henry VII. of England, made the mainland of America.
1498, Sebastian Cabot explored the eastern coast, from Nova Scotia to Cape Hatteras.
1498, Aug. 10, Christopher Columbus first landed on the mainland of America.
1506, Denis, of Honfleur, explored the Gulf of the St. Lawrence River.
1507, Waldseemuller, a German professor of Geography, proposed "America" for the name of the New World.
1510, Vasco Nunez de Balboa planted the first European colony on the Isthmus of Darien.
1512, Easter Sunday, Juan Ponce de Leon found and named Florida.
1518, Baron de Lery attempted a settlement on Sable Island.
1520, Magellan found and named Magellan Strait.
1524, John Verrazano, employed by Francis I. of France, explored the eastern coast, from Newfoundland to Carolina.
1534, April 20, Jacques Cartier left St. Malo.
May 10, Cartier reached Cape Bonavista.
May 27, Cartier entered the Strait of Belle Isle.
July 8, Cartier reached the Bay of Chaleur.
Aug. 15, Cartier sailed for France.

1535, May 19, Cartier, with the "Grand Hermine," the "Petite," and the "Emerillon," the first of which was his flag-ship, the others under Mace Jalobert and Guillaume le Breton Bastille, left St. Malo.
St. Lawrence Day, Cartier entered the Gulf of the St. Lawrence River.
Sept. 1, Cartier reached the mouth of the Saguenay; a few days after he was at Stadacona (Quebec).
Oct. 3, Cartier reached Hochelaga. He called the mountain Mount Royal, Montreal. He returned to Stadacona and wintered over, his men suffering terribly with scurvy.
1536, In the spring, Cartier left Stadacona for France, taking with him Donnacona, whom Cartier had kidnapped.
1540, Jan. 15, Francis I. made Jean François de la Roach, or Roberval, viceroy of the country discovered by Cartier.
Oct. 17, Cartier was made captain-general and pilot of the fleet to go to Canada.
1541, May 23, Cartier, with three ships, left St. Malo, for Canada
Aug. 23, Cartier reached Stadacona.
1542, April 16, Roberval, with three ships and 200 colonists, left Rochelle for Canada.
1542, In July, Roberval and his colonists reached Cape Rouge; but his colony came to nothing.
1557, Sept. 1, Cartier died.
1583, Sir Humphrey Gilbert took possession of Newfoundland.
1585, (Sir Richard Grenville, sent by Sir Walter Raleigh, landed settlers on Roanoke Island.)
1587, Aug. 18, (Birth of Virginia Dare, on Roanoke Island, the first white child born in America.)
1598, The Marquis de la Roche landed forty convicts on Sable Island.
1599, M. Chauvin and M. Pontgrave established a post at Tadoussac, and Chauvin built at Tadoussac the first stone house on the northern continent.
1603, March 15, Pontgrave and Samuel Champlain left Honfleur for Canada.
May 24, Pontgrave and Champlain arrived at Tadoussac.
June 11, Champlain went up the Saguenay.

June 23, Pontgrave and Champlain reached Stadacona.
June 29, Champlain reached and named Lake St. Peter; he then went up as far as the Lachine Rapids.
1604, April 7, De Monts left Havre de Grace for Acadia, followed by Pontgrave.
May 8, Champlain arrived at Cape de la Have.

1605.

De Monts planted a French colony at Port Royal (Annapolis), Nova Scotia, the first permanent settlement in what is now Canada.

1606.

April 10, (James I., of England, gave North Virginia, the territory between 41 degrees and 45 degrees north latitude, to the Plymouth Company; and South Virginia, the territory between 34 degrees and 38 degrees north latitude, to the London Company.)
May 13, Poutrincourt and Lescarbot, in the "Jonas," laden with colonists, left Rochelle for Acadia (Nova Scotia).
July 27, The "Jonas" arrived at Port Royal (Annapolis).

1607.

May 13, (One hundred and five English colonists landed in Virginia and began Jamestown.)

1608.

Jan. 7, The King of France renewed De Monts' monopoly of the fur trade in Canada for one year.
July 3, Champlain founded Quebec.
Sept. 18, Pontgrave sailed for France, leaving Champlain with 28 men to hold Quebec.

1609.

June 18, Champlain ascended the St. Lawrence. At Lake St. Peter he fell in with a band of Hurons and Algonquins, who, with some Montagnais, were preparing to make war against the Iroquois. Champlain joined them
July 30, Champlain helped the Hurons and Algonquins to defeat the Iroquois, near Lake Champlain. He thus brought upon the French the undying hatred of the Iroquois.

1610.

June 24, Father LaFleche baptized Chief Membertou and twenty of his kindred, at Port Royal.

Dec. 27, Champlain entered into a contract of marriage with Helen Boule.

1611

Day of Pentecost, Biencourt, under the patronage of Madame de Guercheville, brought to Port Royal the Jesuits, Fathers Pierre Biard and Enemond Masse.

June 10, Biard and Masse wrote the first letters ever sent to France by the Jesuits from New France.

Henry Hudson was turned adrift in Hudson's Bay by his mutinous crew.

1612.

Jan. 23, A vessel brought succor to the occupants of Port Royal, and also Gilbert du Thet, a lay Jesuit, who came as administrator of Madame de Guercheville.

Oct. 3, Charles de Bourbon, Count de Soissons, was made Governor of Canada, Champlain being lieutenant.

Nov. 1, De Soissons died.

Nov. 22, Henri de Bourbon, Prince de Conde, was made Governor of Canada.

1613.

Jan. 9, Champlain procured a license to print a book that contained his maps.

May 16, Saussaye, a courtier, in command of a vessel of a hundred tons, arrived at La Have, bringing 48 sailors and colonists, and Father Quentin and Du Thet.

May 27, Champlain left the Island of St. Helen, and, with Nicholas de Vignau and three other Frenchmen, went up the Ottawa.

June 7, Champlain lost his astrolabe.

June 17, Champlain returned to Montreal.

> "In 1613, an English ship, under the command of Capt. Samuel Argall, appeared off Mount Desert, where a little company of the French, under the patronage of the Comtesse de Guercheville, had established themselves for the conversion of the Indians. The French were too few to offer even a show of resistance, and the landing of the English

was not disputed. By an unworthy trick, and without the knowledge of the French, Argall obtained possession of the royal commission; and then dismissing half his prisoners to seek in an open boat for succor from any fishing vessel of their own country they might chance to meet, he carried the others with him to Virginia. The same year Argall was sent back by the governor of Virginia, Sir Thomas Dale, to finish the work of expelling the French. With three vessels he visited successively Mount Desert and St. Croix, where he destroyed the French buildings, and then, crossing to Port Royal, seized whatever he could carry away, killed the cattle, and burned the houses to the ground. Having done this he sailed for Virginia, leaving the colonists to support themselves as they best could. Port Royal was not, however, abandoned by them, and it continued to drag out a precarious existence. Seventy-five years later, its entire population did not exceed six hundred, and in the whole peninsula there were not more than nine hundred inhabitants."—Winsor's " Narrative and Critical History of America," IV., p. 141.

1615.

May 25, Champlain, with Fathers Jamay, D'Olban, and Le Caron, and brother DuPlessis, Recollets, arrived at Tadoussac.

June 15, The first church in Quebec, at Cul de Sac, was opened and Mass celebrated.

July 1, Father Joseph Le Caron, accompanied by twelve armed Frenchmen and several Hurons, left Quebec for the Huron country (Simcoe County, Ont.)

July 9, Champlain, with two Frenchmen and ten Indians, left Quebec to join Le Caron.

Aug 12, Father Le Caron said the first Mass in the Huron country; Champlain, his interpreter Etienne Brule, and fourteen other Frenchmen being present.

Sept 8, Champlain set out with a body of Hurons to make war against the Iroquois. They crossed Lake Simcoe, made the portage to Balsam Lake, went down the Trent to Lake Ontario (which Champlain was the first white man to see), and crossed it.

Oct. 10, Champlain and the Hurons attacked an Iroquois town, Onondaga, near Syracuse; but were repulsed, Champlain getting seriously wounded.

Oct. 16, The Hurons began their retreat from Onondaga.

Dec. 20, Champlain and the Hurons reached the Huron towns.

1616.

July 11, Champlain and Father Le Caron reached Quebec, having returned from the Huron country.

1617.

June 14, Louis Hebert, the first farmer in Canada, arrived at Tadoussac.

Pacifique du Plessis began a mission at Three Rivers. Stephen Jonquest and Anne, daughter of Louis Hebert, were married at Quebec by Father Le Caron; this was the first marriage in Canada.

1620.

June 3, The Recollets, in Quebec, "laid the corner-stone of the earliest stone church in French America;" it was the church of Notre Dame des Anges.

July 7, Champlain arrived at Tadoussac, his wife being with him.

Duke of Montmorency was made Viceroy of Canada. Champlain built a fort on the site of Durham Terrace, Quebec.

Dec. 21, (The "Mayflower," carrying the Pilgrims, landed at Plymouth Rock, Massachussetts.)

1621.

The Iroquois obtained firearms from the Dutch.

Sept. 10, The King of England made a grant to Sir William Alexander of "all the territory between the St. Lawrence and the sea, which lies east of the St. Croix River." Then Acadia became Nova Scotia.

1623.

March 19, Violent storm of thunder, lightning, and hail in Canada.

1624.

Aug. 15, Champlain left Canada for France, taking his wife with him

1625.

March 27, (Charles I. began to reign in England.)

Duke of Ventadour was made Viceroy of Canada.

June 19, Charles Lalement, Jean de Brebeuf, Enemond Masse, François Charton, Gilbert Burel, and another

Jesuit, landed at Quebec; these were the first Jesuits to come up the St. Lawrence. Cf. Winsor's "Cartier to Frontenac," p. 129. The Baronets of Nova Scotia were created.

Sept. 1, The Jesuits selected their habitation near the St. Charles River, Quebec.

1626.

Feb. 27, Duc de Ventadour issued a patent to Louis Hebert, giving him, under seignorial tenure, a domain for himself and his heirs

Oct. 18, Father La Roche Daillon, Franciscan, left the Huron country, and went to the Neutral Nation, north of Lake Erie.

Father Nicolas Viel was drowned by Indians at Saut au Recollet, near Montreal.

1627.

Hard winter, snow being four and a half feet deep.

April 19, Cardinal Richelieu signed the charter of "Hundred Associates."

1628.

April 27, Sieur Couillard, the husband of Hebert's second daughter, first used a plough in Canada, oxen drawing it.

May 6, The Council of State ratified the charter of "Hundred Associates."

> "Their capital was 100,000 crowns; their privileges as follows: To be proprietors of Canada; to govern in peace and war; to enjoy the whole trade for fifteen years (except the cod and whale fishery) and the fur trade in perpetuity; untaxed imports and exports. The king gave them two ships of 300 tons burden each, and raised twelve of the principal members to the rank of nobility. The company, on their part, undertook to introduce 200 or 300 settlers during the year 1628, and 16,000 more before 1643, providing them with all necessaries for three years, and settling them afterward on a sufficient extent of cleared land for their future support."—Warburton's "Conquest of Canada," I., p. 93

July 10, Kirke, with an English fleet, summoned Champlain to surrender Quebec; Champlain refused to surrender the place.

July 18, Kirke captured seventeen French ships near Gaspe point.

1629.

May 16, The widow of Louis Hebert married Guillaume Hubou. ("Relations," V., 277.)
A water mill was erected near Quebec.
July 19, Champlain surrendered Quebec to Kirke.
July 20, Kirke took possession of Quebec.

1630.

While the English were in Quebec, they gave Mrs. Hubou a negro boy, the first negro in Canada.
April 30, La Tour and his son received from Sir William Alexander 4,500 square miles in Nova Scotia.

1631.

Feb. 11, The King of France made Charles de St. Etienne Lieutenant-Governor in Acadia.

1632.

March 1, Champlain was appointed the first Governor of Canada.
March 29, By the Treaty of St. Germain-en-Laye, France recovered Canada and Acadia.
April 18, Fathers Le Jeune and De Noue, with a lay brother, left Rouen for Canada.
May 10, Isaac de Razilly, one of "Hundred Associates," was commissioned Lieutenant Governor of Acadia, and instructed to eject all British subjects from his jurisdiction.
May 29, Razilly obtained from the "Hundred Associates" a concession at St. Croix River and Bay, 12 by 20 leagues in extent.
Razilly settled a colony at La Have.
July 5, Emery de Caen arrived at Quebec to take possession of New France, having been given a monopoly of the fur trade for one year, as an indemnity for his losses; Le Jeune and De Noue arrived at the same time.
Aug. 28, Father Le Jeune related his experiences to the provincial of his Order; it was the first letter of "Relations of the Jesuits."

"At this period the fort of Quebec, surrounded by a score of hastily-built dwellings and barracks, some poor huts on the Island of Montreal, the like at Three Rivers and Tadoussac, and a few fishermen's log houses elsewhere on the banks of the St. Lawrence, were the only fruits of the discoveries of Verrazano, Jacques Cartier, Roberval, and Champlain, the great outlay of La Roche and De Monts, and the toils and sufferings of their followers for nearly a century."—Warburton's "Conquest of Canada," I., p. 94.

1633.

March 23, Champlain left France for the last time.
May 22, Champlain arrived at Quebec, bringing with him the Jesuits, Brebeuf, Masse, Daniel, and Davost.
July 28, One hundred and forty canoes, carrying seven hundred Hurons, their peltries and tobacco, came to Quebec to trade.

> "The routine of these annual visits was nearly uniform. On the first day, the Indians built their huts; on the second they held their council with the French officers of the Fort; on the third and fourth, they bartered their furs and tobacco for kettles, hatchets, knives, cloth, beads, iron, arrowheads, coats, shirts, and other commodities; on the fifth, they were feasted by the French; and at day-break of the next morning, they embarked and vanished like a flight of birds."—Parkman.

The Hurons lived in what is now the county of Simcoe, Ontario. In numbers and in bravery they were equal to the Iroquois, with whom they were constantly at war, but in social life, in enterprise, and especially political organization, they were inferior to their great enemy.

In October, Father Le Jeune went with a hunting party of Indians, Montagnais, into the wilderness southeast of Quebec. His purpose was to inculcate the Faith and to learn Algonquin. He had a rough experience.

1634.

Jan. 15, Robert Gifart obtained the seigniory of Beauport. He was the first seignior in Canada.
Feb. 15, The Hundred Associates granted six arpents of land at Three Rivers to the Jesuits.
In April, Father Le Jeune and the Indians returned to Quebec.
July 1, Fathers Brebeuf and Daniel left Three Rivers for the Huron mission.

Robert Gifart built a stone manor house at Beauport. Father Julian Perrault began the Micmac mission on Cape Breton Island.

Aug. 4, Champlain selected a spot for a fort at Three Rivers. The Jesuits built a house for themselves in the Huron country.

> "The house was constructed after the Huron model. It was thirty-six feet long and about twenty feet wide, framed with strong sapling poles planted in the earth to form the sides, with the ends bent into an arch to form the roof,— the whole lashed firmly together, braced with cross poles, and closely covered with overlapping sheets of bark."— Parkman.

1635.

Jan. 15, Charles de St. Etienne was granted the fort and habitation of La Tour, on the River St. John.

About this time a bitter feud originated between Charles La Tour and Charnisay.

Fathers Pijart and Le Mercier went to the Huron mission.

Dec. 25, Samuel Champlain died in Quebec.

> "Christmas Day, 1635, was a dark day in the annals of New France. In the chamber of the fort, breathless and cold, lay the hardy frame which war, the wilderness, and the sea had buffeted in vain. After two months and a half of illness, Champlain, at the age of sixty-eight, was dead. His last cares were for his colony and the succor of its suffering families. Jesuits, officers, soldiers, traders, and the few settlers of Quebec followed his remains to the church; Le Jeune pronounced his eulogy, and the feeble community built a tomb to his honour."—Parkman.

1636.

Jan. 15, The Hundred Associates granted to Antoine Cheffault the seigniory of Cote de Beaupre, having six leagues of river frontage, and embracing all of Montmorency County.

March 10, Montmagny was made Governor of Canada.

June 11, Montmagny arrived at Quebec; several "men of birth and substance" came with him.

Montmagny marked out the Upper Town, Quebec.

July 2, Father Isaac Jogues came to Quebec.

Fathers Jogues, Garnier, and Chatelain went to the Huron Mission.

The Huron towns were visited by a wasting pestilence.

1637.

A settlement of the Montagnais was formed at Sillery, three miles above Quebec.

> "In 1637, a year before the building of Harvard College, the Jesuits began a wooden structure in the rear of the fort [at Quebec]; and here, within one enclosure, was the Huron seminary and the college for French boys."—Parkman's "Jesuits," p. 168.

In May, Father Pijart founded the Mission of the Immaculate Conception, at Ossossane, the largest Huron town.

Aug. 4, The Hurons held a council to inquire into the cause of a terrible disease that was making deadly ravages among their people; they attributed it to the sorceries of the Jesuits, and for a time the lives of the missionaries were in peril.

Aug. 16, The Duchess d'Aiguillon gave 22,400 livres to establish the Hotel-Dieu at Quebec.

1638.

April 14, Two Jesuits took up their abode at Sillery, above Quebec.

Fathers Lalemant and Le Moyne went to the Huron country.

Sept. 29, Father Du Peron landed on the shore of Thunder Bay, fifteen miles from the Huron town of Ossossane.

> "In respect to the commodities of life, the Jesuits were but a step in advance of the Indians. Their house, though well ventilated by numberless crevices in its bark walls, always smelt of smoke, and, when the wind was in certain quarters, was filled with it to suffocation. At their meals, the Fathers sat on logs around the fire, over which their kettle was slung in the Indian fashion. Each had his wooden platter, which, from the difficulty of transportation, was valued in the Huron country at the price of a robe of beaver-skin, or a hundred francs. Their food consisted of sagamite, or 'mush,' made of pounded Indian corn, boiled with scraps of smoked fish. Chaumonot compares it to the paste used for the papering of houses. The repast was occasionally varied by a pumpkin or squash baked in the ashes, or, in the season, by Indian corn roasted in the ear. They used no salt whatever. They could bring their cumberous pictures,

ornaments, and vestments through the savage journey of the Ottawa; but they could not bring the common necessaries of life. By day, they read and studied by the light that streamed in through the large smoke-holes in the roof, at night by the blaze of the fire. Their only candles were a few of wax for the altar. They cultivated a patch of ground, but raised nothing on it except wheat for making the sacramental bread. Their food was supplied by the Indians, to whom they gave in return cloth, knives, awls, needles, and various trinkets. Their supply of wine for the Eucharist was so scanty that they limited themselves to four or five drops for each mass.

"Their life was regulated with a conventual strictness. At four in the morning a bell roused them from the sheets of bark on which they slept. Masses, private devotions, reading religious books, and breakfasting, filled the time until eight, when they opened the door and admitted the Indians. As many of these proved intolerable nuisances, they took what Lalemant calls the honnête liberty of turning out the most intrusive and impracticable, an act performed with all tact and courtesy, and rarely taken in dudgeon. Having thus winnowed their company, they catechized those that remained, as opportunity offered. In the intervals the guests squatted by the fire and smoked their pipes.

"As among the Spartan virtues of the Hurons that of thieving was especially conspicuous, it was necessary that one or more of the Fathers should remain on guard at the house all day. The rest went forth on their missionary labors, baptizing and instructing as we have seen. To each priest who could speak Huron was assigned a certain number of houses,—in some instances, as many as forty; and as these often had five or six fires, with two families to each, his flock was as numerous as it was intractable. It was his care to see that none of the number died without baptism, and by every means in his power to commend the doctrines of his faith to the acceptance of those in health.

"At dinner, which was at two o'clock, grace was said in Huron, for the benefit of the Indians present, and a chapter of the Bible was read aloud during the meal. At four or five, according to the season, the Indians were dismissed, the door closed, and the evening spent in writing, reading, studying the language, devotion, and conversation on the affairs of the mission."—Parkman's "Jesuits," pp. 129-131.

1639.

According to the Jesuits, the Hurons at this time had a population of 20,000.

Aug. 1, Father Vimont, Superior of the Jesuits, Fathers Poncet and Chaumonot, Madame de la Peltrie, Marie de l'Incarnation, Marie de St. Bernard, and another

Ursuline arrived at Quebec. At once the Ursuline Convent, Quebec, was founded, Marie de l'Incarnation being Superior.
Jean Nicollet ascended Green Bay, Lake Michigan, and crossed to the Mississippi.
In the Huron country the Jesuits established Sainte Marie as a central station.
The Hotel-Dieu was founded at Quebec.
Fathers Jogues and Garnier went to the Tobacco Nation, west of the Hurons.

1640.

Except a small clearing on Sieur Giffard's Seigniory at Beauport and another made by M. de Puiseaux between Quebec and Sillery, the country around Quebec was still a forest.
In France, Father Jean Jacques Olier, Baron de Fancamp, Dauversiere, and three others organized the Society of Notre-Dame de Montreal.

Aug. 17, John De Lauson ceded the Island of Montreal to the Society of Notre-Dame de Montreal.
Nov. 2, Fathers Brebeuf and Chaumonot left Sainte Marie to go to the Neutral Nation.
Dec. 17, The Hundred Associates ceded their claim to the Island of Montreal to the Society of Notre-Dame de Montreal.

1641.

Feb. 13, The King of France directed La Tour to return to France, to answer charges made against him.
Now, the Iroquois began war against Canada.
The Iroquois, called by the English the Five Nations, lived in what is now New York State, from the Hudson to the Genesee. They were the Mohawks, Oneidas, Onondagas, Cayugas, and the Senecas,—named in order from east to west. They called their confederacy "The Long House;" the Mohawks guarded the eastern end, the Senecas the western.
Early in the spring Fathers Brebeuf and Chaumonot returned to Sainte Marie.
Fathers Jogues and Raymbault went to the mission at Saut Ste Marie, and "preached the Faith to two

thousand Ojibwas, and other Algonquins there assembled."

Aug. 8, Mademoiselle de Mance arrived at Quebec.

Oct. 14, Maisonneuve took possession of Montreal and then returned to Quebec, where, under the hospitable roof of M. de Puiseaux, he and his colonists, forty men and four women, passed the winter.

Oct. 15, Maisonneuve was declared Governor of Montreal.

1642.

Feb. 21, In Acadia, Charnisay was commissioned to arrest La Tour for contumacy and traitorous conduct.

May 8, Maisonneuve and his colonists, accompanied by Madame de la Peltrie, left Quebec for Montreal.

May 18, Maisonneuve landed at Montreal, when, Jeanne Mance and Madame de la Peltrie having decorated an altar, Father Vimont celebrated mass. The same evening Maisonneuve, guided by two old Indians, ascended the mountain, and from its top surveyed the surrounding country.

Two thousand warriors of the Neutral Nation went into Southern Michigan, and, after besieging a town of the Nation of Fire, defended by nine hundred warriors, took it, tortured many of the defenders to death, and made the rest prisoners.

Aug. 2, Father Jogues and two young Frenchmen, Rene Goupil and Guillaume Couture, were captured by Iroquois, on Lake St. Peter.

Aug. 13, Montmagny, with 100 men, began to erect a fort at the mouth of the Richelieu, to check the Iroquois.

Aug. 15, Feast of the Assumption of the Blessed Virgin was celebrated in the first church in Montreal, a wooden building now opened.

Sept. 29, Goupil, Jogues' companion, was killed by the Mohawks.

Oct. 29, Jean Nicolet was drowned at Sillery.

1643.

Jan. 6, Maisonneuve, bearing a heavy cross, Madame de la Peltrie, and citizens of Ville Marie, or Montreal, walked in procession to the top of the mountain, where Father Du Peron celebrated mass.

"At Quebec, Three Rivers, Montreal, and the little fort of Richelieu, that is to say in all Canada, no man could hunt, fish, till the fields, or cut a tree in the forest, without peril to his scalp. The Iroquois were everywhere and nowhere. A yell, a volley of bullets, a rush of screeching savages, and all was over. The soldiers hastened to the spot to find silence, solitude, and a mangled corpse."—"Jesuits," p. 240.

The people of Montreal, supplied with funds by Madame de Bullion, built a hospital.

"The hospital was intended not only to nurse sick Frenchmen, but to nurse and convert sick Indians; in other words, it was an engine of the mission. From Maisonneuve to the humblest laborer, these zealous colonists were bent on the work of conversion. To that end, the ladies made pilgrimages to the cross on the mountain, sometimes for nine days in succession, to pray God to gather the heathen into His fold. The fatigue was great; nor was the danger less; and armed men always escorted them as a precaution against the Iroquois. The male colonists were equally fervent; and sometimes as many as fifteen or sixteen persons would kneel at once before the cross, with the same charitable petition. The ardor of their zeal may be inferred from the fact, that these pious expeditions consumed the greater part of the day, when time and labor were of a value past reckoning to the little colony. Besides their pilgrimages, they used other means and very efficient ones, to attract and gain over the Indians. They housed, fed, and clothed them at every opportunity; and though they were subsisting chiefly on provisions brought at great cost from France, there was always a portion for the hungry savages who from time to time encamped near their fort If they could persuade any of them to be nursed, they were consigned to the tender care of Mademoiselle Mance; and if a party went to war, their women and children were taken in charge till their return. As this attention to their bodies had for its object the profit of their souls, it was accompanied with incessant catechizing This, with the other influences of the place, had its effect; and some notable conversions were made. Among them was that of the renowned chief, Tessouat, or Le Borgne, as the French called him, a crafty and intractable savage, whom to their own surprise, they succeeded in taming and winning to the Faith. He was christened with the name of Paul, and his squaw with that of Madeleine. Maisonneuve rewarded him with a gun, and celebrated the day by a feast to all the Indians present."—"Jesuits," p. 267-269.

Father Jogues, assisted by Megapolensis, minister of Albany, escaped from the Mohawks and descended the Hudson to New Amsterdam.

Nov. 5, Aided by the Dutch, Father Jogues left New Amsterdam for Europe.

1644.

Feb. 13, The king of France approved the grant of the Island of Montreal to the Society of Notre-Dame de Montreal.

March 30, Maisonneuve beat off a band of skulking Iroquois from Montreal.

April 27, Father Joseph Bressani was captured and terribly tortured by Iroquois near Lake St. Peter.

Wheat was first sown in Canada. (Cf. Garneau' " History of Canada," I., p. 151.)

June 19, The Mohawks, assembled in council, decided to let Father Bressani live, and gave him to an old woman to take the place of a deceased relative; but she, as he was apparently useless, having been so badly tortured and mangled, sold him to the Dutch, who soon gave him a passage to France.

Fathers Brebeuf, Garreau, and Chabanel, escorted by twenty soldiers, went to the Huron country.

1645.

Madame La Tour drove Charnisay from Fort La Tour.

March 6, The Hundred Associates transferred the fur trade and their debts to the people of Canada, but the Associates retained their seignorial rights.

"Early in the spring of 1645, Piskaret (an Algonquin), with six other converted Indians, some of them better Christians than he, set out on a war party, and, after dragging their canoes over the frozen St. Lawrence, launched them on the open stream of the Richelieu. They ascended to Lake Champlain, and hid themselves in the leafless forests of a large island, watching patiently for their human prey. One day they heard a distant shot. 'Come, friends,' said Piskaret, 'let us get our dinner; perhaps it will be the last, for we must die before we run.' Having dined to their contentment, the philosophic warriors prepared for action. One of them went to reconnoitre, and soon reported that two canoes full of Iroquois were approaching the island. Piskaret and his followers crouched in the bushes at the point for which the canoes were making, and, as the foremost drew near, each chose his mark, and fired with such good effect, that, of seven warriors, all but one were killed. The survivor jumped overboard, and swam for the other canoe, where he was taken in. It now contained eight Iroquois, who, far from attempting to escape, paddled in haste for a distant part of the shore, in order to land, give battle, and avenge their slain comrades. But the Algonquins, running through the woods, reached the landing before them, and, as one of them rose to fire, they shot him. In his fall he overset the canoe. The water was shallow, and the submerged warriors, presently finding foothold, waded towards the shore, and made desperate fight. The Algonquins had the advantage of position, and used it so well that they killed all but three of their enemies, and captured two of the survivors. Next they sought out the bodies, carefully scalped them, and set out in triumph on their return. To the credit of their Jesuit teachers they treated their prisoners with a forbearance hitherto without example. One of them who was defiant and abusive, received a blow to silence him; but no further indignity was offered to either."—Parkman's "Jesuits," p. 281.

April 13, Charnisay repeated his attack on Fort La Tour, and succeeded in taking it, its heroic defender, Madame La Tour, dying heart broken three weeks after.

Sept. 17, The Iroquois and Hurons met at Three Rivers and concluded peace.

Sept. 21, Louis Joliet was born in Quebec.

1646.

Jan. 30, Father Anne de Noué left Three Rivers to go to Fort Richelieu, but, losing his way, he perished in the snow.

May 12, Father Enemond Masse died at Sillery, above and near Quebec.

May —, Father Jogues left Three Rivers for the Mohawk country, to hold the Mohawks to the peace lately made and to establish a mission; when, on the eve of Corpus Christi, he reached what is now Lake George, he called it Lac St. Sacrement.

June 27, Father Jogues, having finished his political mission to the Mohawks, reached Fort Richelieu.

About this time the smallpox made dreadful ravages among the Hurons.

Aug. 8, La Tour arrived at Quebec.

Aug. 24, Father Jogues, accompanied by a young Frenchman named Lalande, left Quebec to go to the Iroquois as a missionary, saying "*Ibo et non redibo*" (I will go, but I shall not return).

Aug. 29, Father Gabriel Druilletes left Sillery to go to the Abenaquis Mission on the river Kennebec.

Oct. 17, Father Jogues entered Gandawague, a Mohawk town.
Oct. 18, Father Jogues, the founder of the Mohawk Mission, was martyred
Oct. 19, Lalande was killed by the Iroquois.
Nov. 21, Madame de la Peltrie became a novice in the Ursuline Convent, Quebec.

1647.

April 13, The Hurons sent nine warriors on an embassy to the Andastes, who lived south of the Iroquois, to secure their aid against the Iroquois.
A Council was formed at Quebec to manage the affairs of Canada; its members were the Governor-General, the Superior of the Jesuits, and the Governor of Montreal; this Council was invested with full legislative, judicial, and executive powers.
D'Aillebous: was made Governor of Canada.
June 20, The first horse was landed at Quebec.
Sept. 23, Montmagny left Quebec for France.

1648.

July 4, The Iroquois took the Huron Mission, St. Joseph, and killed Father Daniel.
July 17, Two hundred and fifty Hurons, having ventured to run down the Ottawa, reached Three Rivers to trade; there they were suddenly attacked by a large body of their inveterate enemies, the ubiquitous Iroquois, but the Hurons fought desperately and drove the Iroquois from the place.
A temperance meeting was held at Sillery, the first temperance gathering on the Continent of America.
A small cannon was carried in a canoe up the Ottawa to Sainte Marie in the Huron country.
Nov. 24, The first white child was born in Montreal.
A thousand Mohawks and Senecas took the warpath for the Hurons.

1649.

Jan. 30, (Charles I., King of England, was executed.)
At this time "there were in the Huron country and its neighborhood eighteen Jesuit priests, four lay

brothers, twenty-three men serving without pay, seven hired men, four boys, and eight soldiers."

March 16, The Iroquois took the Huron missions St. Ignace and St. Louis, Fathers Brebeuf and Gabriel Lalemant being made prisoners and tortured to death.

"On the afternoon of the sixteenth,—the day when the two priests were captured,—Brebeuf was led apart, and bound to a stake. He seemed more concerned for his captive converts than for himself, and addressed them in a loud voice, exhorting them to suffer patiently, and promising Heaven as their reward. The Iroquois, incensed, scorched him from head to foot, to silence him; whereupon, in the tone of a master, he threatened them with everlasting flames, for persecuting the worshippers of God. As he continued to speak, with voice and countenance unchanged, they cut away his lower lip and thrust a redhot iron down his throat. He still held his tall form erect and defiant, with no sign or sound of pain; and they tried another means to overcome him. They led out Lalemant, that Brebeuf might see him tortured. They had tied strips of bark, smeared with pitch, about his naked body. When he saw the condition of his Superior, he could not hide his agitation, and called out to him with a broken voice, in the words of St. Paul: 'We are made a spectacle to the world, to angels, and to men.' Then he threw himself at Brebeuf's feet; upon which the Iroquois seized him, made him fast to a stake, and set fire to the bark that enveloped him. As the flame rose, he threw his arms upward, with a shriek of supplication to Heaven. Next they hung around Brebeuf's neck a collar made of hatchets heated redhot; but the indomitable priest stood like a rock. A Huron in the crowd, who had been a convert of the mission, but was now an Iroquois by adoption, called out, with the malice of a renegade, to pour hot water on their heads, since they had poured so much cold water on those of others. The kettle was accordingly slung, and the water boiled and poured slowly on the heads of the two missionaries. 'We baptise you,' they cried, 'that you may be happy in Heaven; for nobody can be saved without a good baptism.' Brebeuf would not flinch; and, in a rage, they cut strips of flesh from his limbs, and devoured them before his eyes. Other renegade Hurons called out to him, 'You told us that the more one suffers on earth, the happier he is in Heaven. We wish to make you happy; we torment you because we love you; and you ought to thank us for it.' After a succession of other revolting tortures, they scalped him; when, seeing him nearly dead, they laid open his breast, and came in a crowd to drink the blood of so valiant an enemy, thinking to imbibe with it some portion of his courage. A chief then tore out his heart and devoured it.

"Thus died Jean de Brebeuf, the founder of the Huron

mission, its truest hero, and its greatest martyr. He came of a noble race, the same, it is said, from which sprang the English Earls of Arundel; but never had the mailed barons of his line confronted a fate so appalling, with so prodigious a constancy. To the last he refused to flinch, and 'his death was the astonishment of his murderers.' In him an enthusiastic devotion was grafted on an heroic nature. His bodily endowments were as remarkable as the temper of his mind. His manly proportions, his strength, and his endurance, which incessant fasts and penances could not undermine, had always won for him the respect of the Indians, no less than a courage unconscious of fear, and yet redeemed from rashness by a cool and vigorous judgment; for extravagant as were the chimeras which fed the fires of his zeal, they were consistent with the soberest good sense on matters of practical bearing.

"Lalemant, physically weak from childhood, and slender almost to emaciation, was constitutionally unequal to a display of fortitude like that of his colleague. When Brebeuf died, he was led back to the house whence he had been taken, and tortured there all night, until, in the morning, one of the Iroquois, growing tired of the protracted entertainment, killed him with a hatchet. It was said that at times he seemed beside himself, then rallying, with hands uplifted, he offered his sufferings to Heaven as a sacrifice. His robust companion had lived less than four hours under the torture, while he survived it for nearly seventeen. Perhaps the Titanic effort of will with which Brebeuf repressed all show of suffering conspired with the Iroquois knives and firebrands to exhaust his vitality; perhaps his tormentors, enraged at his fortitude, forgot their subtlety, and struck too near the life.

"The bodies of the two missionaries were carried to Sainte Marie, and buried in the cemetery there; but the skull of Brebeuf was preserved as a relic. His family sent from France a silver bust of their martyred kinsman, in the base of which was a recess to contain the skull; and, to this day, the bust and the relic within are preserved with pious care by the nuns of the Hôtel-Dieu at Quebec."—Parkman's "Jesuits," pp. 388-391.

March 19, Festival of St Joseph; the Iroquois, seized by a panic, retreated precipitately from the Huron country.

June 14, The Jesuits, at the Huron Mission of Sainte Marie, abandoned their house, and, with their terrified converts, took refuge on St. Joseph Island.

Dec. 7, The Iroquois took the Huron Mission of St. Jean, and murdered Father Charles Garnier; a renegade Huron also murdered Father Noël Chabanel.

"Thus, at the age of forty-four, died Charles Garnier, the favorite child of wealthy and noble parents, nursed in Parisian luxury and ease, then living and dying, a more than willing exile, amid the hardships and horrors of the Huron wilderness. His life and his death are his best eulogy. Brebeuf was the lion of the Huron mission, and Garnier was the lamb; but the lamb was as fearless as the lion."—Parkman's "Jesuits," p. 407.

1650.

May 24, Charnisay perished in the basin at Port Royal; his canoe having overset, he clung to it till the cold overcame him.

June 10, The Jesuits, with a remnant of the Hurons, left the Huron country for Quebec.

July 28, The Jesuits and fugitive Hurons reached Quebec.

"In a former chapter, we followed Father Paul Le Jeune on his winter roamings, with a band of Montagnais, among the forests on the northern boundary of Maine. Now Father Gabriel Druilletes sets forth on a similar excursion, but with one essential difference. Le Jeune's companions were heathen, who persecuted him day and night with their jibes and sarcasms. Those of Druilletes were all converts, who looked on him as a friend and a father. There were prayers, confessions, masses, and invocations of St. Joseph. They built their bark chapel at every camp, and no festival of the church passed unobserved. On Good Friday they laid their best robe of beaver-skin on the snow, placed on it a crucifix, and knelt around it in prayer. What was their prayer? It was a petition for the forgiveness and the conversion of their enemies, the Iroquois. Those who know the intensity and tenacity of an Indian's hatred will see in this something more than a change from one superstition to another. An idea had been presented to the mind of the savage, to which he had previously been an utter stranger. This is the most remarkable record of success in the whole body of the Jesuit 'Relations'; but it is very far from being the only evidence, that, in teaching the dogmas and observances of the Roman church, the missionaries taught also the morals of Christianity. When we look for the results of these missions, we soon become aware that the influence of the French and the Jesuits extended far beyond the circle of converts. It eventually modified and softened the manners of many unconverted tribes. In the wars of the next century we do not often find those examples of diabolic atrocity with which the earlier annals are crowded. The savage burned his enemies alive, it is true, but he rarely ate them; neither did he torment them with the same deliberation and persistency. He was a savage still, but not so

often a devil. The improvement was not great, but it was distinct; and it seems to have taken place wherever Indian tribes were in close relations with any respectable community of white men. Thus Philip's war in New England, cruel as it was, was less ferocious, judging from Canadian experience, than it would have been, if a generation of civilized intercourse had not worn down the sharpest asperities of barbarism. Yet it was to French priests and colonists, mingled as they were soon to be among the tribes of the vast interior, that the change is chiefly to be ascribed. In this softening of manners, such as it was, and in the obedient Catholicity of a few hundred tamed savages gathered at stationary missions in various parts of Canada, we find, after a century had elapsed, all the results of the heroic toil of the Jesuits. The missions had failed, because the Indians had ceased to exist. Of the great tribes on whom rested the hopes of the early Canadian Fathers, nearly all were virtually extinct. The missionaries built laboriously and well, but they were doomed to build on a failing foundation. The Indians melted away, not because civilization destroyed them, but because their own ferocity and intractable indolence made it impossible that they should exist in its presence. Either the plastic energies of a higher race, or the servile pliancy of a lower one, would, each in its way, have preserved them; as it was, their extinction was a foregone conclusion. As for the religion which the Jesuits taught them, however Protestants may carp at it, it was the only form of Christianity likely to take root in their crude and barbarous nature."
—Parkman's "Jesuits," pp. 318-320.

Sept. 1, Father Druilletes left Quebec for Boston: Massachusetts having made advances to the French in Canada for reciprocity in trade, he was sent to conduct negotiations; he had cordial conferences with Winslow, Gov. Dudley, Gov. Bradford, Endicott, and Eliot.

1651.

The Senecas completed the destruction of the Neutrals. Father Druilletes, accompanied by Jean Paul Godefroy, went to New Haven, and explained his mission to the Commissioners of the four English colonies; but, as New England's assistance against the Iroquois was a condition of free trade with Canada, the conference came to nothing.

Oct. 14, M. de Lauson came to Quebec.

La Tour took possession of his old fort at the mouth of the St. John river.

1652.

May 10, Iroquois murdered Father Butéux, north of Three Rivers.
Aug. 19, Du Plessis, Governor of Three Rivers, was killed by the Iroquois.

1653.

Feb. 24, A marriage contract was made by La Tour and the widow of Charnisay.
  The Iroquois captured Father Poncet at Cap Rouge, above Quebec, bore him off, tortured him, and adopted him.
June 26, Sixty Onondagas came to Montreal to sue for peace. They had their hands full of the Eries, with whom they were at war.
Sept. 22, Margaret Bourgeois, who had renounced an inheritance and given all she had to the poor, arrived in Quebec.
  Father Poncet, returning from the Iroquois country, went down the St. Lawrence, being the first white man to glide through the Thousand Islands.
Oct. 21, Father Poncet arrived at Montreal.
Nov. 6, The Iroquois made peace with the French.
Dec. 16, (Oliver Cromwell was made Protector in England.)

1654.

July 2, Father Simon Le Moyne left Quebec to visit the Onondagas, his visit being political.
Aug. 16, Father Le Moyne discovered the salt springs at Onondaga (Syracuse).
Sept. 7, Father Le Moyne reached Montreal.

1655.

Fathers Chaumonot and Dablon, Jesuits, established the mission of St. Mary's of Ganentaa, at Onondaga. The Iroquois exterminated the Eries, who lived south of Lake Erie.

1656.

May 17, Dupuys and a party of Frenchmen left Quebec to form a settlement at Onondaga; this was at the request, the command, of the Onondagas.
May 20, Mohawks made a descent upon Orleans island, and

bore off 80 Hurons, the French at Quebec not daring to attempt a rescue.
July 17, Dupuys and his party arrived at Onondaga.
Aug. 9, La Tour, Thomas Temple, and William Crowne received from Cromwell a large part of Nova Scotia.
An Iroquois shot Father Garreau, near Montreal.

1657.

July 29, Fathers Queylus, Souart, Galinee, and Allet, Sulpitians, sent by M Olier to found a seminary at Montreal and to take charge of the island, arrived at Montreal. The Society had become weary of the Island.
The Archbishop of Rouen made Queylus Vicar-General of Canada.

1658.

March, At Ste. Anne, the church of Ste. Anne de Petit Cap, Bonne Ste. Anne, was begun
March 20, Dupuys and his men at Onondaga, having learned that the Onondagas had made a secret resolve to massacre them, invited the warriors to a feast, and, by urging them to eat more and more, according to the Indian fashion, surfeited them to total insensibility; then the Frenchmen took to their boats, descended the Oswego, and made good their escape to Montreal.
July 11, D'Argenson arrived at Quebec as Governor.
Sept. 29, Margaret Bourgeois, Foundress of the Sisters of the Congregation, accompanied by Mlle. Mance, left Montreal for France to get young girls for teachers.
Dec. 8, Francois de Montmorenci Laval was consecrated Bishop.

1659.

May 14, The King of France ordered Argenson to support Laval against Queylus.
June 16, M. de Laval arrived at Quebec.
The King of France began to aid emigrants for Canada.
Sept. 29, Margaret Bourgeois returned to Montreal.
Oct. 22, Laval sent Queylus to France.

Nov. 25, Margaret Bourgeois began her school in Montreal, in a stable.

1660.

April, Adam Daulac, Sieur des Ormeaux, with a few followers, French and Indians, made a desperate resistance against the Iroquois at the foot of the Long Saut.

May 25, (Charles II. began to reign in England.)
The Hundred Associates sent Peronne Dumesnil to Canada, as controller-general and supreme judge, to inquire into the Company's affairs.

July 21, Father Le Moyne, at the request of the Iroquois, left Montreal to go to Onondaga.

First census of Canada: population 3,418.

1661.

In Canada, two men were shot and one was whipped for selling brandy to Indians.

Aug. 3, Queylus returned to Canada, *incog.*

Aug. 31, D'Avaugour arrived at Quebec.

Father Le Moyne arrived at Montreal, having returned from Onondaga.

Oct. 22, Queylus departed for France.

1662.

Aug. 12, Laval departed for France.

1663.

Feb. 5, The great earthquake began at 5.30 p.m.

"Trees in the forest were torn up and dashed against each other with inconceivable violence; mountains were raised from their foundations and thrown into valleys, leaving awful chasms behind; from the openings issued dense clouds of smoke, dust, and sand: many rivers disappeared, others were diverted from their course, and the great St. Lawrence became suddenly white as far down as the mouth of the Saguenay. The first shock lasted for more than half-an-hour, but the greatest violence for only fifteen minutes. At Tadoussac a shower of volcanic ashes descended upon the rivers, agitating the waters like a tempest. This tremendous earthquake extended simultaneously over 180,000 square miles of country, and lasted for nearly six months, almost without intermission."—Warburton's "Conquest of Canada," I., p. 121.

Feb. 24, Canada was restored to the Crown, the Hundred Associates giving up their charter.

April, Laval secured a royal patent for a Seminary at Quebec ; a tax of one-thirteenth of all taxable property to be paid annually to the directors of the Seminary for its maintenance.
May 1, Sieur de Mésy was made Governor of Canada.
Aug. 18, The Sulpitians acquired the seigniory of Montreal.
Sept. 15, Laval and De Mésy arrived at Quebec.
Sept. 18, The Sovereign Council was formed for the Government of Canada ; it consisted of the Governor, the Bishop, the Intendant, and five Councillors; the Coutume de Paris was made the code of law.
Sept. 28, An edict was issued, forbidding anyone to sell or give liquor to Indians.

1664.

May 28, The West India Company secured a royal grant of all French colonies in America, with the right of appointing governors and all officers.
Sept 8, (Sir Richard Nichols took New Amsterdam, which became New York ; the whole territory of New Netherland, New York State, passing from the Dutch to the English.)
About this time many young men in Canada took to the woods and became " coureurs de bois," hunting, fishing, trapping, and living with the Indians.

1665.

May 5, De Mésy died.
Twelve horses were brought to Canada.
June 30, Marquis de Tracy, Lieutenant-General, arrived at Quebec, four companies of the Carignan regiment having arrived a little before him.
The Iroquois captured and bore off Charles Le Moyne, of Montreal.
Sept. 2, Father Allouez reached Saut Ste. Marie, and, entering Lake Superior, he named it "Tracy" " in acknowledgment of the obligations we are under to that man."
Sept. 23, Sieur de Courcelles was made Governor of Canada.
Sept., Jean Talon arrived in Quebec as Intendant.
Courcelles cut the first road in Canada, from Chambly to Montreal, and erected three forts on the Richelieu.

1666.

Jan. 9, Courcelles, with 100 men, left Quebec to attack the Mohawks.

Feb. 20, Courcelles, having recruited his force on the way, reached the Mohawk towns; he returned, however, without fighting.

La Salle came to Canada; Queylus, Superior of the Sulpitians, gave him a tract of land where Lachine now stands, which La Salle parcelled out to whatever settlers would join him.

July 12, Peace was made with the Mohawks; it was a hollow one.

Sept. 14, Tracy set out with a strong force to chastise the Mohawks.

Oct. 15, Tracy reached the Mohawk towns.

Nov. 5, Tracy reached Quebec.

1667.

Feb. 4, The first ball was held in Canada.

The Mohawks came to Quebec, suing for peace

The mining of iron was begun at Three Rivers.

July 13, The Treaty of Breda; France recovered Acadia.

Fathers Fremin and Perron began missionary work among the Mohawks; Father Bruyas among the Oneidas, and Father Garnier among the Onondagas.

Sept. 26, Rene Gaultier de Varennes and Marie Boucher, daughter of the Governor of Three Rivers, were married. She was twelve years of age. One of their children was Varennes de la Verendrye, discoverer of the Rocky Mountains.

Talon built a ship and sent her with a mixed cargo to the West Indies; he built a brewery; he sent engineers to search for coal, lead, iron, copper, and other minerals; he made tar, and he encouraged settlers to make woollen goods and to grow hemp.

During his administration in Canada, Talon managed to obtain from France several hundred girls as wives for the colonists. They were carefully selected, country girls being preferred, and on their arrival at Quebec were married in batches of twenties and thirties; each received a royal dowry, and a generous one, to begin housekeeping. A royal pension was also offered to the parents of large families; the parents of ten children were to have a pension of three hundred livres a year, and the parents of twelve children four hundred livres a year.

1668.

April 8, Claude de Bouteroue was made Intendant.

Marquette founded the first mission in Michigan, at Saut Ste. Marie.

Oct. 28, Fathers Fenelon and Trouve, Sulpitians, began a mission among the Cayugas settled on Bay Quinte.

Population of Canada, 5,870.

1669.

The Sovereign Council declared wheat a legal tender, three French bushels being equivalent to four francs.

July 6, Dollier de Casson and Galinee, Sulpitians, and La Salle, with seven canoes and twenty-four men, left Lachine to make explorations in the west.

Aug. 2, Father De Casson and La Salle reached Lake Ontario.

Aug. 12, Father Galinee and La Salle left Irondequoit Bay for the chief town of the Senecas.

Sept. 24, Father Galinee and La Salle reached a spot a few miles north of where Hamilton now stands; here La Salle first met Louis Joliet, who was returning from Lake Superior, where he had failed to find what Talon had sent him to find, copper.

Sept. 30, After Father De Casson had said mass, the Sulpitians descended the Grand River to Lake Erie, but La Salle, feigning sickness, held back, and his movements for two years after are not surely known. Catherine Ganneaktena, an Erie girl, who had been adopted by the Iroquois and had become a Christian, began the Iroquois colony, or mission, at La Prairie, opposite Montreal, "probably at the close of 1669," says Shea.

1670.

May 2, Charles II. gave a charter to the Hudson's Bay Company.

Aug. 18, Talon arrived at Quebec as Intendant; with him came Perrot, Governor of Montreal.
In Canada obdurate bachelors were forbidden to hunt, fish, or trade.

1671.
"The winter did not begin till the middle of January, 1671, and ended in the middle of March."—Charlevoix.

June 14, Sieur St. Lusson, attended by Joliet and the Jesuits, Dablon, Druillettes, Allouez, and Andre, on the top of a hill near Saut Ste. Marie, took formal possession of the Great West in the name of the King of France.
Aug. 22, Father Charles Albanel, with two Frenchmen, left Quebec to go up the Saguenay to Hudson's Bay.
The King of France sent 30 single men and 30 single women to Acadia at a cost of 6,000 livres.
Nov. 18, Madame de la Peltrie died in the Ursuline Convent, Quebec.

1672.
April 30, Mother Marie de l'Incarnation, first Superior of the Ursuline Convent, Quebec, died.
June 28, Father Albanel, having gone up the Saguenay route, reached the shore of Hudson's Bay, and, with St. Simon and La Coutre, took ceremonial possession of the district.
Sept. 12, Sieur de Frontenac was made Governor of Canada.
Oct. 23, In the Jesuit church, Quebec, Frontenac convened the three estates of Canada,—nobles, clergy, merchants, and citizens.
Nov. 2, Frontenac wrote to the Minister, "I never saw anything more superb than the position of this town (Quebec). It could not be better situated as the future capital of a great empire."
Nov. 3, Talon, the Intendant, sailed for France.

1673.
May 17, Frontenac sent Louis Joliet to find the Mississippi, Jacques Marquette accompanying him.
June 13, Colbert, the French Minister, disapproved of Frontenac's dividing the people of Canada into three estates, and advised him not to give a corporate form to the people of Canada.

June 17, Marquette and Joliet discovered the Mississippi.
July 13, Frontenac, on La Salle's advice, founded Fort Frontenac at Cataraqui; Raudin, an engineer, began its construction at once.
July 17, Marquette and Joliet, having gone down the Mississippi to an Arkansas village, turned on their homeward voyage.
Aug. 1, Frontenac, returning from Fort Frontenac, reached Montreal, where he quarrelled with Perrot, Governor of Montreal.
Dec. 23, The Seigniory of Terrebonne was granted to Daulier Deslandes, "two leagues frontage upon the Riviere Jesus, formerly called Riviere des Prairies."

1674.

In January, Perrot, Governor of Montreal, and Abbe Fenelon, on snow shoes, walked from Montreal to Quebec.
Cape Breton was joined to Canada.
Charter of West India Company was revoked.
La Salle, well recommended by Frontenac, went to France, and received the Seigniory of Fort Frontenac.
Oct. 1, Laval was made Bishop of Quebec, and Quebec was made a bishopric.
Oct. 3. The members of the Sovereign Council, Quebec, were increased from five to seven.
Nov., Frontenac shipped Perrot and Abbe Fenelon to France.

1675.

May 18, Father Jacques Marquette died on the west shore of Michigan.
Perrot, after being disciplined a little, was restored to the government of Montreal.
Feast of Assumption, mass was first celebrated in the church of Notre Dame de Bon-Secours, the first stone church in Montreal.
Father James de Lamberville began a mission among the Mohawks.
Sept. 25, Jacques Duchesneau arrived at Quebec, as Intendant.

1676.

The Sulpitians began the Mission of the Mountain. Easter Sunday, Father James de Lamberville baptized Catherine Tegahkouita, a Mohawk maiden.

Oct. 26, An assembly, in the Chateau St. Louis, under the direction of the Governor, discussed the propriety or prudence of selling brandy to Indians. "The great majority were for unrestricted trade in brandy; a few were for a limited and guarded trade; and two or three declared for prohibition."—Parkman.

1677.

An Ursuline Convent was established at Three Rivers.

May 1, Colbert wrote to the Intendant, Duchesneau, warning him not to take sides with the Bishop against Frontenac.

May 18, Colbert wrote to Frontenac, exhorting him to live more amicably with the Intendant.

1678.

The stone church at Caughnawaga, opposite Lachine, was finished.

May 12, The King of France issued letters patent, incorporating the Jesuits in Canada.

La Salle obtained a royal patent, allowing him " to build forts through which it would seem that a passage to Mexico can be found."

Sept. 15, La Salle and Tonty reached Quebec.

Nov 18, La Motte and Father Louis Hennepin, under the direction of La Salle, left Fort Frontenac for the west.

Dec. 6, La Motte and Hennepin reached Niagara.

1679.

Jan. 8, By the carelessness of La Salle's pilot, the vessel in which La Salle's men had crossed Lake Ontario, was wrecked east of Niagara; this was almost a calamity, for much of the material for a vessel to be built on Lake Erie was lost.

Jan. 22, La Salle and his men began the construction of a vessel at the mouth of Cayuga Creek, " two leagues above the Falls."

Joliet received a grant of the Mingan Islands as a reward for his discoveries.

Aug. 7, The "Griffon" left the mouth of Cayuga Creek for the west.

Sept. 18, La Salle, at Green Bay, sent the "Gr'ffon," laden with furs, to Niagara. She was never seen nor heard of afterwards.

Nov. 1, La Salle reached the mouth of the St. Joseph River.

1680.

Jan. 1, La Salle and his men celebrated the Feast of the Circumcision at Starved Rock.

La Salle built Fort Crevecœur.

Feb. 28, Hennepin, with two companions, at La Salle's request, went off to explore the Illinois to its mouth.

March 1, La Salle, leaving Tonty with fifteen men to guard the vessel they had built at Fort Crevecœur, started off on foot for Canada.

Father Hennepin discovered St. Anthony's Falls.

April 11, The Sioux captured Father Hennepin.

May 6, La Salle reached Fort Frontenac.

May 29, The King of France granted letters patent, confirming the establishment of the Iroquois mission at Sault St. Louis.

The Iroquois dispersed the tribes of the Illinois.

Aug. 10, La Salle started off again for the west.

Joliet received a grant of the Island of Anticosti.

Du Luth rescued Father Hennepin.

Oct. 29, "Monsieur" was to be given to Frontenac as Governor, to Laval as first Bishop, and to Duchesneau as Intendant of Justice.

Dec , The " Great Comet " appeared, and was visible till the end of Feb., 1681. "No comet has threatened the earth with a nearer approach than that of 1680."

1681.

Joliet, with his wife and six servants, settled on Anticosti Island.

April 30, The King wrote to Frontenac, complaining of his arbitrary conduct, and threatened to recall him unless he mended his ways; he also ordered that whoever went to the woods without a license should be branded and whipped for the first offence, and sent for life to the galleys for the second offence. This was levelled against the " coureurs de bois."

May, La Salle, to his great joy, found Tonty at Mackinaw.

1682.

Feb. 6, La Salle and Tonty issued from the Illinois River upon the Mississippi.

March 31, La Salle and Tonty, with their men, reached the mouth of the Red River.

April 9, La Salle and his men reached the mouth of the Mississippi, when he declared the basin of the river, Louisiana, the territory of Louis the Great.

The King recalled Frontenac and Duchesneau, their disagreements having become intolerable.

"When he [Frontenac] sailed for France it was a day of rejoicing to more than half the merchants of Canada, and, excepting the Recollets, to all the priests, but he left behind him an impression, very general among the people, that, if danger threatened the colony, Count Frontenac was the man for the hour." Parkman's "Frontenac," p. 71.

Aug. 4, At 10 p.m. a great fire broke out in Quebec.

Oct. 9, Sieur de Barre became Governor of Canada, and De Meules became Intendant.

On the top of Starved Rock, Illinois, La Salle and Tonty built Fort St. Louis.

1683.

La Barre sent Chevalier de Baugis, with a competent force, to seize La Salle's Fort St. Louis.

La Barre sent Charles Le Moyne, of Montreal, to Onondaga to prevail on the Iroquois to send forty-three chiefs to Montreal, to meet the Governor.

1684.

Feb., A war party of Senecas and Cayugas was repulsed in an attack on Fort St. Louis, Illinois.

April, A royal order was issued at Quebec, making it death for a Canadian to emigrate to Albany or Manhattan (New York City.)

July 10, La Barre, with 200 men, left Quebec to fight the Iroquois.

"After a long stay at Montreal, La Barre embarked his little army at Lachine, crossed Lake St. Louis, and began the ascent of the Upper St. Lawrence. In one of the three companies of regulars which formed a part of the force was a young subaltern, the Baron la Hontan, who has left a lively account of the expedition. Some of the men were in flat boats, and some were in birch canoes. Of the latter was La Hontan, whose craft was paddled by three Canadians. Several times they shouldered it through the forest to escape the turmoil of the rapids. The flat boats could not be so handled, and were dragged or pushed up in the shallow water close to the bank, by gangs of militia men, toiling and struggling among the rocks and foam. The regulars, unskilled in such matters, were spared these fatigues, though tormented night and day by swarms of gnats and mosquitoes, objects of La Hontan's bitterest invective. At length the last rapid was passed and they moved serenely on their way, threaded the mazes of the Thousand Islands, entered what is now the harbor of Kingston, and landed under the palisades of Fort Frontenac.

"Here the whole force was soon assembled, the regulars in their tents, the Canadian Militia and the Indians in huts and under sheds of bark. Of these red allies there were several hundred : Abenakis and Algonquins from Sillery, Hurons from Lorette, and converted Iroquois from the Jesuit Mission of Saut St. Louis, near Montreal. The camp of the French was on a low, damp plain near the fort ; and here a malarious fever presently attacked them, killing many and disabling many more. La Hontan says that La Barre himself was brought by it to the brink of the grave. If he had ever entertained any other purpose than that of inducing the Senecas to agree to a temporary peace, he now completely abandoned it. He dared not even insist that the offending tribe should meet him in council, but hastened to ask the mediation of the Onondagas, which the letters of Lamberville had assured him that they were disposed to offer. He sent Le Moyne to persuade them to meet him on their own side of the lake, and, with such of his men as were able to move, crossed to the mouth of Salmon River, then called La Famine."—Parkman's "Frontenac," pp. 103-104.

Sept. 4, Treaty of Famine Cove; its terms were humiliating to La Barre.

La Barre was recalled.

Nov. 12, The cathedral chapter, Quebec, twelve canons and four chaplains, was inaugurated.

Nov. 14, Laval left Canada for France.

1685.

Feb. 6, (James II. began to reign in England.)

Feb. 16, La Salle, missing the mouth of the Mississippi, landed his French settlers for Louisiana at Matagorda Bay, Texas, and built Fort St. Louis.

July 29, Denonville, La Barre's successor, and St. Vallier arrived at Quebec.
As it was difficult to keep coin in the country, Meules issued card money.
Dongan, Governor of New York, sent Johannes Rooseboom, an Albany trader, with eleven canoes, to the Upper Lakes, to exchange peltries with the Indians for furs; Rooseboom returned in three months, the venture proving satisfactory to himself and to the Indians.
Population of Canada, 12,263; of New York, 18,000.

1686.

Denonville sent Chevalier de Troyes, with Iberville, Sainte-Helene, Maricourt, and eighty other Canadians, to expel the English from Hudson's Bay; he did so at the request of the Company of the North, just formed in Canada, which desired to secure the Hudson's Bay trade.
Going up the Ottawa, De Troyes and his men crossed the wilderness to Fort Hayes, took it, took Fort Rupert, and Fort Albany, and, leaving Maricourt to command the Bay, returned to Montreal.

> "No Canadian, under the French rule, stands in a more conspicuous or more deserved eminence than Pierre Le Moyne d'Iberville. In the seventeenth century, most of those who acted a prominent part in the colony were born in Old France; but Iberville was a true son of the soil. He and his brothers Longueuil, Serigny, Assigny, Maricourt, Sainte-Helene, and the two Bienvilles, were one and all children worthy of their father, Charles Le Moyne, of Montreal, and favorable types of that Canadian *noblesse*, to whose adventurous hardihood half the continent bears witness."—Parkman's "Frontenac," p. 388.

June 6, Denonville wrote to Du Luth, ordering him to occupy Detroit with fifty "coureurs de bois;" Du Luth quickly did so, and built a stockade to make his occupation good.
June 12, Denonville wrote to the Minister, Seignelay, for troops to humble the Iroquois.
Johannes Rooseboom started with a larger trading outfit for the Upper Lakes.

Canada sent three ships loaded with wheat to the West Indies.

July, Jacques Bochart de Champigny arrived in Canada, as Intendant.

Oct. 15, Denonville wrote to France, "Things grow worse and worse. The English stir up the Iroquois against us, and send parties to Mackinaw to rob us of our trade. It would be better to declare war against them than to perish by their intrigues."

Nov. 16, Denonville wrote to France, " I have a mind to go straight to Albany, storm their fort, and burn everything."

Population of Acadia, 885.

Dongan, Governor of New York, sent a Scotch officer, named McGregory, with fifty men, to join Rooseboom on the Upper Lakes, and to make a treaty of trade and alliance with the Indians.

March 19, La Salle, while trying to make a journey from Fort St. Louis, Texas, to Canada, was murdered near Trinity River by some of his mutinous followers.

Denonville, dissembling his purpose, collected an army for a descent upon the Senecas. His point of departure was Fort Frontenac.

June 20, Champigny, having invited the Iroquois in the neighborhood of Fort Frontenac to a feast, made them prisoners to the number of thirty men and ninety women and children.

July 3, One Perré, with Canadians and Christian Indians, made the Iroquois of Ganneious (near Fredericksburg) prisoners, to the number of eighteen men and sixty women and children.

Some of these captives were distributed among the missions; the others were sent to France to work in the galleys.

July 4, Denonville, with his army, left Fort Frontenac for Irondequoit Bay. Here he was joined by La Durantaye, who brought with him a host of Indians from the West.

July 12, Denonville, with his army, left Irondequoit Bay for the capital of the Senecas.

La Durantaye captured Rooseboom, and, soon after, he and Du Lhut captured McGregory.

July 13, Denonville's vanguard fell into an ambuscade of the Senecas; but, after some disorderly conduct, the main body came to the front, and put the Senecas to flight.

July 14, Denonville's men reached the heart of the Seneca country, but found the "Babylon of the Senecas" in ashes and nobody in sight.

> "The soldiers killed the hogs, burned the old corn, and hacked down the new with their swords. Next they advanced to an abandoned Seneca fort on a hill half a league distant, and burned it, with all that it contained. Ten days passed in the work of havoc. Three neighboring villages were levelled, and all their fields laid waste. The amount of corn destroyed was prodigious. Denonville reckons it at the absurdly exaggerated amount of twelve hundred thousand bushels."—Parkman's "Frontenac," p. 154.

July 24, Denonville returned to Irondequoit Bay; and then proceeded to Niagara, where he built a fort, and left it under Chevalier de Troyes, with 100 men.

Aug. 13, Denonville returned to Montreal.

A mission Indian had told Denonville, that, if he oversets a wasp's nest, he must kill the wasps, or they would sting him. Denonville had overset the Senecas, but he had not even seriously hurt them; they now prepared for revenge.

Oct. 2, Denonville wrote to Dongan, promising to send back McGregory and the other English prisoners; he soon did so.

Oct. 31, Dongan, Governor of New York, wrote to Denonville, demanding that the Iroquois seized at Fort Frontenac and imprisoned in French galleys, be surrendered to the English Ambassador at Paris.

Nov. 10, James II., of England, owned the Iroquois as subjects, and ordered Dongan to protect them.

1688.

Jan. 25, St. Vallier was consecrated Bishop of Quebec. In the spring, the occupants of Fort Niagara were reduced, by want and disease, to ten men.

June 8, Big Mouth, the famous Onondaga orator, with six Onondaga, Oneida, and Cayuga chiefs, arrived at Montreal to confer about peace, Denonville having promised to return the prisoners.

"What had brought the marquis to this pass? Famine, destitution, disease, and the Iroquois were making Canada their prey. The fur trade had been stopped for two years; and the people, bereft of their only means of subsistence, could contribute nothing to their own defence. Above Three Rivers, the whole population was imprisoned in stockade forts hastily built in every seigniory. Here they were safe, provided that they never ventured out; but their fields were left untilled, and the governor was already compelled to feed many of them at the expense of the king. The Iroquois roamed among the deserted settlements, or prowled like lynxes about the forts, waylaying convoys and killing or capturing stragglers. Their war parties were usually small; but their movements were so mysterious and their attacks so sudden, that they spread a universal panic through the upper half of the colony. They were the wasps which Denonville had failed to kill."—Parkman's "Frontenac," p. 167.

When the "Rat," a Huron chief, heard that Denonville, in the prospective peace, was not going to include the Indians allied to the French, he "killed the peace," by intercepting some Iroquois deputies, firing on them, killing some others, and pretending that he had been prompted to it by Denonville.

Aug. 10, Denonville begged the King of France to send back the Indians captured at Fort Frontenac.
Aug. 15, Laval returned to Quebec.
Aug. 20, Denonville promised Dongan that he would demolish Fort Niagara.
Aug. 21, Andros, Governor of New York, wrote to Denonville, forbidding him to molest the Iroquois, as they were British subjects.
Sept. 15, Denonville, at the demand of the Iroquois, abandoned Fort Niagara, and demolished it.

1689.

Feb. 13, (William III. and Mary began to reign in England.) King William's war was begun.
May 8, Nicolas Perrot, Pierre le Sueur being with him, on the Wisconsin side of Lake Pepin, took formal occupation of the country, in the name of the King of France.
May 31, The king recalled Denonville, and made Frontenac Governor of Canada the second time.
Aug. 5, Massacre of Lachine.

THE CARDINAL FACTS OF CANADIAN HISTORY. 47

"On the night before the fourth and fifth of August, a violent hail storm burst over Lake St. Louis, an expansion of the St. Lawrence a little above Montreal. Concealed by the tempest and the darkness, fifteen hundred warriors landed at La Chine, and silently posted themselves about the houses of the sleeping settlers, then screeched the war-whoop, and began the most frightful massacre in Canadian history. The houses were burned, and men, women, and children indiscriminately butchered. In the neighborhood were three stockade forts, called Rémy, Roland, and La Présentation; and they all had garrisons. There was also an encampment of two hundred regulars about three miles distant, under an officer named Subercase, then absent at Montreal on a visit to Denonville, who had lately arrived with his wife and family. At four o'clock in the morning, the troops in this encampment heard a cannon shot from one of the forts. They were at once ordered under arms. Soon after they saw a man running towards them, just escaped from the butchery. He told his story and passed on with the news to Montreal, six miles distant. Then several fugitives appeared, chased by a band of Iroquois, who gave over the pursuit at sight of the soldiers, but pillaged several houses before their eyes. The day was well advanced before Subercase arrived. He ordered the troops to march. About a hundred armed inhabitants had joined them, and they moved together towards Lachine. Here they found the houses still burning, and the bodies of their inmates strewn among them or hanging from the stakes where they had been tortured. They learned from a French surgeon, escaped from the enemy, that the Iroquois were all encamped a mile and a half farther on, behind a tract of forest. Subercase, whose force had been strengthened by troops from the forts, resolved to attack them ; and, had he been allowed to do so, he would probably have punished them severely, for most of them were helplessly drunk with brandy taken from the houses of the traders. Sword in hand, at the head of his men, the daring officer entered the forest : but at that moment a voice from the rear commanded a halt. It was that of the Chevalier de Vaudreuil, just come from Montreal, with positive orders from Denonville to run no risks and stand solely on the defensive. Subercase was furious. High words passed between him and Vaudreuil, but he was forced to obey.

"The troops were led back to Fort Roland, where about five hundred regulars and militia were now collected under command of Vaudreuil. On the next day eighty men from Fort Rémy attempted to join them, but the Iroquois had slept off the effects of their orgies, and were again on the alert. The unfortunate detachment was set upon by a host of savages, and cut to pieces in full sight of Fort Roland. All were killed or captured except Le Moyne de Longueuil, and a few others, who escaped within the gate of Fort Rémy

"Montreal was wild with terror. It had been fortified with palisades since the war began, but, though there were troops in the town under the governor himself, the people were in mortal dread. No attack was made either on the town or on any of the forts, and such of the inhabitants as could reach them were safe, while the Iroquois held undisputed possession of the open country, burned all the houses and barns over an extent of nine miles, and roamed in small parties, pillaging and scalping, over more than twenty miles. There is no mention of their having encountered opposition, nor do they seem to have met with any loss but that of some warriors killed in the attack on the detachment from Fort Rémy, and that of three drunken stragglers who were caught and thrown into a cellar in Fort La Présentation. When they came to their senses, they defied their captors, and fought with such ferocity that it was necessary to shoot them. Charlevoix says that the invaders remained in the neighborhood of Montreal till the middle of October, or more than two months; but this seems incredible, since troops and militia enough to drive them all into the St. Lawrence might easily have been collected in less than a week. It is certain, however, that their stay was strangely long. Troops and inhabitants seem to have been paralyzed with fear.

"At length, most of them took to their canoes, and recrossed Lake St. Louis in a body, giving ninety yells to show that they had ninety prisoners in their clutches. This was not all: for the whole number carried off was more than a hundred and twenty, besides about two hundred who had the good fortune to be killed on the spot. As the Iroquois passed the forts, they shouted, 'Onontio, you deceived us, and now we have deceived you.' Towards evening they encamped on the farther side of the lake, and began to torture and devour their prisoners. On that miserable night, stupefied and speechless groups stood gazing from the strand of La Chine at the lights that gleamed along the distant shore of Châteaugay, where their friends, wives, parents, or children agonized in the fires of the Iroquois, and scenes were enacted of indescribable and nameless horror. The greater part of the prisoners were, however, reserved to be distributed among the towns of the confederacy, and there tortured for the diversion of the inhabitants. While some of the invaders went home to celebrate their triumph, others roamed in small parties through all the upper parts of the colony, spreading universal terror."—Parkman's "Frontenac," pp. 177-181.

Callieres, Governor of Montreal, in France submitted a scheme to the king for the solution of all Canada's difficulties. It was to conquer New York. It could be done, Callieres argued, with the forces in Canada, 1,000 regulars, and 600 militia, and two royal ships of war. The king, after modifying the scheme, adopted it. But delay in fitting out the two ships, and an exceptionally long passage across the Atlantic, caused by head winds, ruined the enterprise.

Sept. 12, Frontenac and Callieres reached Chedabucto.

Oct. 15, Frontenac reached Quebec, bringing with him thirteen Iroquois, taken from the galleys, all that remained of those whom Denonville took at Fort Frontenac.

Nov. 6, Frontenac sent an expedition to succor Fort Frontenac, which soon met De Valrennes, who, having by Denonville's orders destroyed the fort, was returning to Montreal.

By the king's permission a few negroes were brought into Canada for slaves; but slavery never flourished in the colony, the climate being too rigorous for negroes.

1690.

Jan. 22, The Iroquois began a Grand Council at Onondaga, and concluded a treaty of peace with the English and the tribes of the Great Lakes.

Feb. 8, Mantet and Sainte-Helene took Schenectady and massacred nearly all the people, as they were aroused from sleep.

March 28, Hertel took Salmon Falls.

Frontenac sent Captain Louvignay, with 193 Canadians, by way of the Ottawa, to reinforce Mackinaw, where the Indian allies of the French were wavering in their allegiance.

May 11, Menneval surrendered Port Royal to Sir Wm. Phips.

May 28, Portneuf took Fort Loyal.

June 14, Captain Sylvanus Davis, commander of Fort Loyal, arrived at Quebec.

July 31, Frontenac, having left Major Prevost to strengthen Quebec, reached Montreal.

Aug. 9, Sir Wm. Phips, with 32 ships and 2,200 men, left Nantasket, Mass., to take Quebec.

In August, Montreal was thronged with Hurons, Ottawas, Ojibwas, Pottawatamies, Crees, and Nippissings, come to trade; there was a great council and a war-feast, when Frontenac, joining with the Indians in their songs and antics, helped to devour the two oxen and six large dogs that had been minced and boiled with prunes; two barrels of wine and an abundance of tobacco were used in toning down the feast.

Oct. 10, A messenger from Prevost, town-major of Quebec, arrived in Montreal, with a letter to Frontenac, telling him that the English were coming up the St. Lawrence.

Oct. 14, Frontenac arrived in Quebec.

Oct. 16, Sir Wm. Phips entered Quebec harbor, and sent a summons to Frontenac to surrender; Frontenac contemptuously refused.

In the evening, Callieres, Governor of Montreal, arrived at Quebec, bringing 800 soldiers and troops of "coureurs de bois," "all full of fight, singing and whooping with martial glee as they passed the western gate and trooped down St. Louis Street."

Oct. 18, Major Walley landed 1,200 men on Beauport Shore, and Phips began to bombard Quebec.

"Meanwhile, Phips, whose fault hitherto had not been an excess of promptitude, grew impatient, and made a premature movement inconsistent with the preconcerted plan. He left his moorings, anchored his largest ships before the town, and prepared to cannonade it ; but the fiery veteran, who watched him from the Château St. Louis, anticipated him, and gave him the first shot. Phips replied furiously, opening fire with every gun that he could bring to bear ; while the rock paid him back in kind, and belched flame and smoke from all its batteries. So fierce and rapid was the firing that La Hontan compares it to volleys of musketry; and old officers, who had seen many sieges, declared that they had never known the like. The din was prodigious, reverberated from the surrounding heights, and rolled back from the distant mountains in one continuous roar. On the part of the English, however, surprisingly little was accomplished beside noise and smoke. The practice of their gunners was so bad that many of their shots struck harmlessly against the face of the cliff. Their guns, too, were very light, and appeared to have been charged with a view to the most rigid economy of gunpowder ; for the balls failed to pierce the stone walls of the buildings, and did so little damage that, as the French boasted, twenty crowns would have repaired it all. Night came at length, and the turmoil ceased.

"Phips lay quiet till daybreak, when Frontenac sent a shot to waken him, and the cannonade began again. Sainte-Hélène had returned from Beauport; and he, with his brother Maricourt, took charge of the two batteries of the Lower Town, aiming the guns in person, and throwing balls of eighteen and twenty-four pounds with excellent precision against the four largest ships of the fleet. One of their shots cut the flagstaff of the admiral, and the cross of St. George fell into the river. It drifted with the tide towards the north shore; whereupon several Canadians paddled out in a birch canoe, secured it, and brought it back in triumph. On the spire of the cathedral in the Upper Town had been hung a picture of the Holy Family, as an invocation of Divine aid. The Puritan gunners wasted their ammunition in vain attempts to knock it down. That it escaped their malice was ascribed to miracle, but the miracle would have been greater if they had hit it.

"At length, one of the ships, which had suffered most, hauled off and abandoned the fight. That of the admiral had fared little better, and now her condition grew desperate. With her rigging torn, her mainmast half cut through, her mizzen-mast splintered, her cabin pierced, and her hull riddled with shot, another volley seemed likely to sink her, when Phips ordered her to be cut loose from her moorings, and she drifted out of fire, leaving cable and anchor behind. The remaining ships soon gave over the conflict, and withdrew to stations where they could neither do harm nor suffer it."—Parkman's "Frontenac," pp. 272-274.

Oct. 21, At night, Major Walley embarked his men, not being able to touch Quebec.

Oct. 24, Phips retired with his ships behind Orleans Island, where he hove to, to mend rigging and repair his ships. "Quebec was divided between thanksgiving and rejoicing."

Nov. 15, Three supply ships, which had evaded Phips by going up the Saguenay, arrived at Quebec.

1691.

Aug. 10, Peter Schuyler, with 260 men, surprised the French at La Prairie, and then retreated; but, before he reached his canoes on the Richelieu, Valrenne intercepted him and gave him "the most hot and stubborn fight ever known in Canada."

1692.

In February, a young officer, Beaucour, with 300 men, killed or captured a band of Iroquois who were wintering between the St. Lawrence and the Ottawa.

June 10, Portneuf, the Baron de Saint-Castin, and other leaders, with 400 warriors, attacked Castine (Wells), but Capt. Convers beat them off.

During the summer caterpillars destroyed all the crops in Canada; but a prodigious number of squirrels appeared, which the people killed for food.

Oct. 22, The Iroquois attacked Vercheres, but Madeline, the seignior's daughter, fourteen years of age, with two soldiers, two boys, and an old man, held the fort for a week; then help arrived and the Indians were driven off.

1693.

In January, Mantet, Courtemanche, and La Noue, with 625 men, left Chambly, and, on snow shoes, started southward for the Mohawk towns.

Feb. 16, Mantet, Courtemanche, and La Noue took three Mohawk towns, killed several people, and took many to Canada.

Quebec, Montreal, and Three Rivers were strengthened by better fortifications; "a strong stone redoubt, with sixteen cannon," was built upon the summit of Cape Diamond.

By Frontenac's skilful management, two hundred canoes, laden with rich peltries, managed to make a safe descent of the Ottawa. The people called Frontenac, "Father of the People and Preserver of the Country."

Population of Acadia, 1,009.

1694.

Jan. 16, Bishop Saint-Vallier issued two mandates,—one denouncing comedies, especially "Tartuffe," and the other condemning Sieur de Mauriel, a half-pay lieutenant, who had acted the comedian and was booked for a part of "Tartuffe."

Villieu and Thury, with 230 Indians, attacked the settlement of Oyster River, and killed over a hundred people.

"Early in the war, the French of Canada began the merciful practice of buying English prisoners, and especially children from their Indian allies. After the first fury of attack, many lives were spared for the sake of this ransom. Sometimes, but not always, the redeemed captives were made to work for their benefactors. They were uniformly treated well, and often with such kindness that they would not be exchanged, and became Canadians by adoption."—Parkman's "Frontenac," p. 377.

Dec. 8, (Queen Mary, of England, died.)

1695.

In July, Frontenac sent Chevalier de Crisasy, with 700 men, to restore Fort Frontenac.

1696.

July 4, Frontenac, with 2,200 men, left Montreal, to attack the Onondagas.

Aug. 1, Frontenac and his men reached Onondaga. The results of this expedition were similar to Denonville's.

Aug. 15, Villieu, Saint Castin, and Thury took Pemaquid, the commander of the post, Chubb, not being very resolute.

Late, Pierre Le Moyne d'Iberville attacked and overran Newfoundland.

1697.

March 15, Abenakis attacked Haverhill, and carried off Hannah Dustan, Mary Neff, and an English boy; but, while on their way to the Indian village, the three prisoners one night seized hatchets, killed their sleeping captors, scalped them, escaped to Haverhill, and received £50 for their ten scalps.

May 19, Serigny, Iberville's brother, arrived at Newfoundland with five ships of war, bearing orders to Iberville to proceed against the English in Hudson's Bay. In July, Iberville and Serigny, in Hudson's Bay, defeated four English armed merchantmen, and took Fort Nelson.

Sept. 20, Treaty of Ryswick : France recovered Acadia.

1698.

End of May, Major Peter Schuyler, accompanied by Dellius, the minister of Albany, came to Montreal, bearing news of peace.

"Peter Schuyler and his colleague, Dellius, brought to Canada all the French prisoners in the hands of the English of New York, and asked for English prisoners in return; but nearly all these preferred to remain, a remarkable proof of the kindness with which the Canadians treated their civilized captives."— Parkman's "Frontenac," p. 426.

Sept. 23, John Schuyler dined with Frontenac at Quebec.

Nov. 28, Frontenac died.

"He was greatly beloved by the humbler classes, who, days before his death, beset the chateau, praising and lamenting him. Many of higher station shared the popular grief."—Parkman's "Frontenac," p. 428.

1699.

March 2, D'Iberville entered the Mississippi from the sea, the first white man to do so.

April 20, De Callieres, Governor of Montreal, was made Governor of Canada.

Le Moyne d'Iberville built a stockade fort at Biloxi, Mississippi; this was the beginning of Louisiana.

1700.

Jan. 12, Death of Margaret Bourgeois, founder of Sisters of Congregation of Notre Dame.

"To this day, in crowded school-rooms of Montreal and Quebec, fit monuments of her unobtrusive virtue, her successors instruct the children of the poor, and embalm the pleasant memory of Margaret Bourgeois. In the martial figure of Maisonneuve, and the fair form of this gentle nun, we find the true heroes of Montreal."—Parkman's "Jesuits," p. 202.

Sept. 8, De Callieres, at Montreal, signed a treaty of peace with the Iroquois, Abenakis, and Ottawas.

Population of Canada, 15,000.

(Population of New York, 30,000.)

(Population of New England, 100,000.)

1701.

July 24, La Motte-Cadillac, with 100 men, began Detroit.

1702.

March 8, (Queen Anne began to reign in England.)

May 15, England declared war against France; then was begun Queen Anne's War, or the War of the Spanish Succession.

Oct. 5, François de Beauharnois was made Intendant of Canada.

1703.

May 26, M. de Callieres died.

Aug. 1, Marquis de Vaudreuil, Governor of Montreal, was commissioned Governor of Canada.

Oct. 29, The Members of the Sovereign Council were increased from seven to twelve members.

1704.

Feb. 29, Hertel de Rouville, with 50 Canadians and 200 Indians, attacked and burned Deerfield and brought off John Williams, the minister.

In retaliation for Rouville's conduct at Deerfield, Col. Benjamin Church, who had been a prominent fighter in King Philip's War, led an expedition against Acadia, where he committed a few depredations at Grand Pré, but hardly disturbed Port Royal. He returned to Boston.

> "It was a miserable retaliation for a barbarous outrage; as the guilty were out of reach, the invaders turned their ire on the innocent."—Parkman's "Half Century of Conflict," I., p. 120.

1705.

Sept. 6, Jacques and Antoine Raudot, joint Intendants of Canada, arrived at Quebec.

1707.

June 6, Col. March, with 1,500 men from Boston, attempted to take Port Royal.

June 16, Col. March retired from Port Royal. Being reinforced he was ordered to move against Port Royal again.

Aug. 20, Col. Church retreated from Port Royal the second time.

The Intendant granted the porpoise fishery of the seigniory of Rivière Ouelle to six of the *habitans*.

1708.

May 6, Death of Bishop Laval.

In the summer, Hertel de Rouville and Saint Ours de Chaillons led 100 Canadians and 300 Indians against the New England settlements, killed several people, captured many, and burned whatever houses they could.

1709.
Col. Nicholson failed to descend the Richelieu with his provincial levies.
1710.
March 31, Micehl Begon was commissioned Intendant of Canada

Nov. 13, Col. Nicholson took Port Royal.
1711.
In June the Micmacs and Penobscots in Nova Scotia killed or captured seventy English.

July 30, Sir Hovenden Walker, with a fine fleet, left Boston to take Quebec.

Aug 22, Having failed to reach Quebec, Sir Hovenden Walker, through criminal carelessness, lost 10 ships and 884 men in the St. Lawrence, at Isle aux Œufs.
1712.
The Outagamies and Mascoutins besieged Detroit.

May 13, Sieur de Vincennes, with eight Frenchmen, arrived at Detroit from the Miami country.

The French, aided by a strong reinforcement of Indian allies, after fighting for several days, compelled the Outagamies and Mascoutins to surrender.
1713.
April 13, Treaty of Utrecht ; England obtained Acadia.

The Iroquois, or Five Nations, being joined about this time by the Tuscaroras, became the Six Nations.
1714.
April 22, Louis François Duplessis de Mornay was consecrated Bishop of Quebec.

Aug. 1, (George I. began to reign in England.)
Gen. Nicholson was made Governor of Nova Scotia.
1716.
Father Lafitau discovered gensing.
Louvigny defeated the Outagamies at Fox River.
1717.
Gen. Phillips was made Governor of Nova Scotia.
Card money was withdrawn from circulation in Canada.

Merchants' Exchanges were established at Quebec and Montreal.

1720.

The French fortified Louisbourg, Cape Breton Island; they spent £1,500,000 on the work.

Sept. 24, Charlevoix arrived at Quebec.

1721.

June 19, Great fire in Montreal.

The Intendant granted the monopoly of carrying the post, from Quebec to Montreal, to M. Lanouiller; it was the first regular post service in Canada.

1723.

Two men-of-war and six merchantmen were built in Canada.

1724.

Aug. 12, Father Rasles was murdered at Norridgewock.

Col. L. Armstrong was made Governor of Nova Scotia.

1725.

A stone fort was begun at Niagara.

Gov. Burnet, of New York, erected a trading post at Oswego.

Oct. 10, M. de Vaudreuil died.

Dec. 25, Pierre Herman Dosquet was consecrated Bishop of Quebec.

1726.

The French established a permanent garrison at Fort Niagara.

Sept. 2, Marquis de Beauharnois was made Governor of Canada.

Dec. 31, Claude Thomas Dupuy signed his first act as Intendant of Canada.

1727.

June 11, (George II. began to reign in England.)
Dec. 26, Death of Bishop Saint-Vallier.

1728.

Aug 12, Vitus Behring passed through Behring Strait, proving the insularity of America.

1729.

Nov. 22, Gilles Hocquart signed his first act as Intendant of Canada.

1731.

In this year Hocquart received his commission as Intendant.

June 8, Verendrye, equipped by Montreal traders, left Montreal to hunt, trade in furs, and to find the Pacific.

The French erected Fort Frederic, at Crown Point.

1732.

Feb. 19, In Canada, religious houses were forbidden to shelter fugitives from justice.

1733.

The first forge in Canada was set up at St. Maurice.

1734.

A vehicle, on wheels, first went from Quebec to Montreal.

Sazzarin, physician and naturalist, died in Quebec.

1735.

Verendrye built Fort Rouge on the site of the city of Winnipeg.

1737.

April 22, An order-in-council was passed, permitting "La Compagnie des Forges" to work the iron mines at Three Rivers without dues of any kind.

In this year two Christian Brothers came to Canada to promote education.

Nov. 24, Erasmus James Phillips, an officer of the British army, while on a visit in Boston, was made a Freemason.

1738.

Sometime in this year Erasmus James Phillips organized a Freemason Lodge at Annapolis, Nova Scotia. (Cf. "Standard History of Freemasonry," by Emmanuel Rebold and J. F. Brennan, p. 362 and p. 452.) Perhaps this was the first Masonic Lodge in what is now Canada.

Dec. 3, Verendrye entered the village of the Mandans.

1739.

Canadian tobacco was first sent to France.

Dec. 20, François-Louis Pourroy l'Auberiviere was consecrated Bishop of Quebec.

1740.

Capt. P. Mascarene was made Governor of Nova Scotia.

1741.

April 9, Henri-Marie Dubreuil de Pontbriand was consecrated Bishop of Quebec.

1742.

June 29, Joseph La France reached York Factory, having floated down the Nelson River.

1743.

Jan. 1, Chevalier de la Verendrye and his brother saw the Bighorn Range, the first white men to see the Rocky Mountains.

Nov. 25, In Canada an ordinance was published, restraining religious communities from acquiring more land without royal permission.

1744.

King George's War, or War of Austrian Succession, was begun.

Nov. 24, The Bishop of Quebec transferred the observance of several holidays to the following Sunday.

1745.

June 17, William Pepperell, with an American force, took Louisbourg, Cape Breton.

Nov. 29, Marin took Saratoga.

1746.

June 20, Duc D'Anville left Rochelle with a powerful fleet to retake Acadia and Louisbourg.

Aug. 31, Rigaud de Vaudreuil, Major of Three Rivers, took Fort Massachusetts.

Sept. 14, D'Anville's fleet was dispersed by a storm near Sable Island.

Sept. 27, D'Anville died of apoplexy, brought on by suspense and trouble.

1747.

May 10, La Jonquiere, with a formidable fleet for the recapture of Acadia and Louisbourg, sailed from Rochelle.
May 14, Admiral Anson and Rear-Admiral Warren captured La Jonquiere and all the armed ships of his fleet.
Sept 19, Galissonniere arrived at Quebec.

1748.

Jan. 1, François Bigot was commissioned Intendant of Canada. Count Galissoniere advised that 10,000 French peasants be settled in the Ohio valley.
Aug. 25. François Bigot arrived at Quebec.
Sept, Abbe Picquet, a Sulpitian, began a fort at La Présentation (Ogdensburg.)
Oct. 8, Treaty of Aix-la-Chapelle : all conquests were restored.

1749.

May 19, The King of England granted 200,000 acres of land to the Ohio Company, the full grant of 500,000 being promised in seven years if conditions were fulfilled.
June 16, De Celeron, sent west to mark the French occupation by burying leaden plates at particular places, left Lachine.
July 9, Col. Cornwallis landed 2,576 people at Halifax, N.S., founding the city.
Lord Cornwallis was made Governor of Nova Scotia.
July 12, The French reoccupied Louisbourg ; this galled the " Bostonnais."
July 14, The first Council of Halifax met.
July 22, De Celeron reached Lake Chatauqua.
July 29, De Celeron buried the first leaden plate at the confluence of the Conewango and the "Ohio" (Alleghany.)
Aug. 3, De Celeron buried the second leaden plate on the south bank of the Alleghany, nine miles below French Creek.
Aug. 13, De Celeron buried the third leaden plate on the north bank of Wheeling Creek.
Aug. 15, De Celeron buried the fourth leaden plate at the mouth of the Muskingum.
Aug. 16, Sieur de la Jonquiere was made Governor of Canada.

THE CARDINAL FACTS OF CANADIAN HISTORY. 61

Aug. 18, De Celeron buried the fifth leaden plate on the south bank of the Ohio.
Aug 31, De Celeron buried the sixth, the last, leaden plate where the Great Miami joins the Ohio.
Sept 1, De Celeron turned back.
Portneuf, with 15 soldiers, built Fort Rouille, beginning Toronto.
Oct. 6, De Celeron arrived at Detroit.

1750.

Col. Lawrence built a fort at Chignecto.

> "Mr. Bigot, the Intendant of Canada, displayed this year much of that license and prodigality for which he became notorious, and resorted to the most profligate means for the support of his expenses, which were lavished upon a female favorite."—Bouchette's "British Dominions in North America," I., p. 439.

1751.

Early in summer, Abbe Picquet, with six Canadians and five Indians, began the circuit of Lake Ontario.
June 26, Picquet reached Toronto, where he found a band of Mississagas.
June 28, Picquet reached Niagara.
July 12, Picquet reached the mouth of the Genesee, and visited the falls.

1752.

March 28, John Bushell issued the first number of the Halifax *Gazette*, the first newspaper in Canada.
Peregrine T. Hopson was made Governor of Nova Scotia.
May 17, La Jonquiere died in Quebec.
June 21, Charles Langlade, with Ottawas and Ojibwas, took Pickawillany on the Miami, and killed "Old Britain," an Indian chief, and some English traders.
Aug. 7, Marquis du Quesne was made Governor of Canada.
Sept. 2, Great Britain called Sept. 2 Sept. 14, changing Old Style to New.

1753.

Canadians fortified themselves at Presqu'-Isle, Lake Erie, and moved down to Venango.
Gov. Dinwiddie, of Virginia, sent George Washing-

ton to the Upper Ohio, to order the French off British territory.

Major Lawrence was made Governor of Nova Scotia.

Dec. 4, Washington, accompanied by Gist and Half-King, reached Venango, and ordered Capt. Joncaire off British territory : the latter politely but resolutely refused to budge.

1754.

Capt. Trant began to build a fort on the site of Pittsburg, but abandoned it at the command of the French, who finished it, and named it Du Quesne.

May 27, Washington, with 1,500 men, reached the Great Meadows.

May 28, Washington, while fortifying himself on the Monongahela, engaged the French, when M. Jumonville was killed.

May 30, Col. Fry dying, Washington became commander of the English.

July 4, Washington, defeated by De Villiers, abandoned Fort Necessity.

1755.

Feb. 20, Gen. Braddock, with two regiments, arrived in Virginia.

March 16, Bishop Pontbriand visited Detroit.

June 5, In obedience to a proclamation, Acadians to the number of 418 able bodied men met in the church at Grand-Pre, Nova Scotia, when Col. Winslow read "his Majesty's final resolution," which was, that "your lands and tenements, cattle of all kinds, and live stock of all sorts, are forfeited to the Crown, with all your other effects, saving your money and household goods."

June 8, Admiral Boscawen took the French ships, "Lys" and "Alcide," off the coast of Newfoundland.

June 16, Col. Monckton took Fort Beausejour, Nova Scotia.

July 9, Gen. Braddock, with 1,200 men, was defeated and mortally wounded near Fort Du Quesne, by 250 French and Indians under Beaujeu.

July 10, De Vaudreuil was made Governor of Canada.

July 13, Gen. Braddock died.

Gen. Lyman built Fort Lyman, afterwards Fort Edward, on the Hudson.

Aug. 21, Shirley, Governor of Massachusetts, with 2,000 men, reached Oswego, to wait for Braddock.

In Canada provisions were very scarce; the government doled out flour to prevent starvation.

Sept. 8, Gen. Dieskau, commanding a force of French, Canadians, and Indians, was defeated at Lake George by Wm. Johnson. Dieskau was wounded and made a prisoner.

Oct. 21, The Acadians were embarked in transports and taken to the English colonies, where they were thrown upon the hospitality of strangers. This has generally been considered a heartless, inhuman act, but there are defenders of it. It has been hotly discussed, and perhaps the last word has not been spoken yet.

Oct. 24, Shirley left Oswego for home, leaving Col. Mercer to hold Oswego and to strengthen it.

1756.

May 11, Montcalm, De Levis, Bougainville, and Bourlamaque arrived at Quebec.

May 18, England declared war against France.

June 9, France declared war against England.

July 3, Bradstreet, who had taken succor to Oswego and was ascending the Oswego River homeward, beat off Coulon De Villiers, who attacked him.

Aug. 4, Montcalm, with 3,000 men, left Fort Frontenac to take Oswego.

Aug. 10, Montcalm reached Oswego.

Aug. 14, Montcalm took Oswego and 1,400 prisoners, the whole garrison, Col. Mercer being killed.

> "The Canadians and Indians broke through all restraint and fell to plundering. There was an opening of rum barrels and a scene of drunkenness, in which some of the prisoners had their share; while others tried to escape in the confusion, and were tomahawked by the excited savages. Many more would have been butchered but for the efforts of Montcalm, who by unstinted promises succeeded in appeasing his ferocious allies, whom he dared not offend. 'It will cost the king,' he says, 'eight or ten thousand livres in presents.'"—Parkman's "Wolfe and Montcalm," I., p. 413.

Montcalm constructed a road from Laprairie to St. John.

1757.

Jan. 21, Rogers, the ranger, was surprised and beaten outside of Ticonderoga.

March 15, De Rigaud, with 1,400 men, left Carillon, to take Fort William Henry, at the head of Lake George.

March 20, Le Mercier, chief of Canadian artillery, demanded the surrender of Fort William Henry; Major Eyre indignantly refused.

March 23, De Rigaud's men burned the vessels at Fort William Henry, and then retreated.

June 20, Loudon left New York to take Louisbourg, but his expedition was a signal failure.

June 29, (Pitt again became First Minister in England.)

Aug. 1, Montcalm, with 7,606 men, began the siege of Fort William Henry, held by Col. Monroe, who had 2,264 men.

Aug. 3, Col. Monroe sent a messenger to Gen. Webb, at Fort Edward, asking for succor.

Aug. 9, Col. Monroe surrendered Fort William Henry to Montcalm.

Aug. 10, Montcalm's Indians massacred many of the English prisoners, near Fort William Henry.

"To make the capitulation inviolably binding on the Indians, Montcalm summoned their war chiefs to council. The English were to depart under an escort with the honors of war, on a pledge not to serve against the French for eighteen months; they were to abandon all but their private effects, every Canadian or French Indian captive was to be liberated. The Indians applauded; the capitulation was signed. Late on the ninth the French entered the fort, and the English retired to their entrenched camp. Montcalm had kept from the savages all intoxicating drinks, but they obtained them of the English, and all night long were wild with dances and songs and revelry. The Abenakies of Acadia inflamed other tribes by recalling their sufferings from English perfidy and power. At daybreak they gathered round the entrenchments, and, as the terrified English soldiers filed off, began to plunder them, and incited one another to use the tomahawk. Twenty, perhaps even thirty, persons were massacred, while very many were made prisoners. Officers and soldiers, stripped of everything, fled to the woods, to the fort, to the tents of the French. To arrest the disorder, Levi plunged into the tumult, daring death a thousand times. French officers received wounds in rescuing the captives, and stood at their tents as sentries over those they recovered. 'Kill me,' cried Montcalm, using prayers and menaces and promises, 'but spare the English, who are under my protection ;' and he urged the troops to defend themselves. The march to Fort Edward was a flight ; not more than six hundred reached there in a body. From the French camp Montcalm collected together more than four hundred, who were dismissed with a great escort, and he sent Vaudreuil to ransom those whom the Indians had carried away."—Bancroft's "History of the United States," II., p. 467.

Nov 12, Belêtre, with three hundred Canadians and Indians, surprised a German settlement, at the German Flats, on the Mohawk, killed fifty people, made the rest prisoners, and burned the place.

1758.

July 5, Abercromby embarked his army of 15,000 men in 900 small boats and 130 whale boats, on Lake George, and moved down to take Ticonderoga.

July 6, The English army disembarked at the head of the rapids ; the same day, Lord Howe, " the soul of the army," was killed in a skirmish.

July 8, Montcalm drove Abercromby from Ticonderoga with great loss.

"Montcalm saw and was prepared. On the sixth of July, he called in all his parties ; and his whole force, according to his official return, amounted to no more than two thousand eight hundred French, and four hundred and fifty Canadians. On that day he employed the second battalion of Berry in strengthening his post. All the next day, the whole French army toiled incredibly ; the officers giving the example, and the flags being planted on the breastwork. That evening De Levi returned from an intended expedition against the Mohawks, bringing with him four hundred chosen men ; and at night the whole army bivouacked along the entrenchment. On the morning of the eighth, the drums of the French beat to arms, that the troops, now thirty-six hundred and fifty in number, might know their stations, and then they resumed their work ; the right of their defences rested on a hillock, from which the plain between the lines and the lake was to have been flanked by four pieces of cannon ; but the battery could not be finished; the left extended to a scarf surmounted by an abattis. For a hundred yards in front of the intermediate breastwork, which consisted of piles of logs, the approach was obstructed by felled trees with their branches pointing outwards, stumps and rubbish of all sorts. Light troops of the English kept up a sharp discharge of musketry on them from the declivities of Mount Defiance, but they would not stop their work to return it.

"At length the English army, obeying the orders of a commander who remained far behind during the action, rushed forward with fixed bayonets to carry the lines, the regulars advancing through the openings between the provincial regiments and taking the lead. Montcalm, who stood just within the trenches, threw off his coat for the sunny work of the July afternoon, and forbade a musket to be fired till he commanded; then, as the English drew very near, in three principal columns, to attack simultaneously the left, the centre, and the right, and became entangled among the rubbish and broken into disorder by clambering over logs and projecting limbs, at his word, a sudden and incessant fire from swivels and small arms mowed down brave officers and men by hundreds. Their intrepidity made the carnage terrible. The attacks were continued all the afternoon, generally with the greatest vivacity. When the English endeavored to turn the left, Bourlamarque opposed them till he was dangerously wounded; and Montcalm, whose rapid eye watched every movement, sent reinforcements at the moment of crisis. On the right, the Grenadiers and Scottish Highlanders charged for three hours without faltering and without confusion; many fell within fifteen steps of the trench; some, it is said, upon it. About five o'clock the columns which had attacked the French centre and right, concentrated themselves on a salient point between the two; but De Levi flew from the right, and Montcalm himself brought up a reserve. At six, the two parties nearest the water turned desperately against the centre, and, being repulsed, made a last effort on the left. Thus were life and courage prodigally wasted, till the bewildered English fired on an advanced party of their own, producing hopeless dejection; and, after losing in killed and wounded, nineteen hundred and forty-four, chiefly regulars, they fled promiscuously."—Bancroft's "History of the United States," IV., pp. 304-306.

July 9, Abercromby retreated from Ticonderoga.
July 26, General Amherst and Admiral Boscawen, Wolfe assisting, took Louisbourg, the "Dunkirk of America."
Aug. 8, Rogers, Putnam, and Dalzell, with 700 provincials, scattered 450 Canadians under Marin, near Lake George.
Aug. 27, Lieut.-Col. Bradstreet, with 3,000 provincials, took Fort Frontenac.
Sept. 14, Major Grant was defeated near Fort Du Quesne, losing 300 men.

Sept. 18, Abercromby was recalled, Amherst succeeding him.
Oct. 2, The first representative government in Canada met at Halifax.
Nov. 25, Gen. Forbes took possession of Fort Du Quesne, abandoned by the French : he named it Fort Pitt.

1759.

Jan. By a census, the men in Canada capable of bearing arms were 15,229.
June 1, The British fleet, under Admiral Saunders, bearing Wolfe and his army, left Louisbourg for Quebec.
June 26, The British fleet anchored off Orleans Island.
June 27, A storm tossed the British fleet at Quebec.
June 28, Wolfe issued a proclamation to the Canadians.
At night the Canadians sent fire-ships and burning rafts against the British fleet, but the British sailors towed them ashore, where they were soon in cinders.
June 29, Monckton sent a detachment to take possession of Beaumont church.
June 30, Monckton took possession of Point Levis.
July 1, Gen. Prideaux left Oswego to take Fort Niagara.
July 6, Haldimand drove La Corne from Oswego.
July 9, Wolfe landed 3,000 men below the cataract of Montmorenci, who entrenched themselves.
July 12, The British began to bombard Quebec.
At night, Dumas, with sixteen hundred soldiers, mostly boys, crossed the St. Lawrence, intending to surprise the British at Levis ; but, his force marching in two columns, one part in the darkness fired on the other. This fire being returned, a panic ensued, and the enterprise failed. It has been called "The Scholars' Battle," most of the boys being students.
July 18, Two British men-of-war passed above the city of Quebec
July 19, Gen. Prideaux was killed at Niagara, by the premature bursting of a shell from a Coehorn mortar.
July 21, Carleton led an expedition to Point aux Trembles, above Quebec.
July 24, Sir William Johnson crushed a relief party that attempted to succor Niagara, and took Aubry, De

Ligneris, Marin, De Montigny, and Repentigny, all famous bush-fighters, prisoners.

July 25, Pouchot surrendered Niagara to Sir William Johnson.

July 31, Wolfe landed a picked body of men at Montmorenci ; but they were defeated with a loss of over 400.

Amherst took Ticonderoga and Crown Point, about this time.

Aug. 9, De Levis left Quebec to guard the western frontier.

Sept. 2, "In this situation, there is such a choice of difficulties, that I am myself at a loss how to determine. The affairs of Great Britain require most vigorous measures ; but then the courage of a handful of brave men should be exerted only where there is some hope."—Wolfe to Pitt.

Sep, 13, At one o'clock in the morning Wolfe began to land his men at Anse au Foulon (Wolfe's Cove.) They scrambled up the rugged heights, the 78th Highlanders, headed by Captain Donald Macdonald, leading the way ; and soon established themselves on the plateau above, DeVergor not keeping a good lookout. Wolfe soon had 3,800 men in battle array on the Plains of Abraham ; Monckton commanded the right, Murray the centre, and Townsend the left.

"Every officer knew his appointed duty, when, at one o'clock in the morning of the thirteenth of September, Wolfe, with Monckton and Murray, and about half the forces, set off in boats, and, without sail or oars, glided down with the tide. In three-quarters of an hour the ships followed, and, though the night had become dark, aided by the rapid current, they reached the cove just in time to cover the landing. Wolfe and the troops with him leaped on shore ; the light infantry, who found themselves borne by the current a little below the intrenched path, clambered up the steep hill, staying themselves by the roots and boughs of the maple and spruce and ash trees that covered the precipitous declivity, and, after a little firing, dispersed the picket which guarded the height. The rest ascended safely by the pathway. A battery of four guns on the left was abandoned to Colonel Howe. When Townsend's division disembarked, the English had already gained one of the roads to Quebec, and, advancing in front of the forest, Wolfe stood at daybreak with his invincible battalions on the Plains of Abraham, the battlefield of empire.

"'It can be but a small party come to burn a few houses and retire,' said Montcalm, in amazement as the news reached him in his intrenchments the other side of the St. Charles ; but, obtaining better information,—'Then,' he cried, 'they have at last got to the weak side of this miserable garrison ; we must give battle and crush them before mid-day.' And before ten the two armies, equal in numbers, each being composed of less than five thousand men, were ranged in presence of one another for battle. The English, not easily accessible from intervening shallow ravines and rail fences, were all regulars, perfect in discipline, terrible in their fearless enthusiasm, thrilling with pride at their morning's success, commanded by a man whom they obeyed with confidence and love. The doomed and devoted Montcalm had what Wolfe had called but 'five-weak French battalions,' of less than two thousand men, 'mingled with disorderly peasantry,' formed on ground which commanded the position of the English. The French had three little pieces of artillery ; the English one or two. The two armies cannonaded each other for nearly an hour, when Montcalm, having summoned Bougainville to his aid, and dispatched messenger after messenger for De Vaudreuil, who had fifteen hundred men at the camp, to come up, before he should be driven from the ground, endeavored to flank the British and crowd them down the high bank of the river. Wolfe counteracted the movement by detaching Townshend with Amherst's regiment, and afterwards a part of the Royal Americans, who formed on the left with a double front.

"Waiting no longer for more troops, Montcalm led the French army impetuously to the attack. The ill-disciplined companies broke by their precipitation and the unevenness of the ground ; and fired by platoons without unity. The English, especially the forty-third and forty-seventh, where Monckton stood, received the shock with calmness, and, after having at Wolfe's command reserved their fire till their enemy was within forty yards, their line began a regular, rapid and exact discharge of musketry. Montcalm was present everywhere, braving danger, wounded, but cheering by his example. The second in command, De Sennezergues, an associate in glory at Ticonderoga, was killed. The brave but untried Canadians, flinching from a hot fire in the open field, began to waver ; and, so soon as Wolfe, placing himself at the head of the twenty-eighth and the Louisburg grenadiers, charged with bayonets, they everywhere gave way. Of the English officers, Carleton was wounded ; Barre, who fought near Wolfe, received in the head a ball which destroyed the power of vision of one eye, and ultimately made him blind. Wolfe, also, as he led the charge, was wounded in the wrist, but still pressing forward, he received a second ball ; and having decided the day, was struck a third time, and mortally, in the breast. 'Support me,' he cried to an officer near him ; 'let not my brave fellows see me drop.' He was carried to the rear, and they brought him water to quench his thirst. 'They run, they run!' spoke the officer on whom he leaned. 'Who run?' asked Wolfe, as his life was fast ebbing. 'The French,' replied the officer, 'give way everywhere.' 'What,' cried the expiring hero, 'do they run already? Go, one of you, to Colonel Burton; bid him march Webb's regiment with all speed to Charles River to cut off the fugitives.' Four days before he had looked forward to early death with dismay. 'Now, God be praised, I die happy!' These were his words as his spirit escaped in the blaze of his glory. Night, silence, the rushing tide, veteran discipline, the sure inspiration of genius, had been his allies: his battlefield, high over the ocean river, was the grandest theatre on earth for illustrious deeds; his victory, one of the most momentous in the annals of mankind, gave to the English tongue and the institutions of the Germanic race the unexplored and seemingly infinite west and north. He crowded into a few hours actions that would have given lustre to length of life; and filling his day with greatness, completed it before its noon.

"Monckton, the first brigadier, after greatly distinguishing himself, was shot through the lungs. The next in command, Townshend, brave but deficient in sagacity and attractive power, and the delicate perception of right, recalled the troops from the pursuit, and when De Bougainville appeared in view, declined a contest with a fresh enemy. But already the hope of New France was gone. Born and educated in camps, Montcalm had been carefully instructed, and was skilled in the language of Homer as well as in the art of war. Greatly laborious, just, disinterested, hopeful even to rashness, sagacious in council, swift in action, his mind was a well-spring of bold designs; his career in Canada a wonderful struggle against inexorable destiny. Sustaining hunger and cold, vigils and incessant toil, anxious for his soldiers, unmindful of himself, he set, even to the forest-trained red-men, an example of self-denial and endurance; and in the midst of corruption made the public good his aim. Struck by a musket-ball as he fought opposite Monckton, he continued in the engagement, till, in attempting to rally a body of fugitive Canadians in a copse near St. John's gate, he was mortally wounded.

"On hearing from the surgeon that death was certain—'I am glad of it,' he cried; 'how long shall I survive?' 'Ten or twelve hours, perhaps less.' 'So much the better; I shall not live to see the surrender of Quebec.' To the council of war he showed that in twelve hours all the troops near at hand might be concentrated and renew the attack before the English were entrenched. When De Ramsay, who commanded the garrison, asked his advice about defending the city—'To your keeping,' he replied, 'I commend the honor of France. As for me, I shall pass the night with God, and prepare myself for death.' Having written a letter recommending the French prisoners to the generosity of the English, his last hours were given to the hope of endless life, and at five the next morning he expired.

"The day of the battle had not passed when De Vaudreuil, who had no capacity for war, wrote to De Ramsay, at Quebec, not to wait for an assault, but, as soon as his provisions were exhausted to raise the white flag of surrender. 'We have cheerfully sacrificed our fortunes and our houses,' said the citizens, 'but we cannot expose our wives and children to a massacre.' At a council of war, Fiedmont, a captain of artillery, was the only one who wished to hold out to the last extremity : and on the seventeenth of September, before the English had constructed batteries, De Ramsay capitulated."—Bancroft's "History of the United States," Vol. IV., pp. 333-338.

Major Rogers destroyed the Abenakis of St. Francis.
Sept. 21, Gen. Murray was made Governor of Quebec.
Oct. 18, Admiral Saunders, with the British fleet, left Quebec for England; Monckton and Townshend accompanied him ; and the "Royal William" bore the embalmed remains of Gen. Wolfe.
Nov. 28, Eight French ships passed down the river in front of Quebec, at night, and escaped to the ocean.

1760.

April 17, De Levis left Montreal to take Quebec.
April 28, De Levis defeated Murray at Sainte Foye.
May 9, The "Lowestoff," a British frigate, arrived at Quebec.
May 15, Admiral Swanton arrived at Quebec with a British fleet.
May 17, De Levis raised the siege of Quebec.
July 14, Gen. Murray, with 2,200 men, left Quebec for Montreal.
Aug. 10, Gen. Amherst, with 10,000 men, left Oswego for Montreal.
Aug. 16, Gen. Haviland, with 3,500 men, left Crown Point for Montreal.
Aug. 26, Amherst took Fort Levis, a little below La Presentation (Ogdensburg.)
Aug. 29, Gen. Haviland took possession of St. John, deserted by the French.
Sept. 8, At Montreal, Vaudreuil surrendered Canada to Amherst. Military Rule was now begun in Canada.

Sept. 13, Major Rogers, with 200 rangers, left Montreal, by order of Amherst, to take possession of Detroit, Mackinaw, and other western posts.
Jonathan Belcher was made Governor of Nova Scotia.
Sept. 16, Brig.-Gen. Burton was made Governor of Three Rivers.
Sept. 21, General Gage was made Governor of Montreal.
Oct. 25, George III. became king of England.
Nov. 17, Major Rogers had a conference with Pontiac, an Ottawa chief, on the site of Cleveland, Ohio.
Nov. 20, Belêtre surrendered Detroit to Rogers.

1761.

June 6, (John Winthrop, of Harvard, Mass., at St. John's, Newfoundland, observed the transit of Venus over the sun's disk.)
Captain Campbell, commander at Detroit, learned that the Senecas were intriguing with the neighboring Wyandots to destroy him and the garrison.

1763.

Feb. 10, Treaty of Paris: Great Britain obtained Canada, Nova Scotia, and Cape Breton, and the West Indian islands of St. Vincent, Dominica, Tobago, and Grenada; the king of Great Britain was to allow his new Catholic subjects to profess the worship of their religion according to the rule of the Catholic Church as far as the laws of Great Britain would permit; France obtained the Islands of Guadaloupe, Martinique, and St. Lucia, and the right to fish around Newfoundland and in the St. Lawrence Gulf. Maddened by neglect, insult, and loss of territory, several tribes of Indians, under Pontiac, conspired for the destruction of the British in the North-West.
May 6, Gladwyn, commander at Detroit, received secret information that on the next day Pontiac would attempt to capture the fort by treachery.
May 7, Gladwyn admitted Pontiac and sixty of his chiefs into Fort Detroit; they had their shortened guns concealed under their blankets; but Gladwyn expos-

ed their meditated treachery and dismissed them in contempt.

Col. M. Wilmot was made Governor of Nova Scotia.

May 9, Pontiac attacked Detroit.
May 16, Indians took Fort Sandusky.
May 25, Indians took Fort St. Joseph, near head of Lake Michigan.
May 28, Lieutenant Cuyler's relief detachment for Detroit was surprised and overpowered at Point Pelee.
June 1, Indians took Ouatanon, on the Wabash.
June 4, Indians, beguiling the garrison of Mackinaw with a game of lacrosse, at a concerted signal, when the soldiers were off their guard and the gates of the fort open, rushed inside and began an indiscriminate massacre, Captain Etherington, the commander, escaping the slaughter.
June 17, Indians took Presqu'-Isle.
June 19, Indians took Le Bœuf and Venango.
June 24, A schooner, having beaten off a horde of Indians at Turkey Island, in Detroit River, brought men, amunition, and provisions to Detroit.
July 27, Indians began the siege of Fort Pitt.
July 31, Captain Dalzell was defeated and killed at Bloody Run, near Detroit.
Aug. 5, Colonel Bouquet, leading an army to relieve Fort Pitt, was, early in the afternoon, attacked by Indians at Bushy Run, Pa., who fought the weary soldiers till night.
Aug. 6, At daylight, the Indians renewed the fight at Bushy Run; at ten o'clock, by a masterly stratagem conceived on the spot, Bouquet drew out the Indians, threw a body of men on their flank, and utterly routed them.
Aug. 10, Bouquet relieved Fort Pitt
Aug. 13, The schooners "Beaver" and "Gladwyn" left Detroit to get provisions.
Sept. 14, A train of waggons and pack horses, escorted by 24 soldiers, returning from Fort Schlosser to Fort Niagara, were, at the Devil's Hole, surprised and massacred or driven over the precipice by the Senecas; two companies of light infantry that hurried to the spot were similarly destroyed.

Oct. 7, By royal proclamation, the Treaty of Paris went into effect in Canada; Cape Breton and St. John's Island were "annexed with the lesser islands adjacent thereto to our government of Nova Scotia;" and the king gave to "such reduced officers and soldiers as have served in North America during the late war and are actually residing there," wild lands in the following proportions:—every field officer, 5,000 acres; every captain, 3,000 acres; every subaltern, 2,000 acres; every non-commissioned officer, 200 acres; and every private, 50 acres.

Oct. 21, Gen. Murray was appointed Governor-General of Canada.

1764.

June 21, Messrs. Brown and Gilbert issued the first number of the "Quebec Gazette," half in French and half in English; this was the first newspaper in provincial Canada. It began with 150 subscribers.

Bradstreet left Albany with an army for the Upper Lakes.

July, Sir William Johnson held a great council at Niagara, and made treaties with various tribes of Indians.

Aug. 10, Gen. Murray took office as Governor-General of Canada. Military Rule in Canada was now ended.

Aug. 13, Bradstreet, near Presqu'-Isle, made an unauthorized treaty with the Delawares and Shawnees.

Aug. 26, Bradstreet relieved Detroit, and sent Capt. Howard to repossess Mackinaw.

Aug. 31, Bradstreet superseded Gladwyn at Detroit.

Oct., Captain Holland began the survey of St. John's Island.

Nov., Colonel Bouquet led an army into the country of the Delawares and Shawnees, humbled them, and forced them to return all white prisoners.

1765.

March 22, (The Stamp Act received royal assent; by this Act "all instruments in writing were to be executed on stamped paper, to be purchased from agents of the British Government," to go into effect Nov. 1, same year.)

A catechism was published in Quebec; it was the first book printed in Canada.

Rev. George Henry, a Presbyterian minister, began to preach in Quebec; his "services were conducted in an apartment in the Jesuit college."

1766.

Lord W. Campbell was made Governor of Nova Scotia.

March 18, (The House of Commons repealed the Stamp Act.)

April 28, Gov.-Gen. Murray left Canada, deputing his functions to Lieut.-Col. Æmilius Irving.

July 23, Pontiac met Sir Wm. Johnson at Oswego, and confirmed his assent to peace.

Sept. 23, Governor Carleton arrived at Quebec, to be Lieut.-Gov. and acting Gov.-Gen.

1767.

June 10, The "Hope," sent by the Philadelphia Company, entered Pictou harbor, Nova Scotia, bringing the "Pictou Colony."

Island of St. John (Prince Edward Island) was granted to proprietors.

1768.

An Illinois Indian, bribed by an English trader, assassinated Pontiac, at Cahokia, opposite St. Louis.

Oct. 25, Gen. Carleton, Lord Dorchester, became Governor-General of Canada.

1770.

Prince Edward Island was separated from Nova Scotia and made an independent province.

Walter Patterson was made the first Governor of Prince Edward Island.

July 3, In Halifax, the Presbyterian ministers, Lyon and Murdoch, and the Congregational ministers, Seccombe and Phelps, ordained Mr. Bruin Romcas Comingoe to the ministry; this was the first Presbytery and the first Presbyterian ordination in Canada.

Aug. 13, Gov. Carleton left Canada to visit England, leaving Hector Theophile Cramahe to administer the government.

1771.

Samuel Hearne discovered the Coppermine River.
Sir Gordon Drummond was born in Quebec.

1773.

Francis Legge was made Governor of Nova Scotia.

1774.

May 2, The Earl of Dartmouth introduced the Quebec Act into the House of Lords.

June 22, Quebec Act received royal assent: it extended the boundaries of Canada westward to the Mississippi, and southward to the Ohio; it assured to Catholics the free exercise of their religion, and it declared that "the clergy of the Catholic Church may hold, receive and enjoy their accustomed dues and rights with respect to such persons only as shall profess the said religion"; the Custom of Paris was to be continued in disputes relative to property and civil rights, but in criminal matters the law of England was to hold; the Government was to be an Executive Council of not more than twenty-three members nor less than seventeen.

Sept. 5, (The First American Congress met in Carpenters' Hall, Philadelphia.)

Oct. 26, The American Congress invited the Canadians to send delegates to represent their province in the "Continental Congress."

1775.

April 19, (Skirmish at Lexington, the beginning of the American Revolution.)
May 1, Quebec Act went into force.
May 10, Ethan Allan took Ticonderoga.
May 29, Congress issued an address to the Canadians.
    Rev. Wm. Black settled at Amherst, Nova Scotia.
    In this year the curious disease, "St. Paul's Bay disease," attained serious prominence in Canada.
June 17, (Battle of Bunker Hill or Breed's Hill.)
Aug. 2, Sir Guy Carleton was made Commander of the forces in Canada.

Sept. 18, Benedict Arnold, with 1,200 men, embarked at Newburyport for the Kennebec River, beginning his expedition to Quebec.
Sept. 25, Ethan Allan was taken prisoner while trying to take Montreal.
Oct. 31, Gen. Montgomery took St. John's.
Nov. 3, The Americans took Chambly.
Nov. 8, The American Congress sent Robert R. Livingston, John Langdon, and Robert Treat Paine, to examine the fortifications of Ticonderoga, and "to use their endeavors to procure an accession of the Canadians to a union with these colonies."
Nov. 9, Arnold, having led an army through the wilderness of Maine, arrived at Point Levis.
Nov. 11, Carleton left Montreal for Quebec.
Nov. 13, Carleton entered Quebec, having adroitly eluded the Americans in his flight from Montreal.
Arnold, with 650 men, crossed the St. Lawrence to Wolfe's Cove and led his men up to the Plains of Abraham.
Montgomery took Montreal.
Nov. 14, Arnold attacked the Gate of St. Louis, Quebec, but was speedily repulsed.
Dec. 1, Gen. Montgomery joined Arnold at Point aux Trembles.
Dec. 20, Lord Mansfield, in the House of Lords, declared that he "ever since the peace of Paris always thought the Northern Colonies were meditating a state of independency of Great Britain."
Dec. 31, Montgomery and Arnold made careful preparations to assault Quebec.

1776.

Jan. 1, At 4 a.m the Americans began the assault of Quebec; Montgomery was killed; Arnold's men, to the number of 431, surrendered at Sault-au-Matelot, and Arnold was severely wounded.

"When Gen. Montgomery was killed he had in his pocket a watch which Mrs. Montgomery was very desirous to obtain. This was made known to Gen. Arnold, and he applied to Governor Carleton, offering any price for the watch, which he might choose to demand. Carleton immediately sent it out, but would suffer nothing to be received in return."— Jared Sparks' "Life of Arnold," p. 54.

Jan. 29, Gen. Schuyler took Johnson Hall, New York, the home of Sir Wm. Johnson.

April 1, The American General, Wooster, arrived at Quebec and superseded Arnold.

April 29, Benjamin Franklin, Chase, Carroll, and Rev. John Carroll arrived at Montreal ; they were sent by Congress to induce Canadians to rebel against Great Britain.

May 1, Gen. John Thomas took command of the Americans at Quebec.

May 6, Carleton, having received reinforcements, drove Gen. Thomas and his men in headlong flight from Quebec.

May 19, Major Isaac Butterfield, American, surrendered the post at the Cedars and 390 men to Captain George Foster.

June 2, Gen. Thomas died of small pox and was succeeded in command by Gen. John Sullivan.

June 7, Richard Henry Lee, of Virginia, said, in Congress, "Resolved that these United States are, and of right ought to be, free and independent states." John Adams, of Massachusetts, seconded it.

June 8, The Americans under Col. St. Clair, were defeated at Three Rivers.

> "The American loss in the battle of Three Rivers was about two hundred prisoners and twenty-five killed, most of the latter being from Wayne's and Maxwell's divisions, who had borne the brunt of the fight. Chaplain McCalla, of the 1st Pennsylvania, was among the prisoners. The British loss was eight killed, including a sergeant of the 31st, and three men of the 20th Regiment, and nine wounded, eight of whom were of the 62nd regiment."—Jones' "Campaign for the Conquest of Canada."

June 11, An American Order of the Day at Sorel : "Every non-commissioned officer or soldier who shall come to the parade dirty, with a long beard, or his breeches knees open, shall be mulcted of a day's allowance of provision, and do a double tour of duty."

June 13, Arnold, at Montreal, wrote to Gen. Sullivan, "The junction of the Canadas with the colonies is now at an end. Let us quit them, and secure our own country before it is too late."

June 15, Canadians re-took Montreal.

July 4, The American Congress adopted the Declaration of Independence.

1777.

May 6, Gen. Burgoyne arrived at Quebec.
May 20, Carleton wrote to Lord Germain, defending his military conduct in Canada, and submitting to being superseded by Burgoyne.
June 27, Carleton left Canada.
July 6, Burgoyne took Ticonderoga, abandoned by the Americans.
Sept. 13, Burgoyne crossed the Hudson.
Oct. 17, Burgoyne surrendered to Gen. Gates at Saratoga.

1778.

March 7, Capt. James Cook touched the west coast in latitude 44 degrees north.
June 3, The *Montreal Gazette* first appeared.
June 26, Gen. Frederic Haldimand arrived at Quebec, as Governor-General of Canada.
Rev. Raphael Cohen settled in Montreal, the first Rabbi in Canada.
Robert Land settled on the site of Hamilton, Ont.
Nov. 19, Charles Michel d'Irumberry de Salaberry was born at Beauport, Lower Canada.
Dec. 17, Henry Hamilton, Governor of Detroit, took Vincennes.

1779.

Feb. 24, Geo. Rogers Clark took Vincennes, making Hamilton prisoner and securing for the U.S. the district of Michigan, Indiana, etc.

1780.

May 19, " Dark Day." at 10 a.m. darkness began to shadow the country; at 2 p.m. no one could see without artificial light. In New England the people supposed the day of judgment had come.
Mr. Tuffey, a commissary of the 44th regiment, and a Methodist, began to preach in Quebec.
Oct. 31, The " Ontario," a new vessel of 16 guns, with a full crew and thirty men of the 34th regiment, left Niagara. She was seen near the north shore of

Lake Ontario a day or two later, but she and all on board were lost.

1781.

July 9, Articles of Confederation were ratified by the United States Congress.

Oct. 19, Cornwallis surrendered at Yorktown.

1782.

June 11, Rev. William Black preached the first Methodist sermon in Halifax.

John Parr was made Governor of Nova Scotia.

1783.

Jan. 20, An armistice, declaring a cessation of hostilities between Great Britain and the United States, was concluded.

May 4, Four hundred and seventy-one families of United Empire Loyalists, from New York, landed at Shelburne, Nova Scotia.

May 18, United Empire Loyalists from New York landed at the mouth of the St. John River, New Brunswick, and began Parrtown (St. John.)

Sept. 3, Treaty of Paris: by this treaty Great Britain recognized the independence of the United States, admitted the right of the people of the United States "to enjoy unmolested the right to take fish of every kind on the Grand Bank and on all the other banks of Newfoundland, also in the Gulf of the St. Lawrence, and at all the other places in the sea where the inhabitants of both countries used at any time heretofore to fish." This was signed by David Hartley for Great Britain, and by John Adams, Benjamin Franklin, and John Jay for the United States.

In the fall, many United Empire Loyalists came to Canada, and wintered, before settling on their grants.

1784.

United Empire Loyalists settled along the St. Lawrence River and on the Bay of Quinte. Butler's rangers settled near Niagara.

June 2, Rev. John Stuart, "the father of the Upper Canada Church," began pastoral duties.

May 22, At Niagara, Sir John Johnson purchased the Grand River Reserve from the Mississagas.

Aug. 16, New Brunswick was detached from Nova Scotia and made an independent province. Thomas Carlton was the first Governor of New Brunswick.

Oct. 1, La Corne de St. Luc died in Montreal.

Oct. 25, At Quebec, Governor Haldimand, in the name of the Crown, granted to the Mohawks and others of the Six Nations the tract of land "upon the banks of the river Ouise, commonly called Grand River, running into Lake Erie, of six miles breadth from each side of the river, beginning at Lake Erie and extending in that proportion to the head of said river; which the Mohawks, and others of the Six Nations who had either lost their possessions in the war, or wished to retire from them to the British, with their posterity, were to enjoy forever."

Nov. 15, Governor Haldimand went to England, leaving Henry Hamilton to administer the government.

1785.

Feb. 22, The laws of England were declared to be in force in Cape Breton Island.

May 18, Parrtown was incorporated and named St. John; this was the first town in Canada to be incorporated. Rev. Dr. Stuart opened a classical school at Kingsston; it was the first school in Upper Canada.

Oct. 9, At 4 p.m., a sudden darkness overspread the country, "partaking of a fiery yellow colour;" a storm followed.

Oct. 15, At 3 p.m., there was another period of darkness, followed by a storm.

Nov. 2, Hamilton resigned, and Hope assumed the administration of the government in Canada.

1786.

The Mohawks, on the Grand River, built the first church in Upper Canada.

Gen. Neal entered the Niagara district.

Seven counties were formed in New Brunswick.

Oct. 7, Louis Joseph Papineau was born in Montreal.

Geo. E. Fanning was made Governor of Prince Edward Island.

Oct. 23, Carleton, Lord Dorchester, arrived as Governor-General of Canada the second time.
The Government of New Brunswick moved to St. Anne's Point, beginning Fredericton.

1787.

About this time the "St. Paul's Bay disease" disappeared.

Aug. 12, Rev. Charles Inglis, at Lambeth, was consecrated the first Anglican Bishop of Nova Scotia, with jurisdiction over the other North American provinces.
Rev. John Bethune, Presbyterian, settled at Williamstown, Upper Canada.

Sept. 17, (Congress adopted the Constitution of the United States.)

Oct. 1, Joseph Remi Valliers de St. Real, jurist, was born in Markham, Upper Canada, or in Quebec.

1788.

July 24, Lord Dorchester divided Upper Canada into four judicial districts: Lunenberg, from the river Ottawa to Gananoque; Mecklenburg, from Gananoque to Trent; Nassau, from Trent to Long Point; and Hesse, from Long Point to Lake St. Clair; he appointed a judge and sheriff to administer justice in each district.

This has been called the "Hungry Year," the people being barely able to subsist.

Nov. 1, Under the direction of Bishop Inglis an academy was opened at Windsor, Nova Scotia; it was the beginning of King's College.

1789.

June 11, Bishop Inglis arrived at Quebec.
A dockyard was established at Kingston, Upper Canada.

Aug. 5, The "first episcopal conference of the Protestant Church" was held in the Recollets' Church, Quebec.

Nov. 9, By an Order in-Council it was declared that every son of a Loyalist should have, when of age, 200 acres of land; that every daughter of a Loyalist should have, when married, 200 acres of land; and that the descendants of those who had been loyal to Great Britain in the Revolutionary War should have their names distinguished from the names of other people by the letters " U. E."

1790.

Rev. Lossee, the first regular minister of the Methodist Church in Upper Canada, began to preach in the Bay of Quinte district.

1791.

Feb. 20, The first regular class (Methodist) in Upper Canada was organized at Adolphustown.

March 7, Mr. Pitt introduced a Bill into the House of Commons to divide Canada into two provinces.

March 14, The Constitutional Act became law : it divided Canada into two parts, Lower and Upper ; each province was to have an Executive Council crown appointed, Lower Canada to have no fewer than fifteen members and Upper Canada no fewer than seven members, and each was to have a Legislative Assembly, the members for Lower Canada to be no less than fifty and for Upper Canada to be no less than sixteen : and it granted one-seventh of the crown lands in each province " for the support and maintenance of a Protestant clergy within the same."

July 26, Birth of John Beverley Robinson

Aug. 17, Lord Dorchester returned to England, leaving Major-General Clarke to administer the government.

Nov. 18, By a royal proclamation, made at Quebec, it was declared that the Constitutional Act should go into effect, Dec. 26, 1791.

Dec. 26, The Constitutional Act went into effect.

1792.

May 7, Lower Canada was divided into fifty counties.

> " The Montreal congregation (Presbyterian) erected the church known afterwards as St. Gabriel Street Church, accommodation having been furnished up to that time in a church belonging to the Order of the Recollets."—Robertson's " History of Presbyterian Missions in Canada."

July 8, Lieut. Col John Graves Simcoe was sworn in as Lieut.-Gov. of Upper Canada.

July 29, Hon. William Osgoode was made Chief Justice of Upper Canada.

Sept 15, The Methodist Church in Upper Canada was organized at Bay Quinte.

Rev. Mr. Addison opened a school at Newark (Niagara.)

Sept. 17, Lieut.-Gov. Simcoe convened the first parliament of Upper Canada at Newark. In a month it introduced English law, established trial by jury, regulated millers' tolls, legislated for the recovery of small debts, for erecting a jail and court-house in each district, and for re-naming the districts, for the regulation of weights and measures, for regulating the court of common pleas, and to prevent accidents by fire.

Nineteen counties were formed in Upper Canada.

John Wentworth was made Governor of Nova Scotia.

Oct. 16, In Upper Canada, Hesse was changed to Western District, Nassau to Home District, Mecklenburg to Midland District, aud Lunenburg to Eastern District.

Dec. 17, The first parliament of Lower Canada met in Quebec.

Dec. 18, M. J. A. Panet was elected President of Lower Canada Parliament.

Population of Upper Canada 20,000.

Population of Lower Canada 130,000.

Dec. 20, A fortnightly mail was established between Canada and the United States.

1793.

April 1, Brant obtained for the Mohawks the Bay of Quinte Reserve.

April 18, The first number of the *Upper Canada Gazette* appeared at Niagara ; it was the first newspaper in Upper Canada. Its size was fifteen by nine and a half inches; its price $3 a year.

June 14, Lieut.-Gov. Simcoe gave the Mohawks, and others of the Six Nations, an official patent to their reserve on the Grand River.

July 7, The Archbishop of Canterbury, the Bishop of London, the Bishop of Bangor, and the Bishop of St. David's consecrated Dr. Jacob Mountain, Bishop of Quebec.

July 9, By an Act of the Legislature of Upper Canada, all slave children born in Upper Canada after this date shall be free at the age of 25.
July 22, On the Pacific Coast, Mackenzie wrote in letters of red vermilion, on a bold rock, "Alexander Mackenzie, from Canada by land, the twenty-second of July, one thousand seven hundred and ninety-three."
Aug. 27, Toronto became York, the change of name being proclaimed by the first royal salute from the garrison.
Joseph Bouchette surveyed the harbour of York, Upper Canada.
Some of Lord Selkirk's settlers began "Baldoon," Kent, Upper Canada.
Rev. Jabez Colver settled in Norfolk, Upper Canada.
Nov. 1, Lord Dorchester arrived in Quebec.

1794.

A Baptist Church was organized at Caldwell's Manor, Lower Canada.
Captain Samuel Ryerson settled in Norfolk, Upper Canada.
Rev. Robert Dunn settled near Niagara.
May 31, The Alien Act was passed in Upper Canada.
Sept. 14, William Osgoode was sworn in Chief Justice of Lower Canada.
Nov. 19, A Treaty of amity, commerce, and navigation, "Jay's Treaty," was concluded between Great Britain and the United States.
Dec. 5, Lieut.-Gov. Simcoe went from York to Kingston in an open boat.

1795.

Sept. 5, Etienne Paschal Tache, statesman, was born at St. Thomas, Lower Canada.

1796.

Jan. 29, The last English Court of General Quarter Sessions was held in Detroit.
Augustus Jones, surveyor, reported: "Went to the garrison, York, and waited on His Excellency the Governor, and informed him that Yonge Street

is opened from York to the Pine Fort Landing, Lake Simcoe."

A part of the North-West Company formed an independent trading company, which became known as the X. Y. Z. Company.

Mr. Silas Knowlton, of Vermont, settled in the township of Stukeley, Lower Canada.

July 9, Lord Dorchester left Canada.

Rev. John Bethune, at Williamstown, built the first Presbyterian Church in Upper Canada.

500 Maroons were brought from Jamaica to Nova Scotia.

April 27, Major-General Prescott became Governor-General of Canada.

Upper Canada Parliament moved from Newark to York.

July 21, David McLane was executed at Quebec, for conspiring against the Government.

1798.

April 20, Sir William Edmond Logan, geologist, was born in Montreal.

Newark became Niagara.

Dec. 1, The *Gazette and Oracle*, at York, said :

> "Last Monday William Hawkins was publicly whipped, and Joseph McCarthy burned in the hand, at the market place, pursuant to their sentence."

1799.

March 2, The *Gazette and Oracle*, at York, said :

> "Married on Tuesday last, by William Willcocks, Esq., Sergeant Mealy, of the Queen's Rangers, to Miss M. Wright, of this town." Mr. Willcocks was a layman.

June 3, By proclamation Ile Saint Jean became Prince Edward Island.

July 31, Mr. Ralph Merry, of Massachusetts, settled on 1,000 acres of land at Magog Outlet, Lower Canada.

Dec. 31, John Strachan arrived at Kingston.

The Danforth road was finished from York to Hope Township, sixty miles.

Jan. 3, Behind the government building in York, John White, Attorney-General, and John Small, Clerk of the

Executive Council, fought a duel, the former being mortally wounded.

March 15, Father Jean Joseph Casot, the last Jesuit in Canada, died in Quebec; then the Crown appropriated the remaining possessions of the Order in Canada.

March 20, The *Quebec Gazette* said :

"On Sunday last, the 15th inst., died the reverend father Jean Joseph Casot, priest, of the company of Jesus, procurer of the missions and colleges of the Jesuits in Canada, the last of the Jesuits of this Province. The immense charities which he bestowed assure him for a long time the blessing of the poor. He was one of those men whose life is a hidden treasure, and his death is a public calamity."

The Maroons, not doing well in Nova Scotia, were shipped to Sierra Leone.

Lieut.-Governor Simcoe granted 8,000 acres of land in the County of York, U.C., to Timothy Rogers, a Quaker.

The first Baptist Association in Canada was organized at Granville, L.C.

July 18, College of New Brunswick, Fredericton, was chartered.

Dec. 4, Sir William Fenwick Williams, the defender of Kars, was born at Annapolis Royal, Nova Scotia.

Mr. David Thompson, of Montreal, crossed the Rocky mountains, in latitude 51 degrees north.

1801.

Jan. 25, Joseph Octave Plessis was consecrated Bishop of Quebec.

Mr. Sawyer built the first Methodist church in Upper Canada.

Mr. Ogilvie erected a flour mill at Jacques Cartier, near Quebec.

Rev. Daniel W. Eastman settled near Niagara.

Rev. Mr. Benton organized the first Congregational church in Quebec.

1802.

Jan. 3, The *Niagara Herald* announced :

"For sale : A negro man slave, 18 years of age, stout and healthy; has had the small-pox, and is capable of service either in the house or out of doors. The terms will be made

easy to the purchaser, and cash or new lands received in payment. Enquire of the printer."
Three hundred Highlanders settled at Sydney, Cape Breton Island.

1803.

March 24, Adolphus Egerton Ryerson was born in Charlotteville, Norfolk County, U.C.
Dr. McCulloch came to Nova Scotia.
May 21, Thomas Talbot began his settlement at Port Talbot, U.C.
Chief Justice Osgoode, in Montreal, declared slavery inconsistent with the laws of Canada.
July 12, Augustin Norbert Morin was born in St. Michel, L.C.
August, Eight hundred colonists from Skye, Uist, Ross, Argyle, and Inverness, under the direction of Lord Selkirk, landed on Prince Edward Island.

1804.

March 2, Four mutineers and three deserters, of the 6th, 41st, and 49th regiments were executed at Quebec early in the morning. It was a revolting spectacle, being badly managed.
Rev. Alexander Macdonald settled Glengarry.
Sedition Act was passed in Upper Canada.
Oct. 8, The Government schooner, "Speedy," was lost on Lake Ontario; all her passengers were also lost, namely, Mr. Justice Cochrane; Robert J. D. Gray, Solicitor-General; Angus Macdonell, member of Assembly; Mr. Jacob Herchmer, merchant; Mr. John Stegman, surveyor; Mr. George Cowan, Indian interpreter; James Ruggles, Mr. Anderson, Mr. John Fisk, and an Indian, who was being taken to Newcastle to be tried for murder.
Dec. 13, Joseph Howe, statesman and orator, was born near Halifax.

1805.

Jan. 1, First number of Quebec *Mercury* was issued.
Col. Des Barres was made Governor of Prince Edward Island.
April 19, Rev. Reuben Garlick, the first clergyman of the English Church in the Eastern Townships, died at Waterloo, L.C.

The North-West Company and the X.Y.Z. Company amalgamated.
Dec. 25, John Anthony Baptist Ferland, priest and historian, was born in Montreal.

1806.

May 16, (Great Britain passed Orders-in-Council declaring a blockade of the European coast from the Elbe to Brest.)
The first timber raft was floated down the Ottawa River.
Sept. 27, Colonel Brock took command of the forces in Canada.
Oct. 10, William Weeks, member of Assembly for York, Durham, and Simcoe, was killed at Niagara by Mr. Dickson in a duel.
Nov. 21, (Napoleon, at Berlin, declared British ports blockaded.)
Nov. 22, *Le Canadien*, the first French newspaper in Canada, appeared.

1807.

June 1, Rev. Dr. Okill Stuart opened the "Home District School," on King Street, the first public school in Toronto.
June 22, (The British frigate "Leopard" fired into the American "Chesapeake," and took four seamen from her. Soon after, England made ample reparation for the "outrage.")
The Parliament of Upper Canada made provision for eight Grammar Schools, the master of each school to receive an annual salary of £100.
In August, Joseph Willcocks began *The Upper Canada Guardian, or Freeman's Journal* in Toronto.
Oct. 24, Sir James H. Craig began his duties as Governor-General of Canada.
Nov. 24, Joseph Brant died at Burlington, U.C.
Dec. 22, (The American Congress passed "Jefferson's Embargo," forbidding any vessel to leave an American port.)

1808.

Jan. 15, Sir George Prevost was made Lieut.-Governor of Nova Scotia.

March 2, John Henry wrote his first letter to Sir James Craig, through H. W. Ryland, Craig's Secretary, from Swanton, Vt., describing the condition of the country and the feeling of the people.

April 25, Malcolm Cameron was born in Three Rivers, L. C.

June 14, Governor Craig took from Lieut-Col. T. A. Panet, Capt. Bedard, Aide-Major Taschereau, Lieut. Borgia, and Surgeon Blanchet, their militia commissions. He did so, he said, because he considered them proprietors of *Le Canadien*, a seditious paper.

The first Methodist Church in Montreal was erected.

1809.

Jan. 9, Jonathan Sewell was made speaker of the Legislative Council, Lower Canada.

Jan. 31, Lemuel Allan Wilmot was born in Sunbury County, New Brunswick.

March 3, (The American Congress repealed the Embargo Act, and passed the Non-Intercourse Act, forbidding Americans to trade with Great Britain or France.)

June 15, François Xavier Garneau, historian, was born in Quebec.

Nov. 3, John Molson, of Montreal, sent the "Accommodation," the first steamboat on the St. Lawrence, from Montreal to Quebec ; she made the trip in 36 hours.

1810.

March 17, A magistrate, two constables, and a party of soldiers, suppressed *Le Canadien* in Quebec : it was a very arbitrary proceeding.

March 19, Messrs. Bedard, Blanchet, and Taschereau were arrested in Lower Canada for alleged seditious tendencies.

Barnabas Bidwell and his son, Marshall Bidwell, came from the United States and settled in the County of Addington, U.C.

Rev. Dr. Kier settled at Princetown, Prince Edward Island, and took charge of the first Presbyterian congregation on the Island.

The *News*, Kingston, U.C., now appeared.

1811.

May 16, (The " President " fired into the " Little Belt.")
June 12, The Earl of Selkirk, for 10 shillings, purchased from the Hudson's Bay Company 116,000 square miles of land in the Red River district.
Bishop Asbury, Methodist, came to Upper Canada. Sir John C. Sherbrooke was made Lieut.-Gov. of Nova Scotia.
June 19, Governor Craig embarked for England, leaving Mr. Dunn to administer the Government in Canada.
Sept. 12, Sir George Prevost landed at Quebec.
Oct. 9, Sir Isaac Brock assumed the Government of Upper Canada.
Captain Miles McDonell landed the first contingent of Selkirk's settlers at York Factory.

1812.

Feb. 10, President Madison gave John Henry $50,000 for the correspondence between Henry and Sir Jas. Craig, which Henry pretended contained evidence of British attempts to corrupt the loyalty of New Englanders.
Feb. 21, The Lower Canadian Parliament met, and soon granted £12,000 for drilling the militia, £20,000 for means of defence, and £30,000 for the Governor's use, should war be declared.
March 9, Henry's correspondence was read in Congress.
May 28, Lower Canada passed a general order, to embody four regiments of militia.
June 18, The United States declared war against Great Britain.

> " In June, 1812, the reasons for declaring war on Great Britain, though strong enough, were weaker than they had been in June, 1808, or in January, 1809. In the interval the British Government had laid aside the arrogant and defiant tones of Canning's diplomacy, had greatly modified the Orders-in-Council, had offered further modifications, and had atoned for the Chesapeake outrage."—Adams' " History of U.S.," VI., p. 225.
>
> The Orders-in-Council which almost ruined the foreign trade of the United States and the searching of American ships by British men-of-war for deserters, were intolerable to the Americans ; and were, if

impossible to adjust by negotiation, seemingly good reasons for war; but the "war hawks," the Calhouns, Clays, etc., disclosed the great reason for the declaration of war when they averred that Canada could be conquered in a short campaign by raw American militia. The time was opportune, for Great Britain was in a death struggle in Europe. Still the Americans were at their wits' end to give a decent pretext for declaring war.

"In the war message of June 1, these charges (British intrigues disclosed by Henry's letters) are repeated as among the reasons for an appeal to arms. . . . The Henry affair was declared an 'act of still greater malignity' than any of the other outrages against the United States of which Great Britain had been guilty, and that which 'excited the greatest horror.' . . . It was easy, therefore, to alarm the public with confessions of a secret emissary, as he pretended, who had turned traitor to the government which had employed him, and to the conspirators to whom he had been sent; and the more reprehensible was it, therefore, in a President of the United States, to make the use that was made of this story, which an impartial examination would have shown was essentially absurd, and infamously false. Mr. Madison's intelligence is not to be impugned. He was too sagacious, as well as too unimpassioned a man to be taken in by the ingenious tale of such an adventurer as Henry. . . . He accepted, then, the Henry story, in spite of his deliberate opinions, as a help to invoke the country in a party war."— Gay's "Life of Madison," pp. 309-315.

But, be it remembered, if Great Britain had been somewhat high-handed, the Americans had not been passive sufferers.

"The fitting out of privateers, and the capture of prizes by these privateers, as well as the seizure of British vessels within our waters, all leading to expostulation and demands for redress on the part of the English minister, confronted the administration in a constant succession of cases."— Lodge's "Life of Alex. Hamilton," p. 157.

June 23, Great Britain repealed the Orders-in-Council.

When it was known that war was declared, Lower Canada passed a Bill to legalize the issue of Army Bills to the amount of £250,000.

At this time the population of Canada was about 400,000; the population of the United States was fully 8,000,000.

A college was established at St. Hyacinthe, L.C.

July 3, Lieut. Rolette, at Malden, seized Gen. Hull's schooner "Cayahoga," which carried "his most valuable papers," plan of his campaign, etc.

July 3, All Americans were ordered to leave Canada.

July 12, Gen. Hull, with 2,500 Americans, crossed from Detroit to Sandwich.

July 15, Col. Lewis Cass vainly tried to pass the River aux Canards, below Sandwich.

July 17, Captain Roberts, with 33 Royal Veterans and 160 Canadian voyageurs, took Mackinaw.

July 19, The Americans were again foiled at River aux Canards.

July 24, The Americans were the third time checked at River aux Canards.

Aug. 5, Brock left York for Fort George, on his way to Amherstburg.

Aug. 8, Hull re-crossed to Detroit.

Aug. 13, Brock, with 300 men, reached Amherstburg, having traversed Lake Erie in open boats.

Miles McDonell and his settlers arrived at Red River.

Aug. 14, Tecumseh, the Shawnee Chief, met Brock at Amherstburg.

Aug. 16, Hull surrendered Detroit to Brock on summons; by the terms of the capitulation, Brock obtained possession of Detroit, Michigan, the "Adams" brig of war, 2,500 prisoners, 33 cannon, a large quantity of stores, the military chest, and what was especially valuable, 2,500 stand of arms.

> Adams' "Hist. of U.S.," VI., p. 333, gives the following from the evidence of Major Snelling, at Hull's court-martial in Albany. It refers to Hull's conduct while he considered Brock's summons to surrender:
> "He unconsciously filled his mouth with tobacco, putting in quid after quid more than he generally did; the spittle, colored with tobacco juice, ran from his mouth on his neck cloth, beard, cravat and vest."

Aug. 19, The "Constitution" captured the "Guerriere" on the ocean. Although this occurrence is not strictly Canadian, yet as Americans are steadily mindful of the circumstance and even speak of it sometimes, it may not be amiss to present the rough particulars of it.

The comparative forces of the two ships is given by

Roosevelt, "Naval War of 1812," p. 92, as follows: "Constitution," 1,576 tons, 27 guns, 684 lbs. broadside, 456 men.

"Guerriere," 1,338 tons, 25 guns, 556 lbs. broadside, 272 men.

This preponderance of force should have been sufficient to ensure a victory for the "Constitution" in any water or weather; but she had an advantage still greater. She had 17 twenty-four pounders, long guns, against the 14 eighteen pounders, long guns of the "Guerriere," and, by standing off beyond the range of the eighteen pounders, she overcame the "Guerriere." In the same way the "United States" defeated the "Macedonian," and the "Constitution" the "Java." But during the whole war of 1812, when the conditions were equal, the Americans never won a single encounter.

Aug. 20, Mr. Molson, at Montreal, launched the "Swiftsure," his second steamer on the St. Lawrence.

Aug. 24, Brock reached Fort George, having left Proctor in command at Detroit.

Sept. 1, Commodore Isaac Chauncey was appointed commander of the U.S. naval forces on the Great Lakes. He made Sackett's Harbor his headquarters.

Oct. 10, Isaac Brock was made Knight of the Bath.

Oct. 13, Gen. Van Rensselaer, before daybreak, sent 600 men across the Niagara River to Queenston. Captain Denis with a few men tried in vain to prevent their landing. After the Americans were heavily reinforced, Gen. Brock came up from Fort George, and while charging up Queenston Heights was shot, and also Lieut.-Col. McDonell. In the afternoon Gen. Roger H. Sheaffe drove some of the Americans over the Heights, and took the rest, 900 men, prisoners.

In the afternoon Fort George and Fort Niagara exchanged a heavy fire of big guns.

"The Americans lost this day about 90 killed, and 100 wounded; nearly 900 prisoners surrendered. The British loss in killed, wounded, and prisoners was about 130."—Schouler's "Hist. of U.S.," II., p. 360

"The military importance of the Heights, of which Wool

was thus left in quiet possession [between the death of Brock and the arrival of Sheaffe] was the assistance the battery could give to the army in its advance on Queenston. But the army made no such advance. Indeed, save about six hundred militia and three hundred and fifty regulars, not a man crossed the river. Officer after officer came to the bank and shouted and beckoned to them to come over. Van Rensselaer [a cousin of the Gen.], wounded though he was, crossed and implored them to be men. Some well-known politicians, who were present, went about entreating them to fight. But it was of no avail. No sooner did the militia behold a real battle, no sooner did they see the dead brought back in boats, and hear the groans of the wounded, than fear overcame them, and they refused to cross. Soldiers who the day before were clamorous to be brought face to face with what they called the British hirelings now stood on their constitutional rights and refused to help their fighting countrymen. They were, they said, militia, and the only services for which the militia could be called out were to uphold the laws, to put down insurrection, to repel invasion. The Constitution did not give the President power to send them out of the United States, and they would not go. Holding such views, they stood quietly on the American side, saw the British gather in force, and march up the hill, saw their countrymen overwhelmed by numbers driven back foot by foot to the edge of the cliff and down the side to the river bank, where, as no one would row a boat across, the little band of six hundred threw down their arms and surrendered. With them was captured some three hundred skulkers and cowards, who had been crouching at the river edge all day."—McMaster's "History of People of United States," IV., p. 12.

Oct. 25, The "United States" took the "Macedonian" on the ocean.

Roosevelt, "Naval History of 1812," p. 112, gives their forces as follows:

"United States," 1576 tons, 27 guns, 786 lbs. broadside, 478 men.

"Macedonian," 1325 tons, 25 guns, 547 lbs. broadside, 301 men.

"United States" had 17 twenty-four pds. long guns, and the "Macedonian" 14 eighteen pds. long guns.

Nov. 7, Louis V. Sicotte, jurist and statesman, was born at St. Famille, L.C.

Commodore Chauncey, an American, on Lake Ontario took a schooner, on which was Capt. Brock, of the 49th, a brother of Sir Isaac, and the plate and effects of the dead General. Chauncey generously paroled his prisoner and restored the property.

Nov. 20, Gen. Dearborn, with nearly 2,000 Americans, attacked Odelltown, but Major de Salaberry drove him back to Champlain.

Nov. 28, Gen. Smyth, successor of Van Rensselaer, on the Niagara, said to his army of 4,500 men, " Come on, my heroes, and when you attack the enemy's batteries, let your rallying word be ' The cannon lost at Detroit—or death ;' " then he sent his men into Canada, and instantly called them back. The people of Buffalo hooted and pelted him ; his government cashiered him.

Dec. 8, Gen. Porter and Gen. Smyth, Americans, fought a duel on Grand Island ; but, as their seconds had carefully drawn the balls from their pistols, both generals survived the encounter.

Dec. 12, John Sandfield Macdonald was born at St. Raphael's, Upper Canada

"The Loyal and Patriotic Society of Upper Canada" was formed to care for the wounded, help destitute families, and provide comforts for the soldiers.

Dec. 29, The Legislature of Lower Canada met, and soon renewed the Army Bill Act, which authorized the circulation of £500,000 ; a grant of £15,000 was made to equip the militia, £1,000 to provide hospitals, and £25,000 for general purposes of defence.

The "Constitution" took the "Java" on the ocean. Roosevelt, "Naval History of 1812," p. 126, gives their forces as follows :

"Constitution," 1,576 tons, 654 lbs. broadside, 475 men.

" Java," 1,340 tons, 576 lbs. broadside, 426 men.

The "Constitution" had 17 twenty-four pds. long guns ; the "Java" had 14 eighteen pds. long guns.

"Though the thrilling sensation of touching an enemy's soil had been repeatedly felt, it took the fruitless campaign of this first year to teach our people that the British Provinces could not be carried at a dash, nor Canada pierced by an army of raw, though enthusiastic recruits, officered by political generals and the invincibles of peace."—Schouler's " Hist. of U.S.," II., p. 361.

1813.

Heretofore, only Madison's party, the Republicans, had been zealous in prosecuting the war; but now that the honour of the nation was at stake, that a national disgrace had to be wiped out, all the people of the United States were hot belligerents. New England had been opposed to the war, because it was unjust; but, says Gay, "Life of Madison," "Massachusetts contributed, in the second campaign, more recruits than any other single State, and New England more than all the Southern States together."

Jan. 22, Colonel Proctor, with 500 soldiers and 800 Indians, under Roundhead, defeated Gen. Winchester at Frenchtown, on the Raisin river, and made him and 495 of his men prisoners.

Feb. 6, Captain Forsythe crossed from Ogdensburg to Brockville (Elizabethtown), and carried off 52 people.

Feb. 22, Major Macdonnell, with 480 men, crossed from Prescott to Ogdensburg, and, after a sharp fight, took the place. It was defended by Forsythe, who had 500 men and eleven guns. Macdonnell secured the cannon and a large amount of military stores, and burned four war vessels. Macdonnell's men were mostly Glengarry men.

Feb. 25, Gen. Sheaffe convened the Legislature of Upper Canada, which made the Army Bills issued in Lower Canada a legal tender, prohibited the export of grain, and restrained distillation.

March, The 104th regiment, New Brunswick regulars, marched from Fredericton to Quebec through the snow-covered wilderness.

March 27, Commodore Oliver H. Perry arrived at Erie, Pa., to fit out a squadron.

April 27, The Americans took York, Upper Canada, the American General, Pike, being killed by an accidental explosion.

"The fleet and army arrived at York early in the morning of April 27. York, a village numbering in 1806, according to British account, more than three thousand inhabitants,* was the capital of Upper Canada, and contained the

---

*Kingsford, "History of Canada," VIII., p. 253, says, "Bishop Bethune tells us that seven years later it did not exceed 1,000."

residence of the Lieutenant-Governor and the two brick buildings where the Legislature met. For military purposes the place was valueless, but it had been used for the construction of a few war vessels, and Chauncey represented through Dearborn, that 'to take or destroy the armed vessels at York would give us the complete command of the lake.' The military force at York, according to British account, did not exceed six hundred men, regulars and militia; and of these, one hundred and eighty men, or two companies of the eighth or King's regiment, happened to be there only in passing. Under the fire of the fleet and riflemen, Pike's brigade was set ashore; the British garrison, after a sharp resistance, was driven away, and the town capitulated. The ship on the docks was burned; the ten gun brig, 'Gloucester,' was made prize; the stores were destroyed or shipped; some three hundred prisoners were taken; and the public buildings, including the Houses of Assembly, were burned."—Adams's "Hist. of U. S.," VII., p 154.

May 1, Proctor, with 1,037 regulars and 1,500 Indians, began to attack Fort Meigs, on the Maumee, defended by Gen. Harrison. Proctor displayed poor generalship, failed to take the place, and incurred the deadly enmity of the Americans by alleged connivance at the massacre of forty prisoners by his Indians. Tecumseh stopped the massacre.

May 5, Sir James Yeo, with 450 seamen, arrived at Quebec.

May 8, The Americans left York.

May 27, Chauncey and Gen. Dearborn, with 7,000 men, took Fort George, Gen. Vincent retreating towards Burlington with what were left of his 1,400 men.

May 29, Gov. Prevost and Sir James Yeo assaulted Sackett's Harbor; but, as Prevost checked an assured success by an order to retreat, the expedition was a disgraceful failure.

"If the enemy had persevered twenty minutes longer, the sloop of war, 'General Pike,' and our depot at Sackett's Harbor would have fallen into their hands.... If the enemy had prevailed, and the sloop of war 'Pike' had been destroyed, we must have taken a long farewell of the superiority on Lake Ontario."—Wilkinson's "Memoirs," I., pp. 585-586.

McMaster, "Hist. of People of U.S.," IV., 46, says: "Prevost was far from being a bold and energetic commander. But the sight of Sackett's Harbor, with its naval stores, its military stores, its shipyard, with the twenty-eight gun ship, 'General Pike,' on the stocks almost ready to be launched, was too tempting, and he determined to attack the place. On the night of May twenty-sixth, accordingly, at the very time that Chauncey was making his soundings off Fort George, Prevost embarked eight hundred men on board the fleet of Sir James Yeo, sailed from Kingston, and soon after daybreak on May twenty-eighth sighted Sackett's Harbor. Had he entered the harbor boldly, landed his troops without a moment's delay, and stormed the forts, the place would have been his by noon. But he waited twenty-four hours; the militia of the neighborhood rushed in, and, what was far more important, Jacob Brown had arrived and taken command."

Adams's, "Hist. of U.S.," VII., 169-170, says: "Whatever were the true causes of Prevost's failure, Americans could not admit that an expedition which cost the Americans so much, and which so nearly succeeded, was discreditable to the British governor-general, or was abandoned without sufficient reason."

But some Americans say that, had Prevost remained fifteen minutes longer, he and all his men would have been captured.

June 3, Major Taylor captured two American vessels, the "Growler" and the "Eagle," on Lake Champlain.

June 5, Colonel Harvey, under General Vincent, defeated the Americans at Stony Creek, and captured two American Generals,—Winder and Chandler.

"After the capture of Fort George, the Americans invaded Canada; but their advance guard, 1,400 strong, under Generals Chandler and Winder, was surprised in the night by 800 British, who, advancing with the bayonet, broke up the camp, capturing both the generals and half the artillery." —Roosevelt's "Naval War of 1812," p. xvii., 5th edition.

Adams's, "Hist. of U.S.," VII., 160, says: "The whole American force, leaving the dead unburied, fell back ten miles, where Major-General Lewis took command in the afternoon of June 7. An hour later the British fleet under Sir James Yeo made its appearance, threatening to cut off Lewis' retreat. Indians hovered about. Boats and baggage were lost. Dearborn sent pressing orders to Lewis directing him to return, and on the morning of June 8 the division reached Fort George."

June 10, The de Watteville regiment arrived in Canada.

June 19, Maj.-Gen. De Rottenburg took command of the forces in Upper Canada, Sheaffe being transferred to Montreal.

June 24, Lieutenant Fitzgibbon captured Colonel Boerstler, and his men at Beaver Dam (Thorold.)

"Galled by complaints of the imbecility of the army, Boyd, with Dearborn's approval, June 23, detached Colonel

Boerstler, of the 14th infantry, with some four hundred men and two field pieces, to batter a stone house at Beaver Dam, some seventeen miles from Fort George. Early in the morning of June 24, Boerstler marched to Beaver Dam. There he found himself surrounded in the woods, by hostile Indians, numbering, according to British authority, about two hundred. The Indians, annoying both flank and rear, caused Boerstler to attempt retreat, but his retreat was stopped by a few militiamen, said to number fifteen. A small detachment of 150 men came to reinforce Boerstler, and Lieutenant Fitzgibbon, of the British 49th regiment, with forty seven men, reinforced the Indians. Unable to extricate himself, and dreading dispersion and massacre, Boerstler decided to surrender; and his five hundred and forty men accordingly capitulated to a British lieutenant with two hundred and sixty Indians, militia, and regulars."—Adams's "Hist. of U.S.," VII, p. 162-163.

We must not forget that Mrs. Secord, the wife of a wounded Canadian militiaman, at great personal risk, had walked 20 miles through the woods to apprise Lieut. Fitzgibbon of Boerstler's approach.

July 4, Lieut.-Col. Thos. Clark, of the 2nd Lincoln Militia, with 40 of his men, crossed from Chippewa to Fort Schlosser, surprised and took the place, and recrossed the river, having secured a six pound (brass) gun, several stands of arms, 15 prisoners, and a large quantity of pork and flour.

July 11, Col. Bisshopp was killed in an attack upon Black Rock.

July 31, Commodore Chauncey visited York again, "set fire to the barracks and public store-houses, liberated the prisoners in jail, ill-treated some of the inhabitants, and retired with the few stores he could find." Such is said; but, if true, it was exceptional conduct for Chauncey, who, in his general undertakings, was a respectable enemy.

At this time, on Lake Ontario, Chauncey had 14 ships, 114 guns, and 1,193 seamen; Yeo had 6 ships, 92 guns, and 717 men.

July 31, Col. Murray took Plattsburg, and Capt. Everard and Capt. Pring destroyed four American vessels outside of Burlington, Vt.

Aug. 2, Col. Proctor was repulsed in an attempt to take Fort Stephenson on the Sandusky River, Major Croghan defending it.

Aug. 10, Yeo and Chauncey had a running fight on Lake Ontario, Yeo capturing the "Julia" and the "Growler." (This is Roosevelt's date ; some put it Sept. 4.) To prevent further loss, Chauncey took shelter under the guns of Niagara.

> Roosevelt, "Naval War of 1812,' pp. 240-241, says : "The British had acted faultessly and the honor and profit gained by the encounter rested entirely with them. On the contrary, neither Chauncey nor his subordinates showed to advantage. . . . . . . As it was, the British commander had attacked a superior force in weather that just suited it, and yet had captured two of its vessels without suffering any injury beyond a few shot holes in the sails."

Aug. 20, Gen. Hampton, with 5,000 men, entered Canada.

Sept. 10, Commodore Perry defeated Captain Barclay, on Lake Erie.

In Roosevelt's "Naval History of War of 1812," p. 260, the comparative strength of the two fleets is given as follows :

BARCLAY'S SHIPS.

"Detroit," 19 guns, throwing a broadside of 138 lbs.
"Queen Charlotte," 17 guns, throwing a broadside of 189 lbs.
"Lady Prevost," 13 guns, throwing a broadside of 75 lbs
"Hunter," 10 guns, throwing a broadside of 30 lbs.
"Chippeway," 1 gun,   "   "   9 "
"Little Belt," 3 guns, "   "   18 "

Total   -   -   -   -   -   459 "

PERRY'S SHIPS.

"Lawrence," 20 guns, throwing a broadside of 300 lbs.
"Niagara," 20   "   "   " 300 "
"Caledonia," 3   "   "   "   80 "
"Ariel," 4 guns   "   "   "   48 "
"Scorpion," 2 guns   "   "   "   64 "
"Somers," 2   "   "   "   "   56 "
"Porcupine," 1 gun   "   "   "   32 "
"Tigress," 1 gun   "   "   "   32 "
"Trippe," 1 gun   "   "   "   24 "

Total   -   -   -   -   936

"The superiority of the Americans in long-gun metal was therefore nearly as three is to two, and in carronade metal greater than two to one. . . . The 'Niagara' might be considered a match for the 'Detroit,' and the 'Lawrence' and 'Caledonia' for the five other British vessels ; so the Americans were certainly very greatly superior in force."—Roosevelt's "Naval War of 1812," p. 261.

"In number of guns the British fleet was superior to the American. But in other respects—in ships, in tonnage, in men, in weight of metal thrown in a broadside, whether at long range or at short range—Perry had a most decided advantage."—McMaster's "History of People of U.S.," IV., 36.

"Perry's superiority was decided, as it was meant to be. The Americans had thirty-nine thirty-two pound carronades ; the British had not a gun of that weight, and only fifteen twenty-four pound carronades. The lightest guns on the American fleet were eight long twelve-pounders, while twenty-four of the British guns threw only nine pound shot, or less. The American broadside threw at close range about nine hundred pounds of metal ; the British threw about four hundred and sixty. At long range the Americans threw two hundred and eighty-eight pounds of metal ; the British threw one hundred and ninety-five pounds. In tonnage the Americans were superior as eight to seven. In short, the Navy Department had done everything reasonably necessary to insure success."—Adams's "Hist. of U.S.," VII., 120.

Barclay, however, lost the battle solely for the want of seamen to work his ships. England's sailors were too much needed in Europe at this time to be spared for service in America.

On the other hand, the Americans had an abundance of young, active seamen anxious for service.

"Her [U.S.] commerce being temporarily suspended to a large degree, there was an abundance both of ships and sailors, from which to build up a navy and fit out a fleet of privateers."—Rossiter Johnson's "War of 1812," p. 23.

Kingsford, "Hist. of Canada," VIII., p. 313, says, that Barclay lost 38 killed and 85 wounded out of a total of 384 men, and that Perry lost 27 killed and 96 wounded out of a total of 650 men.

Sept. 26, Proctor left Sandwich, beginning his retreat.

Sep. 27, Gen. Harrison landed 5,000 men near Amherstburg.

Sept 28, Yeo and Chauncey had an indecisive action on Lake Ontario.

Oct. 2, Harrison, with 4,000 men, began to pursue Proctor.

Oct. 4, Harrison captured all of Proctor's ammunition and stores.

Oct. 4, John Armstrong, U.S. Secretary of State, wrote to McClure, commanding the U.S. troops at Fort George:

> "Understanding that the defence of the fort committed to your charge may render it proper to destroy the town of Newark, you are hereby directed to apprise the inhabitants of the circumstance, and to invite them to remove themselves and their effects to some place of greater safety."

Oct. 5, At Moravian Town, Harrison, with 3,500 men, defeated Proctor, with 407 soldiers and 800 Indians under Tecumseh. Tecumseh was killed.

> Major Richardson, "Operations . . . . Division," p. 123, speaking of his experience in the battle of the Thames, says: "In this affair I had an opportunity of witnessing the cruel dexterity and despatch with which the Indians use the tomahawk and scalping knife. A Kentucky rifleman, who had been dismounted within a few yards of the spot where I stood—and the light company, to which I was attached, touched the left flank of the Indians—was fired at by three warriors of the Delaware tribe. The unfortunate man received their several balls in his body, yet, although faint from loss of blood, he made every exertion to save himself. Never was fear so strongly depicted on the human countenance, and the man's hair (for he was uncovered) absolutely seemed to me to stand on end, as he attempted to double a large fallen tree, in order to elude the weapons of his enemies. The foremost of his pursuers was a tall, powerful man—a chief whom I well knew, having, only a few days before we commenced our retreat, obtained from him a saddle in exchange for a regimental coat, purchased at the sale of the effects of Lieut. Sutherland, wounded at Maguaga. When within twelve or fifteen paces of the rifleman, he raised and threw his tomahawk, and with such precision and force, that it immediately opened the skull, and extended him motionless on the earth. Laying down his rifle, he drew forth his knife, and after having removed the hatchet from the brain, proceeded to make a circular incision throughout the scalp. This done, he grasped the bloody instrument between his teeth, and placing his knees on the back of his victim, while at the same time he fastened his fingers in the hair, the scalp was torn off without much apparent difficulty, and thrust, still bleeding, into his bosom. The warrior then arose, and after having wiped his knife on the clothes of the unhappy man, returned it to its sheath, grasping at the same time the arms he had abandoned, and hastening to rejoin his comrades. All this was the work of a few minutes."

> Drake, "Life of Tecumseh," p. 198, says: "Mr. James asserts that Tecumseh was not only scalped, but that his body was actually *flayed*, and the skin converted into razor-straps by the Kentuckians. We fear there is too much truth in this statement. It is confirmed by the testimony of several American officers and privates, who were in the battle of the Thames."
>
> "He [Proctor] was tried by court-martial for his share in this disaster, and sentenced to be suspended from rank and pay for six months. He was reinstated, commanded again during the war, and rose to the rank of Lieutenant-General. He was much admired by the people of Canada, and the sentence that was passed upon him was regarded as arbitrary and unmerited."—Appleton's Biog. Dict.

Proctor's bravery, despite the insinuations of hostile critics, was unquestioned; but that he was more solicitous for the safety of his family and personal effects than for success in the field, may be a just charge. He might have made a better retreat perhaps, and a better disposition of his force for battle, but, with his few worn-out men, he could not possibly have withstood Harrison's army.

Oct. 6, Harrison burned Moravian Town.

> "Harrison destroyed Moravian Town the day after the battle, and then marched back to Detroit."—Rossiter Johnson's "War of 1812," p. 147.

Oct. 26, At Chateauguay, Lieut.-Colonel De Salaberry, with a handful of men, threw Hampden's army into headlong flight by a chilling blast of trumpets and a few shots.

> "The defeat of three thousand five hundred by the three hundred and fifty was overwhelming in its completeness. The victory of Chatueguay, let it be remembered, was a victory of the French-Canadian militia led by their own officers, and it was perhaps the most glorious in the whole course of a war which brought much glory to our arms."—Roberts' "History of Canada," p. 245.
>
> "A few hundred Canadian militia, with a handful of regulars, stopped this army of more than four thousand men with ten pieces of artillery, so that it was forced, with a loss of but thirty men killed, wounded and missing, to retreat twenty-four miles along the road it had cut with so much labor through the forest."—Headley's "The Second War with England," I., 295.
>
> Kingsford says, "With the exception of Colonel McDonnell, Captain Ferguson, and three or four others, there was not a person of British blood in the field."

Nov. 1, Gen. Wilkinson, with 8,000 men in batteaux, left Sackett's Harbor to descend the St. Lawrence, form a junction with Hampden, and then take Montreal.
Nov. 11, Col. Morrison defeated Gen. Boyd at Chrystler's Farm, and the American General, Covington, was killed.

"A council of war was now called to consider what to do, for new dangers sprang up at every step. Chauncey, who had been left to blockade the entrance to the river, did his duty so badly that Captain Mulcaster, of the British navy, ran the blockade and hung upon the rear of the army with his gun-boats. Joined by eight hundred men from Kingston and Prescott, who lined the bank at every narrow pass and fired on the flank of the army with musketry and artillery, while the gun-boats threatened its rear, Mulcaster became a dangerous enemy. At White House, therefore, twelve hundred men were landed on the Canadian shore with orders to drive him away. The council, meantime, having decided to push on, General Brown with more troops was landed and ordered to march ahead of the fleet and clear the bank, while General Boyd, with the remainder of the troops, protected the rear. In this manner, the expedition went slowly down the river, making not more than twelve miles a day, till the night of November 10th, when it halted at a place called Chrysler's Farm. On the following morning, just as Brown sent word that the river bank was clear ahead, a messenger hurried in from Boyd, declaring that the British were advancing in column. But, as Wilkinson and Lewis were sick, and Brown and Scott far in advance, Boyd was left to fight as he pleased, and after a stubborn resistance his force of two thousand men, beaten and almost routed by Mulcaster and his eight hundred, fled over the river in the dusk of the evening, and, without waiting for orders, clambered on board the ships. Next day the flotilla ran the Long Saut Rapids, joined Brown at Cornwall, and so terrified the army that within twenty-four hours the entire expedition had fled up the Salmon River, and was safe within the United States"—McMaster's "History of People of U.S.," IV., 51.

"The flotilla stopped, on the night of Nov. 10th, near a farm called Chrysler's on the British bank, and the next morning. Nov. 11th, at half past ten o'clock, Brown having announced that all was clear below, Wilkinson was about to order the flotilla to run the rapids, when General Boyd sent word that the enemy in the rear were advancing in column Wilkinson was on his boat, unable to leave his bed ; Morgan Lewis was in no better condition ; and Boyd was left to fight a battle as he best could. Boyd never had the confidence of the army ; Brown was said to have

threatened to resign rather than serve under him, and Winfield Scott, who was that day with Macomb and Brown in the advance, described Boyd as amiable and respectable in a subordinate position, but 'vacillating and imbecile beyond all endurance as a chief under high responsibilities.' The opportunity to capture or destroy Mulcaster and his eight hundred men was brilliant, and warranted Wilkinson in turning back his whole force to accomplish it. Boyd actually employed three brigades, and made an obstinate but not united or well-supported attempt to crush the enemy. Colonel Ripley, with the 21st regiment, drove in the British skirmishers, and at half-past two o'clock the battle became general. At half-past four, after a stubborn engagement, General Covington was killed; his brigade gave way, and the whole American line fell back, beaten and almost routed. This defeat was the least creditable of the disasters suffered by American arms during the war. No excuse or palliation was ever offered for it. The American army consisted wholly of regulars, and all the generals belonged to the regular service. Wilkinson could hardly have had less than three thousand men with him, after allowing for his detachments, and was alone to blame if he had not more. Boyd, according to his own account, had more than twelve hundred men and two field-pieces under his immediate command on shore. The reserve, under Col. Upham of the 11th regiment, contained six hundred rank-and-file, with four field-pieces. Wilkinson's official report admitted that eighteen hundred rank-and-file were engaged; Col. Walbach, his Adjutant-General, admitted two thousand, while Swartwout thought that twenty-one hundred were in action. The American force was certainly not less than two thousand, with six field-pieces. The British force, officially reported by Lieut.-Col. Morrison of the 89th regiment, who was in command, consisted of eight hundred rank-and-file and thirty Indians. The rank-and-file consisted of three hundred and forty-two men of the 49th regiment, about as many more of the 89th, and some Canadian troops. They had three six-pound field-pieces, and were supported on their right flank by gun-boats. On the American side the battle was ill fought both by the generals and by the men. . . . . The American loss was twice that of the British, and Wilkinson's reports were so little to be trusted that the loss might well have been greater than he represented it."
—Adam's "History of U.S.," VII., 188-190.

"It [invasion of Canada] was mismanaged in every possible way and was a total failure; it was attended with but one battle, that of Chrysler's Farm, in which 1,000 British, with a loss of less than 200 men, beat back double their number of Americans, who lost nearly 500 men, and also one piece of artillery."—Roosevelt's "Naval War of 1812," p. xviii.

"The loss of the British in this engagement [Chrystler's Farm] was 22 killed, 150 wounded, and 15 missing. The Americans lost 102 killed, and 237 wounded."— Lossing's (American) "War of 1812," p. 654.

Dec. 11, Gen. McClure, at Fort George, fearing the approach of the British, burnt Newark and crossed to Fort Niagara. He burned 149 houses, compelling 400 women and children to seek shelter in the woods.

"McClure, at Fort George, hearing that Murray had approached within ten miles, evacuated the post and crossed the river to Fort Niagara; but before doing so he burned the town of Newark and as much as he could of Queenston, turning the inhabitants, in extreme cold, into the open air."—Adams's "History of U.S.," VII., 202.

Dec. 18, Colonel Murray, with 550 men, crossed the Niagara River and took Fort Niagara.

Dec. 19, General Riall, with 500 men, crossed to Lewiston, took it, burned it, and also Youngstown and Manchester.

Death of James McGill, founder of McGill University, Montreal.

In December, Lieutenant Medcalf, of the Norfolk militia, having learned that an American marauding party of U.S. regulars was stationed at a farm house near the River Thames, hastily collected 28 militiamen and made a forced march to attack the enemy. Sergeant McQueen broke in the door of the barricaded house with the butt of his musket; the Norfolk militia rushed in, killed two Americans and took 41 prisoners, Lieutenant Larwell, the American officer included. Only two Americans escaped. —Cf. Kingsford's "History of Canada," VIII., p. 445.

Dec. 30, Riall crossed the Niagara to Black Rock, routed the opposing forces, and the next day burned Buffalo.

"The final military operations of this year on the northern border were the most disappointing, and on the whole the most disgraceful, of any that had been undertaken."— Rossiter Johnson's "History of War of 1812," p. 149.

"All that the Americans had gained on the northern frontier during the year 1813, with the exception of the territory of Michigan, restored by Harrison's victory, had now been lost, and, on New Year's Day of 1814, the settlers along the whole length of the Niagara—those of them who survived—were shivering beside the smouldering embers of their homes."—Rossiter Johnson's "History of War of 1812," p. 167.

"New Year's Day found the Cross of St. George floating over Fort Niagara, and the whole American side of the river a ruined country."—McMaster's "History of People of U.S.," IV., 54.

1814.

Feb., A part of the 8th regiment marched from Fredericton, New Brunswick, to Quebec.

March 15, The Governor, at the Castle of St. Louis, Quebec, had a "Talk," a conference, with chiefs and warriors of the Mohawks, Ottawas, Chippewas, Sacs, Foxes, Shawnees, Kickapoos, and Winabagoes. When they departed for the West they were loaded down with presents.

March 30, Gen. Wilkinson, with 4,000 men, crossed the boundary line to La Colle Mill; but Major Hancock, with 340 men, compelled him to retreat to Plattsburg.

April 15, The "Prince Regent," 58 guns, and the "Princess Charlotte," 42 guns, were launched at Kingston.

A printing press for Upper Canada was purchased at Ogdensburg, for £84 7s. 6d., to replace the one destroyed by the Americans at York in 1813.

May 3, Sir Adams Geo. Archibald, jurist, was born in Truro, N.S.

May 6, Sir James Yeo and Gen. Drummond took Oswego.

May 15, A Canadian squadron bombarded Charlotte, at the mouth of the Genesee.

May 15, Col. Campbell, of the 11th U.S. infantry, with 500 men, crossed from Erie, Pa., and, after robbing the people of Port Dover, burned the place, "a sawmill and tannery, 5 distilleries, 6 stores, 13 barns, 3 gristmills, 19 dwelling houses." Col. Winfield Scott called the performance an "error of judgment."

May 30, Sir James Yeo sent two gun-boats up Sandy Creek to capture naval material on the way to Sackett's Harbor; but the Americans captured them.

July 1, Adams' "History of U.S." says, that on this day Gen. Brown's army in Buffalo consisted of Ripley's brigade, 1,415 men all told; Porter's brigade, 830 men all told; Scott's brigade, 2,122 men all told, and Hindman's artillery, 413 men all told. Total, 4,780 rank and file, all told.

July 3, Gen. Brown led his army across the Niagara to Fort Erie, which he soon took.

July 5, Gen. Brown defeated Riall at Chippewa or Street's Creek. Riall, although a Ney in a fight, was an indifferent general. With only 1,800 men he abandoned a strong position and attacked Brown's entire army, which was advantageously posted and defended by powerful artillery.

> "No one could have been more surprised than Brown or more incredulous than Scott, at Riall's extraordinary movement. The idea that a British force of two thousand men at most should venture to attack more than three thousand, with artillery, covered by a deep, miry creek, had not entered their minds."—Adams' "History of U.S ," VIII., 41.

The British lost 511 killed and wounded; the United States over 308.

July 11, Sir Thomas Hardy and Col. Pilkington took Moose Island.

July 12, Gen. John Swift, American, was killed in a skirmish near Fort George. There is credible authority for the statement, that the best spoons of the Niagara peninsula, mostly silver, were found in his pockets. During Brown's short campaign on the peninsula, the border men that were in his army, all crack shots, suffered at the hands of the Canadian Militia, who were their equals with the rifle, and altogether their superiors at individual tactics in the woods.

July 15, Gen. Brown began the investment of Fort George.

July 19, The Americans burned St. Davids, 40 houses, near Queenston.

July 20, Gen. Brown, not being aided by Chauncey in an attack on Fort George, retired to Queenston.

Eight traitors, Americans who had settled in Upper Canada, were hanged at Ancaster.

July 24, In the afternoon Gen. Drummond left York on the "Netley," arriving at Niagara the next morning.

July 25, At daybreak, Col. Tucker, with 1,500 men, crossed the Niagara and took Lewiston, destroying the public stores. At six o'clock p.m. the battle of Lundy's Lane was begun; Drummond, with 2,800 men, defeated Gen. Brown with 4,000 Americans. This battle, which ended at midnight, was the most stubborn and sanguinary contest, in proportion to the numbers engaged, that has ever been fought in America, and ever since the engagement two facts have been stoutly disputed, the number of men in each army and the result of the contest.

(I.) The British army was 2,800 men; the American was 4,000 men or more.

Gen. Drummond, in a letter of July 27, two days after the battle, which is given in Dodsley's "Annual Register," says:

"The darkness of the night, during this extraordinary conflict, occasioned several uncommon incidents; our troops having for a moment been pushed back, some of our guns remained for a few minutes in the enemy's hands; they were, however, not only quickly recovered, but the two pieces, a six pounder and a five and a half inch howitzer, which the enemy had brought up, were captured by us, together with several tumbrils, and in limbering up our guns at one period, one of the enemy's six pounders was put, by mistake, upon a limber of ours, and one of our six pounders limbered on one of his, by which means the pieces were exchanged, and thus, though we captured two of his guns, yet, as he obtained one of ours, we have gained only one gun. . . . . . The enemy's efforts to carry the hill were continued until about midnight, when he had suffered so severely from the superior steadiness and discipline of his majesty's troops that he gave up the contest, and retreated with great precipitation to his camp beyond the Chippewa. On the following day he abandoned his camp, threw the greatest part of his baggage, camp equipage and provisions into the rapids, and having set fire to Streets' Mills and destroyed the bridge at Chippewa, continued his retreat in great disorder towards Fort Erie. . . . . The number of troops under my command did not for the first three hours exceed sixteen hundred men, the addition of the troops under Col. Scott did not increase it to more than two thousand eight hundred of every description."

"At five o'clock, July 25, the British army was nearly concentrated. The advance under Riall at Lundy's Lane numbered nine hundred and fifty rank and file, with three field pieces which had been in the battle of Chippewa, and either two or three six pounders. Drummond was three miles below with eight hundred and fifteen rank and file, marching up the river, and Col. Scott, of the one hundred and third regiment, with twelve hundred and thirty rank and file and two more six pound field pieces, was a few miles behind Drummond. By nine o'clock in the evening the three corps, numbering three thousand rank and file, with eight field pieces, were to unite at Lundy's Lane."—Adams' "Hist. of U.S.," VIII., 50.

THE CARDINAL FACTS OF CANADIAN HISTORY. 111

This, for an U. S. estimate, is almost satisfactory; Riall's force, though, was exactly 825 men.
But Drummond's statement of his own force should be final - 2,800 men.
Brown's force was 4,000 or more. He entered Canada July 3 with all his men, nearly 5,000 He lost some at Chippewa, some in scouting, and some may have deserted. But he had been reinforced too. On July 24 he was joined by 520 men from Fort Erie, etc. He must, then, have had 4,000 or more at Lundy's Lane.

"The Americans engaged in the battle numbered about four thousand; their loss in killed, wounded and missing was more than eight hundred."—Ridpath's "Popular History of United States," p. 408.

(II.) The Canadians won the battle.

"It is proper here to mention that having received advices as late as the 20th from Gen. Gaines that our fleet was then in port, and the commodore sick, we ceased to look for co-operation from that quarter, and determined to disencumber ourselves of baggage and march directly for Burlington Heights. To mask this intention, and to draw from Schlosser a small supply of provisions, I fell back upon Chippewa."—Extract from Gen. Brown's report of the battle of Lundy's Lane, given in Niles' "Weekly Register," No. 26 of Vol. VI.

Why, then, after the battle, did not Gen. Brown march to Burlington Heights? It was because Drummond compelled him to flee to Fort Erie.

"Across the river, at Chippewa, and next at Niagara Falls, or Lundy's Lane, were famous victories, the latter a conquest, however, only by the arithmetic of slaughter. The field and captured cannon were not retained, for which reason the British have claimed the fight as theirs ever since."—Schouler's "Hist. of U.S.," II., 405.

This is really an admission that the Americans lost the battle, for even the "arithmetic of slaughter" was against them

Rossiter Johnson, "Hist. of War of 1812," p. 244, says that in the battle of Lundy's Lane the Americans lost 174 killed and 565 wounded, and that the British lost 84 killed and 557 wounded, which is almost correct for the British side.

"Nearly eight hundred Americans and as many English had fallen on and around that single hill."—Headley's "Second War with England," II., 95.

"To hold out longer was impossible, and about midnight Brown led his troops back in good order to camp."—McMaster's "Hist. of People of U.S." IV., 60.

"The time was then about 11 o'clock, and everyone felt that the army must soon retreat. Farther in the rear Gen. Brown met Major Hindman of the Artillery, who was bringing up his spare ammunition wagons. Brown ordered Hindman to collect his artillery as well as he could, and retire immediately; 'we shall all march to camp.' He said that they had done as much as they could do; that nearly all their officers were killed or wounded; that he was himself wounded, and he thought it best to retire to camp."—Adams's "History of U.S.", VIII., 58. On page 64, same volume, Adams says that Brown ordered Ripley, morning of the 26th, to return to Lundy's Lane, "to regain a battlefield which Brown had felt himself unable to maintain at midnight."

Roosevelt, "History of Naval War of 1812," p. 21, says, "it is equally beyond question that it was a defeat and not a victory for the Americans. They left the field and retired in perfect order to Fort Erie, while the British held the field and the next day pursued their foes."

If the Americans captured the British guns, they neither took them off, destroyed them nor spiked them; they left their dead and wounded on the field; and, to expedite their flight to Fort Erie, they threw camp equipage and provisions into the Niagara. Instead of going to Burlington, as Brown had intended, he was forced to make all speed in an opposite direction.

Aug. 4, Capt. Sinclair, Commander of American vessels on Lake Erie, attempted to take Mackinaw, but was driven off with loss.

In July and August, 16,000 regulars arrived in Canada.

Aug. 12, Captain Dobbs, who had carried boats overland from Ontario to Erie, captured the U.S. schooners "Ohio" and "Somers" at Fort Erie.

Aug. 15, Gen. Drummond assaulted Fort Erie, but the accidental explosion of an ammunition chest nearly destroyed the storming party, and failure ensued. His nephew, Col. Drummond of the 104th, was killed.

Aug. 24, Gen. Ross took Washington and burned the public buildings. Some writers, British and American, have used "vandalism" in speaking of this exploit. It was a justifiable offset to the burning of Newark, York, St. Davids, Moravian Town, and Port Dover.

Sept. 3, Lieutenant Worsley captured the American vessel "Tigress," off Nottawassaga.

Sept. 6, Lieutenant Worsley captured the American vessel "Scorpion," off Nottawassaga.

George Etienne Cartier, statesman, was born at St. Antoine, Lower Canada.

Sept. 11, Capt. Downie was defeated and killed at Plattsburg, and Gov. Prevost made a hasty retreat from the same place.

"The squadron which the British vessels were now bearing down to attack was much their superior in men, tonnage and weight of metal, besides being supported by powerful land batteries. Still Downie relied upon Prevost's assurance that the enemy's position would be assailed by land while he attacked his fleet, and bore gallantly down to action. But, instead of supporting this movement, Prevost directed his men to cook their breakfasts. The result was what might naturally be expected. After a desperate battle the 'Confiance,' 'Linnet' brig, and 'Chub' sloop were compelled to strike their colours. The 'Finch' struck on a reef, and was of no use during the action, and nine of the gunboats fled. Prevost at length put his attacking columns in motion, but, on finding that he could not expect succor from the fleet, he immediately withdrew them and resolved to retreat. The works would have been easily carried; a success in this way would have been a set-off to the disaster of the fleet, and nothing could have equalled the indignation of the troops when they were ordered to retreat. Many of the officers indignantly broke their swords, declaring they would never serve again, and the army sullenly retraced its way to the Canadian frontier, undisturbed by the enemy. The disgraceful course pursued on this occasion effectually destroyed the military reputation of the Governor-in-Chief, and as he died before he could be tried by court-martial, the stain still rests on his memory."—McMullen's "Hist. of Canada," p. 314.

McMullen gives the following, as the comparative strength of the fleets engaged at Plattsburg:

	British.	American.
Vessels	8	14
Broadside guns	38	52
Weight of metal, lbs.	765	1,194
Aggregate of crews	537	950
Tons	1,425	2,540

> "He [Macdonough] forced the British to engage at a disadvantage by his excellent choice of position, and he prepared beforehand for every possible contingency."—Roosevelt's "Naval War of 1812," p. 398.
>
> "Madonough anchored his four large vessels across Plattsburg Bay, where it was a mile and a half wide, and placed his gunboats in their rear to fill the gaps. Cumberland Head, on his left and front, and Crab Island on his right, obliged the enemy to enter in a line so narrow that Downie would find no room to anchor on his broadside out of carronade range, but must sail into the harbor under the raking fire of the American long guns, and take a position within range of the American carronades."—Adams's "Hist. of U.S.," VIII, 107.

Sept. 17, The Americans made a useless sortie from Fort Erie.

Sept. 29, Sir James Lucas Yeo wrote to the Secretary of the Admiralty, submitting the correspondence between Prevost and Downie, which showed that Prevost had urged Downie into action too soon, and had not, simultaneously with the naval action, assaulted Plattsburg, as he had promised.

Oct. 10, The "St. Lawrence," 100 guns, was launched at Kingston. Yeo then commanded Lake Ontario.

Nov. 5, The Americans evacuated and destroyed Fort Erie and re-crossed the Niagara River.

Gen. Drummond wrote to Prevost concerning the conduct of the Americans on the Niagara peninsula:

> "The wanton outrages, robberies and excesses lately committed by the enemy's army on this frontier demand a severe retaliation, and I would recommend to your Excellency to make the necessary communications to Sir Alexander Cochrane on the subject, unless you would prefer that it should be inflicted on the opposite frontier, a service which I consider this division is perfectly equal at any time effectually to perform."

Dec. 21, Col. Proctor was tried by court-martial in Montreal.

> "But of all these sanguinary conflicts the miserable recompense was the capture of the one British fort opposite Buffalo, which Izard, who arrived with reinforcements in September to assume command, had to abandon and blow up, after in vain offering battle to the enemy, for it was certain that the American army could not safely quarter for the winter on the Canada side. 'The most that can fairly be hoped,' wrote Madison gloomily in October, 'is that the campaign may end where it is.'"—Schouler's "Hist. of U.S.," II., 405.

Dec. 24, Treaty of Ghent; this diplomatically ended the war between Great Britain and the United States.

It is supposed by some people that, on the whole, the war resulted favorably to the United States; such, however, is not an easy inference from the sober statements of the best American historians.

"While the bells were ringing and the cannon booming, none, save a few old Federalists, thought it necessary to stop and enquire what the terms of the treaty might be. The feelings of the people, as expressed in their actions, were: We have peace, and peace is all we want. But now that the treaty was made public, and the first outburst of joy had subsided, the terms were read by the Federalists with shouts of exultation, by the Republicans with humiliation and shame. 'Bad as it is,' said the Federalist journals, 'we hail it with delight. To our country, pining for peace, it is a sweet restorative. To our people, harassed by war and impoverished by taxes, it is a welcome relief. To our bankrupt treasury, whose every resource was gone, it is a happy escape. In truth, it is not too much to say that the coming of peace has saved the country and the Government from disunion. But when the sweet delirium we now all enjoy has passed away the day of reckoning will come, and we shall then hear asked on every hand, What have we gained by war? Can Mr. Madison tell us? Into that war he dragged us in defence of Free Trade and Sailors' Rights. Have they been secured? No! Are they reserved for future negotiation? No! Are they silently surrendered, and with them, according to the declaration of war, the honor and independence of the nation? They are, indeed. But we also fought against certain doctrines of Great Britain in the matter of paper blockades, which were too outrageous to be borne any longer. These surely have been settled in our favor? No, not a word is said about them. But those impressed sailors, those sixty-two hundred and fifty-seven American citizens shut up in the "floating hells of England," have they been relieved and compensated? No, they are not even alluded to. Well, at all events, we have lost nothing. Not so; we have lost much. We have lost Moose Island; we have lost our rights to the fisheries claimed by us in the treaty of 1783 and recognized by it; we have lost the West India trade, and, most shameful of all, we have submitted the boundaries of the United States to the revision of monarchical umpires, sceptered brothers of the British King. The limits of our republic now depend on the honesty of kings!' The Republicans, on the other hand, had nothing to say in defence. They contented themselves, therefore, with dwelling on the blessings of peace, on the happy result of the war, on the great lessons it had taught the people and the world, and on the bright era of prosperity that seemed to be at hand."—McMaster's "Hist. of People of U.S.," IV., 276.

"Never before was an administration so loudly called upon to ask that public thanks might be offered for deliverance from great perils."—Headley's "Second War with England," II., 190.

"In America so great was the universal joy that the Federals and Democrats forgot their differences and their hates, and wept and laughed by turns in each other's arms and kissed each other like women."—Gay's "Life of Madison," p. 331.

"It [peace] was welcome to the Administration, whose inexperience in the conduct of the war had involved it in great financial straits, to the Federalists, who considered the war iniquitous, and even to the war party, who had begun to anticipate a single contest with England. Therefore, the peace, which actually secured not one of the objects for which war had been declared, occasioned rejoicings which would have been more appropriate for a more successful termination of the war."—Johnston's "American Politics," p. 85.

"Great Britain, after the war, though not bound by the Treaty to do so, put a stop to the irritating and unjust practice of searching vessels flying the American flag. And warlike Americans, from that day to this, have not dreamed of easily conquering any part of the British provinces."—Ed. Eggleston's "Life of Tecumseh," p. 319.

Yes, Great Britain ceased the practice of search, not on account of the war nor of the Treaty, but because the necessity of doing so had passed away, the European wars being over.

1815.

Jan. 8, Gen. Pakenham was defeated and killed at New Orleans.

Jan. 30, Bishop Strachan, of York, wrote his famous letter to Thos. Jefferson, Esq., of Monticello, ex-president of the United States.

March 3, The United States repealed the Non-intercourse and Non-importation Acts.

March 27, The entire amount of Army Bills outstanding was £1,249,996.

April 3, Sir George Prevost left Quebec, Gen. Drummond assuming the government.

May 22, Fort Niagara was restored to the Americans.

Sept. 16, The *Montreal Herald* said : "Yesterday between the hours of 9 and 10, pursuant to their sentences, Andre Latulippe, Henry Leopard, and John Quin received 39 lashes each, in the new Market Place."

1816.

Jan. 8, Sir Geo. Prevost died in England.
Feb. 5, Day named for Prevost's trial.
May 22, Gen. Drummond went to England, leaving Maj.-Gen. Wilson administrator.
Myer's Creek became Belleville.
Shipman's Corners became St. Catharines.
June 18, Mr. Semple, Governor of Hudson's Bay Company, and some of his men, were fiercely attacked by employees of the North-West Company, at "Seven Oaks," Red River, and Mr. Semple was killed.
Earl Dalhousie was made Gov.-Gen. of Nova Scotia.
The Durham boat came into use in Canada.
July 13, Sir John Sherbrooke was made Lieut. Gov. of Canada.
Aug., The Earl of Selkirk, with De Meuron's regiment, took possession of Fort William and its contents, the property of the North-West Company.
Sept. 7, At Earnestown, U.C., the "Frontenac" was launched, the first Canadian steamer on Lake Ontario.
Sept. 20, A stage began to run from York to Niagara.
Nov. 7, A constable and twelve men, with warrants from Upper Canada, attempted to arrest Selkirk and his officers at Fort William, but Selkirk withstood the constable, seiz'd him, and imprisoned him.

1817.

Jan., Samuel Purdy put on the first stage from Kingston to York.
April 29, Mr. Bagot, for Great Britain, and Mr. Rush, for the United States, made an agreement for their respective governments that each nation should maintain "on Lake Ontario one vessel not exceeding one hundred tons burden, and armed with an eighteen pound cannon. On the Upper Lakes two vessels not exceeding the like burden each, and armed with like force, and on the waters of Lake Champlain one vessel not exceeding like burden and armed with like force."

April 30, A mandamus was issued which gave Mgr. Plessis a seat in the Legislative Council as Catholic Bishop of Quebec.
Robert Gourlay came to Canada.
June 23, The Bank of Montreal was founded; its capital was limited to £250,000 currency.
July 3, The Synod of the Presbyterian Church of Nova Scotia was formed.
July 12, Samuel Jarvis killed John Ridout in a duel in Toronto.

1818.

Jan. 17, Antoine Aime Dorion, statesman, was born in Ste. Anne de la Perade, L.C.
May 2, Bishop Plessis sent Fathers Provencher and Dumoulin to Red River.
May 8, Samuel Leonard Tilley, statesman, was born at Gagetown, N.B.
June 9, Quebec Bank was founded; its capital was limited to £75,000 currency.
In this year the first Methodist Church in Toronto was built.
It is said that wolves and fallow deer were unknown in New Brunswick before this year.
July 5, Father Edmund Burke, western missionary, was consecrated Bishop of Halifax, N.S.
July 15, The first of a series of letters on agriculture, by "Agricola" (John Young), appeared in the Acadian Recorder. They gave an impetus to farming.

> "There are Junius like touches in the letters of Agricola, which are rarely met with even in the best authors, and which would have done credit to an Addison or a Macauley, and have all the more merit as coming from a merchant who wrote only during his leisure hours."—Campbell's "History of Nova Scotia," p. 223.

July 18, The first shower of grasshoppers fell in Red River; they hid the sun and devoured every green thing.
July 29, Duke of Richmond arrived in Canada as Governor-General.
Aug. 15, Robert Gourlay, a Scotch immigrant, who made himself too inquisitive about public matters, to suit the upper-crust people of Upper Canada, was tried

"for libel" in Kingston; but, being a capable man, he argued out his dismissal.

Sept. Earl of Selkirk was tried in Sandwich for breaking into Fort William and for resisting arrest.

Oct. 20, Frederic John Robinson and Henry Goulbourn, for Great Britain, and Albert Gallatin and Richard Rush, for the United States, signed a convention, "London Convention," which restored to the United States the right to fish around Newfoundland, and to cure fish on any of the unsettled bays or harbors; and made, provisionally, the 49th parallel of north latitude the boundary from Lake of Woods to the Stony Mountains; a joint occupation of Oregon was also agreed on.

Dec. 15, A Provincial Agricultural Society was formed in Nova Scotia, the Governor of the province, Lord Dalhousie, being president.

1819.

Jan. 4, Robert Gourlay was put in Niagara gaol.

Jan. 12, Father Alexander Macdonell was made Vicar-Apostolic of Upper Canada. St. Boniface College, Red River, was founded. Upper Canada Association of Baptists was formed.

July 12, The Bank of Kingston was incorporated.
Locusts devoured every green thing in the Red River district.

Aug. 28, The Duke of Richmond died from the effects of a fox-bite, the fox being afflicted with hydrophobia. Mr. Monk assumed the government.

Nov. 15, The Law Officers of the Crown, the question having been referred to them, decided that the Church of Scotland had a claim for a share of the rents and profits of the Clergy Reserves, but no claim for parochial endowments.

1820.

Jan. 29, Geo. IV. began to reign.
The Bank of New Brunswick was founded.
About this time the "Family Compact" is said to have been formed in Upper Canada.

June 18, Earl Dalhousie assumed the Government of Canada. Sir J. Kempt was made Lieut.-Gov. of Nova Scotia.
July 22, Sir Oliver Mowat, statesman, was born in Kingston, U.C.
Aug, 28, The Montreal Bible Society was established.
    Rev. Mr. West, Anglican, settled at Red River, the first Protestant clergyman in the country.
    The *Recorder*, Brockville, U.C., now appeared.
Oct. 9, Cape Breton was reunited to Nova Scotia.
Oct. 13, Sir John William Dawson, geologist, was born at Pictou, Nova Scotia.
Dec. 24. The Army Bill Office was closed, the Army Bills being redeemed.
Dec. 31, Father Alexander Macdonell received Episcopal consecration in Quebec, Bishop of Regiopolis (Kingston.)

1821.

March 26, The Hudson's Bay Company and the North-West Company amalgamated.
March 31, McGill College, Montreal, obtained a royal charter.
April 21, The Bank of Upper Canada was incorporated by proclamation.
June 6, Corner-stone of Montreal General Hospital was laid.
July 2, Sir Charles Tupper was born at Amherst, N.S.
July 17, Ground was broken for the Lachine Canal, Telford being the engineer.
Nov. 14, Thos. C. Keefer, engineer, was born in Thorold, Upper Canada.

1822.

May 1, The General Hospital, in Montreal, was opened; it had accommodation for 80 patients.
June 20, A Bill was introduced into the Imperial Parliament, to facilitate trade in, and with, Canada, "Canada Trade Act," and to incorporate the legislatures of Lower and Upper Canada. The Trade Act passed; the second clause was defeated.
    The Law Society of Upper Canada was incorporated.
July 16, Charles Sangster, author, was born in Kingston, U.C.
    Father Provencher was made Bishop of Red River.

Sept. 3, The Bank of Kingston failed.
Oct. 2, Matthew Crooks Cameron, jurist, was born in Dundas, U.C.

1823.

During this year, Nova Scotia, the first of the Provinces to issue coinage, issued a penny and a half-penny.

June 12, The steamer "De Salaberry," which left Quebec at 2 a.m. for Montreal, took fire off Cape Rogue, but of 240 passengers only 6 were lost.

Oct. 17, Samuel Sobieski Nelles was born at Mount Pleasant, Upper Canada.

Nov. 23, Receiver General Caldwell, Lower Canada, being £96,000 in arrear, was suspended from office.

Dec. 4, The following professors were appointed for McGill College: Rev. G. J. Mountain, D.D., Principal and Professor of Divinity; Rev. J. L. Mills, D.D., Professor of Moral Philosophy and Languages; Rev. J. Strachan, D.D., Professor of History and Civil Law; Rev. G. J Wilson, M A., Professor of Mathematics and Natural Philosophy; Thomas Fargues, M.D., Professor of Medicine.

1824.

Jan. 4, Peter Mitchell, statesman, was born in Newcastle, N.B.

Jan. 6, The Historical Society of Quebec first met, Lord Dalhousie presiding.

March 9, "An Act to promote the progress of useful arts in this Province," Canada, received royal assent. It was the beginning of the patent system in Canada. Common School Act passed in Upper Canada.
The "Fabrique Act" was passed in Lower Canada, empowering the priest and church-wardens of every parish to provide a school for every 100 families.

May 18, Wm Lyon Mackenzie issued the first number of the *Colonial Advocate*, at Queenston, U.C.

June 1, The foundation stone of Brock's monument was laid with Masonic honors, Wm. Lyon Mackenzie acting a foremost part, and putting a copy of his *Advocate* in the hollow of the foundation stone; when Sir

Peregrine Maitland heard of it, he ordered that the *Advocate* be extracted; Mackenzie took it out.

June 8, Noah Cushing, of Quebec, received a patent for a washing and fulling machine; it was the first patent issued by Canada.

Sept. 1, The foundation stone of Notre Dame Church, Montreal, was laid.

Sept. 13. The remains of Sir Isaac Brock and Lieut. Col. McDonell were deposited in the vault beneath the monument on Queenston Heights.

Nov. 25, Wm. Lyon Mackenzie, having moved from Queenston to York, first published the *Advocate* in York.

1825.

Jan. 24, James MacPherson Le Moine, author, was born in Quebec.

Feb. 28, Great Britain and the United States made a treaty, agreeing that fishing, navigation, and trade be free, "in any part of the ocean commonly called the Pacific Ocean."

June 16, Bishop Mountain died at Marchmont, near Quebec.

July 22, Lord Bathurst, Colonial Secretary, wrote to Sir Peregrine Maitland, Upper Canada, authorizing him to erect a parsonage in every parish, and to endow it with a land grant proportionate to its importance.

July 23, It was determined, under the terms of the Canada Trade Act, "that for the four years next succeeding the 1st July, 1824, one-fourth part of the duties levied in the Province of Lower Canada, under the authority of any act or acts passed therein, upon goods, wares, and commodities imported therein by sea, shall be paid to the province of Upper Canada, as the proportion of the same duties arising and due to the said province."

Lachine Canal was completed.

Directed by Hon. Peter Robinson, 415 Irish families came from Cork, and settled in the Newcastle district of Upper Canada, Peterboro'.

Oct 7, Miramichi Fire.

"In the autumn of 1825, a terrible disaster overwhemed the province [New Brunswick.] A long drought had

parched the forest to tinder. For two months not a drop of rain had fallen, and the streams were shrunken to rivulets. Numerous fires had laid waste the woods and farms, and filled the air with stifling smoke. The Government House at Fredericton was burned. But a still greater calamity was impending. On the 7th of October a storm of flame swept over the country for sixty miles, from Miramichi to the Bay of Chaleurs. A pitchy darkness covered the sky, lurid flames swept over the earth, consuming the forest, houses, barns, crops, and the towns of Newcastle and Douglas, with several ships upon the stocks. Resistance was in vain and escape almost impossible. The only hope of eluding the tornado of fire was to plunge into the rivers and marshes, and to cower in the water or ooze till the waves of flame had passed. The roar of the wind and fire, the crackling and crashing of the pines, the bellowing of the terrified cattle, and the glare of the conflagration, were an assemblage of horrors sufficient to appal the stoutest heart. When that fatal night had passed, the thriving towns, villages and farms over an area of five thousand square miles were a charred and blackened desolation. A million dollars worth of accumulated property was consumed, and the loss of timber was incalculable. One hundred and sixty persons perished in the flames or in their efforts to escape, and hundreds were maimed for life. The generous aid of the sister provinces, and of Great Britain and the United States, greatly mitigated the sufferings of the hapless inhabitants, made homeless on the eve of a rigorous winter."
—Withrow's "History of Canada," pp. 502 503.

1826.

Anticosti was re-annexed to Canada.

Jan. 27, The Pope set off Upper Canada as a separate diocese, making Kingston the See.

Feb. 14, Bishop Macdonell took charge of his See at Kingston, U.C.

Col. John By came to construct the Rideau Canal.

Peterboro, Upper Canada, was laid out.

June 8, A "genteel mob" wrecked Mackenzie's *Advocate* in York.

June 11, James Colledge Pope, statesman, was born in Bedeque, Prince Edward Island.

Aug. 19, The Canada Company was chartered; its capital was £1,000,000 in nearly 3,000,000 acres of land in Lower and Upper Canada, conditional to road making and general development.

Aug 26, Sir Hector Louis Langevin was born in Quebec.

1827.

March 15, A royal charter was obtained for establishing at York, U.C., a college, with the privileges of a university, to be called King's College.

Shade's Mill became Galt.

April 23, John Galt began Guelph, U.C.

Goderich, U.C., was laid out.

The first steam engine in Nova Scotia.

The Shubenacadie Canal was begun, to connect Halifax Harbor with the Bay of Fundy.

Nov. 20, The corner-stone of Wolfe's and Montcalm's monument was laid at Quebec, Earl Dalhousie directing it.

Dec. 3, The Presbyterians in Montreal made application to the home government for a share of the clergy reserves; their demand was soon granted.

1828.

April 10, While Francis Collins, editor of the *Freeman*, in York, was explaining to Judge Willis, in open court, the reasons why Attorney-General Robinson had preferred indictments for libel against him, a bitterness originated between the Judge and the Att.-Gen.

June 6, Judge Willis was suspended by the Imperial Government.

July 11, Judge Willis left York for England.

The Methodists of Upper Canada separated from the Methodist Church of the United States.

Sept. 8, Earl Dalhousie departed for England, and Sir James Kempt assumed the government.

1829.

Jan. 8, In Upper Canada, Messrs. Bidwell, Perry, Rolph, Matthews, and Dr. Baldwin took seats on the Opposition benches

Feb. 14, Mr. Robert Christie, member for Gaspe, was expelled from the Assembly of Lower Canada " for having advised the dismissal of a number of magistrates from the Commission of the Peace on account of their votes and speeches in the Assembly." He was expelled several times afterwards on the same allegations.

Heretofore only clergymen of the English Church could legally perform the marriage ceremony in Upper Canada; but in this year Marshall Bidwell passed a Bill that empowered any Christian clergyman to perform the marriage rite.

June 7, Notre-Dame Church, Montreal, was dedicated; it is the largest church in America, having a seating capacity of 10,000.

Thomas Chandler Haliburton wrote "History of Nova Scotia."

The wheat midge first appeared in Lower Canada.

Nov. 21, The *Christian Guardian*, Methodist, first appeared, Rev. Adolphus Egerton Ryerson, editor.

Nov. 30, The Welland Canal was formally opened.

1830.

Jan. 1, In Brockville, Upper Canada, Ogle R. Gowan opened the first Orange Lodge, No. 1, L.O.L., in Canada.

Jan. 8, Upper Canada College, York, was opened.

June 26, William IV. began to reign.

Oct. 13, Lord Aylmer arrived at Quebec.

Oct. 20, Sir James Kempt went to England, transferring the Government to Lord Aylmer.

1831.

Jan. 10, The King of the Netherlands gave his decision on the "Maine Boundary," to which the United States would not submit.

Feb. 3, Lord Aylmer was made Governor-General.

March 26, John Herbert Sangster, scientist and author, was born in London, Upper Canada. In this year 34,000 immigrants came to Canada. The "Royal William" was built at Quebec; she was the first steamship to cross the Atlantic.

Dec. 12, William Lyon Mackenzie was expelled from the House of Assembly, Upper Canada, for libel.

1832.

Jan. 2, Wm. L. Mackenzie, in York, was presented with a gold medal, worth £60, by his constituents of York, "as a token of their appreciation of his political career."

Jan. 8, Wm. L. Mackenzie was expelled from the Upper Canada Assembly, the second time for libel.
April 5, Brockville, U.C., was incorporated into a town.
May 2, First Protestant church in Red River, St. Andrew's, was opened at Grand Rapid.
May 21, Election riot in Montreal.
May 29, The propeller "Pumper" made the first trip through the Rideau canal from Bytown (Ottawa) to Kingston.
New School Act was passed in Lower Canada.
London district, U.C., was now settled.
During this year some prominent men of Upper Canada urged that the Island of Montreal be added to Upper Canada, so that a seaport could be secured for the younger province.
The quarantine station, Grosse Isle, was established.
"The Tallow Company" was organized at Red River, to raise cattle and export hides and tallow.
June 7, The corner stone of Upper Canada Academy (Methodist) was laid in Cobourg.
June 9, The cholera reached Quebec, brought by the ship "Carrick" from Dublin.
June 10, The cholera reached Montreal.
Oct. 4, Felix P. C. Geoffrion, statesman, was born in Varennes, Lower Canada.

1833.

Gov. Simpson, Red River, advised his people to engage in stock-raising, especially sheep.
June 2, Hector Cameron was born in Montreal.
June 5, The corporation of the city of Montreal first met, Mr. Jacques Viger, mayor.
The penitentiary, Kingston, U.C., was first opened.
Aug. 5, The "Royal William" left Quebec for London; this was the first ship, depending on the motive power of steam alone, that crossed the Atlantic.
Oct. 13, Edward Blake was born in Adelaide, Middlesex county, Upper Canada.
Nov. 2, Wm. L. Mackenzie was expelled from the U.C. Assembly, the third time.
Nov. 7, Louis François Roderique Masson, statesman, was born in Terrebonne, L.C.

Quebec, Lower Canada, was incorporated as a city, Mr. Elzear Bedard first mayor.
Dec. 16, Wm. L. Mackenzie was re-elected by York.
Dec. 17, Wm. L. Mackenzie was re-expelled from the Assembly for "publishing a false and scandalous libel."

1834.

Jan. 23, The Chateau, St. Louis, Quebec, was burned.
Feb. 11, Wm. L. Mackenzie, having taken the oath prescribed for members of the Legislature, entered the House, but the serjeant-at-arms forcibly ejected him.
Feb. 21, Mr. Bedard, in L.C. Assembly, introduced ninety-two resolutions, expressing grievances against the Government.
March 6, York was made a city and re-named Toronto.
March 27, Wm. L. Mackenzie was elected first mayor of Toronto.
April 15, Mr. Roebuck, in the Imperial Parliament, moved for a select committee to enquire into the political conditions of the Canadas, adding that these Provinces, in consequence of continuous bad Government, are in a state approaching to open revolt.
Aug. 4, Mr. Hume presented to the Imperial Parliament, Mr. Bedard's ninety-two resolutions, signed by 18,083 people.
Aug. 23, Lord Gosford arrived at Quebec.
Quit Rents were commuted in Nova Scotia.
The *Whig*, Kingston, U.C., now appeared.
Aug. 26, Louis François George Baby, statesman, was born in Montreal.
Nov. 4, The last number of the *Colonial Advocate* appeared.
Nov. 20, The Constitutional Society of Montreal framed an address, expressing the political views of the ultra British element.
Dec. 9, The "Canadian Alliance Society" was formed in Toronto, an organization with democratic tendencies.

1835.

"Sam Slick," the clockmaker, written by Judge Haliburton, appeared in the *Nova Scotian*.
Lord Aylmer erected a monument to Wolfe on the Plains of Abraham, and a slab to the memory of Montcalm in the Ursuline Convent, Quebec.

Aug. 23, Lord Gosford arrived at Quebec.
Hudson's Bay Company paid the Earl of Selkirk £84,000 for the land the Company had granted in 1811 to Thomas, Earl of Selkirk, and for costs of settlers and settlements.
Aug. 23, Samuel Hume Blake was born in Toronto.
The settlers at Red River began to complain against the monopoly and the oppressive rule of the Hudson's Bay Company.
Sept. 15, Lord Aylmer went to England.
Dec. 4, Sir Richard John Cartwright, statesman, was born in Kingston.

1836.

Jan. 15, Sir John Colborne, at the instance of the Executive Council of Upper Canada, created and endowed forty-four rectories in U.C.
Feb. 6, John A. Macdonald was called to the degree of barrister-at-law.
Feb. 14, Rev. George Jehosophat Mountain was made the first Anglican bishop of Montreal.
Feb 20, Sir Francis Bond Head called Messrs. John Henry Dunn, Robert Baldwin, and John Rolph to the Executive Council of Upper Canada.
March 4, Messrs. Dunn, Baldwin, Rolph, Peter Robinson, Geo. H. Markland, and Joseph Wells resigned from the Executive Council of Upper Canada.
A horse railway was put in operation between Laprairie and St. John's, L.C.
June 30, A meeting of rural Reformers, at Lloydtown, U.C., resolved that as oppression could not be constitutionally resisted, every Reformer should arm himself to defend his rights.
Aug. 20, Thomas Moss, jurist, was born in Cobourg, U.C.
Aug. 27, The Upper Canada Academy, Cobourg, was opened.
Sept. 8, Jean Jacques Lartigue was made the first Catholic bishop of Montreal.
Oct. 3, The Assembly of Lower Canada, in an address to the Governor, declined to vote a supply for government expenses, until there was an elective legislative council and other reforms.

1837.

March 6, Lord John Russell laid before the House of Commons his Ten Resolutions.

March 8, The Bank of British North America was opened in Montreal.

May, The banks of Lower Canada suspended specie payment; it was due to the financial panic in the United States. Gen. Sir J. Harvey was made Lieut.-Gov. of New Brunswick.

June 21, Queen Victoria began to reign.

July 28, At a meeting of Reformers, held in John Doel's brewery, Toronto, Wm. L. Mackenzie moved, seconded by Dr. Morrison, "that the thanks of the Reformers of Upper Canada be tendered to Hon. L. J. Papineau and his compatriots for their devoted, honorable, and patriotic opposition to the oppressive rule of the Imperial Government."

Locomotives began to be used on the railway from Laprairie to St. John's.

Oct. 24, Bishop Lartigue, of Montreal, issued a *mandament*, to be read in the churches, condemning all revolutionary proceedings.

Nov. 6, Thomas Storrow Brown led the "Sons of Liberty" in an attack upon members of the Doric Club, in Montreal; it was the beginning of the Rebellion in Lower Canada.

The office of the *Vindicator*, a patriot paper, was wrecked in Montreal.

Nov. 16, Warrants were issued for the arrest of Papineau, Brown, O'Callaghan, and others.

Nov. 23, Col. Gore attacked Dr. Nelson at St. Denis, but was forced to retire. The rebels brutally murdered Lieutenant Weir.

Nov. 25, Col. Wetherall drove Brown out of St. Charles.

Dec. 2, Col. Gore entered St. Denis, Nelson having withdrawn.

Dec. 4, About 800 rebels collected on Yonge Street, north of Toronto; Col. Moodie was shot.

Dec. 5, The Governor declared the district of Montreal under martial law.

Dec. 7, Sir Francis Head and Col. McNab, with 500 militia, marched from Toronto to Montgomery's Tavern on

Yonge Street, when, after driving off 800 rebels, they burned the tavern; William Lyon Mackenzie took to flight.

A reward of £1,000 was offered for the apprehension of Mackenzie, and £500 for that of Gibson, Lount, Jesse Lloyd, and Silas Fletcher.

Dec. 11, Mackenzie reached Buffalo.

Dec. 12, Mackenzie addressed a large audience in Buffalo, appealing for help.

Dec. 14, Sir John Colborne crushed a large gathering of rebels at St. Eustache, Lower Canada.

Dec. 29, Lieutenant Drew, directed by Col. McNab, cast the "Caroline," which had carried munitions and stores from the United States to the rebels on Navy Island, over the Niagara Falls.

1838.

Jan 5, President Van Buren issued a proclamation forbidding Americans to aid "patriot" Canadians.

Feb. 10, The Imperial Government suspended the constitution of Lower Canada.

March 1, Six hundred "patriots" under Dr. Nelson, surrendered in Vermont to Gen. Wool, of U.S. army.

March 26, Lount and Matthews, in Toronto, were arraigned before Chief Justice Robinson for participation in the rebellion.

March 29, Lount and Matthews were condemned to death.

April 12, Lount and Matthews were executed in Toronto.

May 27, Lord Durham arrived in Canada as High Commissioner.

May 29, Members of "Hunter's Lodges," an American organization in sympathy with Canadian rebels, burned the steamer "Sir Robert Peel" on the St. Lawrence. The Bank of Montreal issued a penny, now a very rare coin.

June 28, Lord Durham, by an ordinance of a special council created by himself, sent Wolfred Nelson, R. S. M. Bouchette, and other rebels to Bermuda, making death the penalty for returning; Louis Joseph Papineau, Dr. O'Callaghan, George Etienne Cartier, and thirteen others, who had fled to the United States, were to get the death penalty if they returned of their own accord. The Imperial Government promptly disallowed the ordinance. Lord Durham soon went to England, and during the passage he made his famous "Report" on Canadian affairs.

July 14, Allan Napier MacNab was knighted.
Nov. 1, Colborne began to administer the government.
Nov. 3, Rebels at Beauharnois attacked the steamer "Henry Brougham."
Nov. 4, Rebels attacked Caughnawaga Village, while the Indians were in church ; but the Iroquois rushed out, seized their arms, and put the rebels to flight.
Mr Hincks began the *Toronto Examiner*, having for its motto, "Responsible Government and the Voluntary Principle."
Nov. 9, Col. Charles C. Taylor defeated Nelson and 800 rebels at Odelltown.
Nov. 11, William Von Schoultz landed a body of men at Prescott, and took possession of a wind-mill.
Nov. 13, Col. Young forced Von Schoultz and his men to surrender.
Dec. 4, "Gen." Bierce led 400 men from Detroit to Windsor, where they burned a steamer, several houses, and killed some unarmed people ; Col. Prince, with 170 militia, hurried up from Sandwich, killed 24 of the filibusters, and took four prisoners whom he immediately shot. He was sharply reprimanded for doing so however.
Dec. 8, Von Schoultz was executed at Kingston.
Dec. 21, In Montreal, two rebels, Joseph Narcisse Cardinal and Joseph Duquette, were hanged

1839.

Jan. 17, Sir John Colborne took the oath of office as Gov. General of Canada.
Jan. 18, Decoigne, two Sanguinets, and Hamelin, rebels, were hanged in Montreal.
Jan. 31, Lord Durham issued his report in London.
Owing to the undecided boundary between New Brunswick and Maine, the New Brunswick and Maine lumbermen came to blows. Gov. Fairfield, of Maine, called on the State militia ; Sir John Harvey, Governor of New Brunswick, sent two regi-

ments to the Aroostook. War seemed imminent. But, in a short time, Sir John Harvey and Gen. Scott compromised the matter. It has been called the "Aroostook War."

Feb. 11, Lord Melbourne laid Lord Durham's report on the table of the House of Commons.

Feb. 25, Lorimer, Hindenlang, Narbonne, Nicholas, and Daunais, rebels, were hanged in Montreal.

Aug. 4, In the chapel of Lambeth Palace, the Archbishop of Canterbury, the Bishop of London, the Bishop of Chichester, and the Bishop of Nova Scotia consecrated Rev. John Strachan Bishop of Toronto, his diocese being Upper Canada.

Aug. 15, Gov. Colborne, under the seal of the province, issued letters patent, constituting Mgr. Jean Jacques Lartigue Bishop of the Catholic diocese of Montreal, with perpetual succession for him and his successors.

Oct. 17, Mr. Charles Poulett Thomson, Lord Sydenham, arrived in Canada, to obtain the concurrence of the Canadians to a reunion of the two provinces, in which after a fashion he succeeded.

Nov. 12, Jonathan Sewell, jurist, died in Quebec.

Nov. 16, Louis Honore Frechette, author, was born in Levis, Lower Canada.

1840.

Feb. 10, In the Chapel Royal, the Archbishop of Canterbury, at 10 a.m., married Prince Albert of Saxe-Coburg-Gotha and Queen Victoria.

March 31, William Meredith, jurist, was born in Westminster, Upper Canada.

April 17, Benjamin Lett, a renegade Canadian, blew up Brock's Monument

July 4, The "Brittania," the pioneer of the Cunard steamship line, left Liverpool for Halifax and Boston.

July 7, James Bethune, jurist, was born in Glengarry, Upper Canada.

July 23, Lord John Russell's Bill, "An Act to reunite the provinces of Upper and Lower Canada, and for the Government of Canada," Act of Union, received Royal assent.

"The Act provided for a legislative council of not less than twenty members, and for a legislative assembly in which each section of the united provinces would be represented by an equal number of members—that is to say, forty-two for each, or eighty-four in all. The Speaker of the Council was appointed by the Crown, and ten members, including the Speaker, constituted a quorum. A majority of voices was to decide, and in case of an equality of votes, the Speaker had a casting vote. A legislative counsellor would vacate his seat by continuous absence for two consecutive sessions. The number of representatives allotted to each province could not be changed except with the concurrence of two-thirds of the members of each house. The quorum of the assembly was to be twenty, including the Speaker. The Speaker was elected by the majority, and was to have a casting vote in case of the votes being equal on a question. No person could be elected to the assembly unless he possessed a freehold of lands and tenements to the value of five hundred pound sterling over and above all debts and mortgages. The English language alone was to be used in the legislative records. A session of the legislature should be held once, at least, every year, and each legislative assembly was to have a duration of four years, unless sooner dissolved."
—Bourinot's "Constitution of Canada," p. 35.

Aug. 9, Royal assent was given to an act which empowered the Governor of Canada to sell certain of the Clergy Reserves, and to apply the proceeds for the benefit of the Churches of England and Scotland.

In this year, the *Advertiser* was begun in Montreal, the first daily newspaper in Canada.

Sept. 21, Chas. Mair, poet, was born in Lanark, Upper Canada.
Oct. 15, Honore Mercier was born in St. Athanase, Lower Canada.

Population of Upper Canada, 465,000.
Population of Lower Canada, 691,000.

Nov. 12, Alexander McLeod was arrested in Lewiston, N.Y., for the murder of Durfee, when the "Caroline" was sent over the Falls, and for arson.

The Imperial Government established a magnetical and metereological observatory at Toronto.

1841.

Feb. 5, A proclamation was issued, declaring a reunion of Lower and Upper Canada.
Feb. 10, Lord Sydenham, in Montreal, after taking the oath of office, proclaimed the reunion of the two provinces.

Feb. 13, Lord Sydenham, after making Kingston the capital of Canada, named Messrs. Sullivan, Dunn, Ogden, Draper, Baldwin, Day, Daly, and Harrison for his Council.

Mar. 12, Mr. Fox, British Minister, demanded McLeod's release

Mar. 17, Mr. H. H. Killaly was added to Lord Sydenham's Council.

April 6, Steps were taken to organize a Board of Trade in Montreal, Hon. Peter McGill in the chair.

April 10, Halifax, N.S., received a city charter.

May 17, Thirty-two people were killed in Quebec by a landslide from the Citadel Rock.

June 14, The first Parliament of Canada met in Kingston. The members of the Executive Council were William Henry Draper, Attorney-General, and Robert Baldwin, Solicitor-General.

Mr. Baldwin's suggestion that French Canadians be included in the Ministry being rejected, he resigned.

July 14, Mr. Harrison presented the Municipal Act to the Assembly.

July 30, Sir Geo. Arthur presided over a meeting of 8,000 people beside the ruined monument of Gen. Brock, to restore the monument at public expense.

Aug. 10, James David Edgar, statesman, was born in Hartley, L.C.

Aug. 19, The Municipal Act passed its third reading.

Aug. 27, Upper Canada Academy, by royal charter, became Victoria College, and endowed with university powers.

Sept. 3, Resolutions were passed in the Canadian Parliament recognizing responsible government.

Sept. 4, Lord Sydenham had a leg broken, by the falling of his horse.

Sept. 18, An Act for the establishment and maintenance of public schools in Canada, introduced by Solicitor-General Day, was assented to ; it provided that an annual sum of $80,000 be appropriated for schools in Upper Canada, and $120,000 for schools in Lower Canada.

Sept. 18, Royal assent was given to Canadian Copyright Act.

Sept. 18, Canadian Parliament was prorogued.
Sept. 19, Lord Sydenham died.
Oct. 4, Alex. McLeod was put on trial in Utica, N.Y.; after eight days he was discharged.
Oct. 16, Queen's College, Kingston, received a royal charter.
Oct. 21, Victoria College, Cobourg, was opened by its principal, Rev. Egerton Ryerson, D.D.
Nov. 9, Birth of the Prince of Wales.
Nov. 20, Sir Wilfrid Laurier was born at St. Lin, Lower Canada.

Sixty-four seagoing vessels, with an aggregate of 23,-122 tons, were built in Quebec during the year.

Dec. 1, The first copyright was granted by Canada; it was for the "Canadian Spelling Book," prepared by Alex. Davidson, Niagara district, and published by Henry Roswell, King St., Toronto.

1842.

Jan. 1, The Municipal Act went into force.
Jan. 10, Sir Charles Bagot arrived at Kingston.
Jan. 12, Chief Justice Robinson and two puisne judges—Jonas Jones and Archibald Maclean,—swore Sir Chas. Bagot into office.

John Ings began the *Islander*, a newspaper, in Prince Edward Island.

March 7, Queen's College, Kingston, was opened.
April 23, Sir Charles Bagot, in Toronto, laid the foundation-stone of King's College.
May 8, Rev. Michael Power was made the first Catholic bishop of Toronto.
May, The Jesuits, Fathers Chazalle, Martin, Tellier, Hanipaux, Luiset, and Duranquet, came to Canada, "renewing the tradition of their name in Canada."
May, Jean Baptiste Meilleur was made Superintendent of Education in Lower Canada.
June 9, Mr. Hincks was made Inspector-General of Public Accounts.
July 9, The steamer "Shamrock" was lost in the St. Lawrence, twelve miles above Lachine, and many people, mostly immigrants, were lost.
July 23, Mr. Henry Sherwood was made Solicitor-General for Upper Canada.

Aug. 9, Lord Ashburton and Daniel Webster, at Washington, concluded the "Ashburton Treaty," which fixed the boundary line between New Brunswick and Maine and re-affirmed its continuation westward to the Rocky Mountains ; and provided for the extradition of criminals "charged with the crime of murder, or assault with intent to commit murder, or piracy, or arson, or robbery, or forgery, or the utterance of forged paper, committed within the jurisdiction of either." Lord Palmerston called it the "Ashburton Capitulation."

Sept. 8, Parliament met in Kingston.

"In Canada, so recently as on Sept. 8, 1842, the Governor-General, in his speech from the Throne at the opening of the Legislature, announced that the Imperial Parliament had framed a tariff for the British possessions in North America, which, it was anticipated, would promote essentially their financial and commercial interests. But this was the last instance of Imperial interference in a matter so vitally affecting the welfare and internal development of the Canadian people."—Todd's "Parliamentary Government in the British Colonies," p. 176.

Sept., Mr. Lafontaine got a seat in the Cabinet, the first French-Canadian to enter the Cabinet since the Re-union.

Oct. 5, Rampant ruffianism defeated Mr. Baldwin's election in Hastings County.

Oct. 12, Mr. Draper having tendered his resignation, the Canadian Government was reconstructed as follows :
Hon. L. H. Lafontaine, Att.-Gen. for Lower Canada.
" Robt. Baldwin, Att.-Gen. for Upper Canada.
" R. B. Sullivan, President of the Council.
" J. H. Dunn, Receiver-General.
" Dominick Daly, Provincial Secretary for Lower Canada.
" S. B. Harrison, Provincial Secretary for Upper Canada.
" H. H. Killaly, President of Department of Public Works
" F. Hincks, Inspector-General of Public Accounts.
" T. C. Aylwin, Solicitor-General for Lower Canada.

Hon. J. E. Small, Solicitor General for Upper Canada.
" A. N. Morin, Commissioner of Crown Lands.
This was the first Lafontaine Baldwin Ministry.

1843.

Jan. 19, William Mulock, statesman, was born in Bond Head, U.C.
Mount Allison College, Sackville, N.B., was opened.
Jan. 30, Mr. Baldwin was elected by Rimouski County, L.C.
March 15, Father Bolduc landed on Vancouver Island, the first priest on the island.
March 16, James Douglas, with 15 men, began the first settlement work on Vancouver Island, the building of Fort Camosun (Victoria.)
March 29, Charles Theophilus Metcalfe, in Kingston, was sworn in as Governor of Canada.
July 4, Lord Stanley's Bill, to reduce the admission of Canadian wheat into the English market from 5s. a quarter to 1s. a quarter, was passed by the Imperial Parliament.
July 12, At the Governor's request, the Orangemen did not parade in Kingston, but at night repealers attacked the lodge rooms, when Robert Morrison was shot.
The first issue of the *Chronicle*, Halifax, N.S., appeared.
Aug. 18, George Brown and his father began the *Banner*, a free church paper, in Toronto.
Aug. 28, With respect to Dr. Nelson, Dr. E. B O'Callaghan, and Thomas S. Brown, a *nolle prosequi* was entered in the Court of Queen's Bench, in Montreal.
Sept. 1, John A. Macdonald married Miss Isabella Clark.
Sept. 28, Parliament met in Kingston.
Nov. 26, As the Governor held that appointments to office, without consulting his Council, was his prerogative, thus acting in the face of responsible government, the Ministry, except Mr. Daly, resigned. Then " Dominick Daly was the Ministry and the Ministry was Dominick Daly."
Dec. 9, Bishops' College, Lennoxville, L.C., was incorporated.
Dec. 9, Parliament of Canada was closed.

1844.

About this time Lieut.-Gov. Falkland resisted the principles of responsible government in Nova Scotia against Messrs. Howe, Uniake, and McNab.

March 5, George Brown issued the first number of the *Globe*, in Toronto.

The Government moved from Kingston to Montreal, the Governor changing Alvington House, Kingston, for Monklands, Montreal.

May 16, Sir Charles Bagot died

May 30, Mr. Roebuck, in the House of Commons, condemned Sir Charles Metcalfe's administration in Canada.

July 1, Parliament met in Montreal.

July, In Kingston, 68 Presbyterian ministers held to the Scottish establishment; 23 formed themselves into the Free Church Synod.

Rev. Egerton Ryerson was made Chief Superintendent of Education for Upper Canada.

Sept. 23, Parliament was dissolved.

Oct. 14, John A. Macdonald was elected Member of Parliament by Kingston.

Nov. 5, Knox College, Toronto, was opened.

Nov. 10, John Sparrow David Thompson was born in Halifax, N.S.

Nov. 12, General election in Canada; "such an election has never been witnesssed in Canada."

Nov. 28, Parliament met in Montreal.

1845.

Feb. 13, Mr. Draper, having resigned his seat in the Legislative Council to be Government leader in the Assembly, was elected by London.

March 29, Parliament was prorogued in Montreal.

"About this time the French press of Lower Canada began to seriously advocate an idea which eventually came to be known as 'the double majority principle.' The existing Government, ever since its formation, had been kept in power by a large Upper Canada majority, acting in concert with a small minority from Lower Canada. It was now proposed that it should be recognized as a vital principle of the constitution that a Government, in order to its continuance in power, must be sustained, not merely by a majority of votes in the entire Assembly, but by a majority of votes from each section of the Province. The object sought to be attained was to prevent either section of the province from imposing unpalatable legislation upon the other. There were repeated attempts to apply this principle, but contrary to what is asserted in most histories of Canada, it did not obtain general recognition until more than ten years subsequent to the date at which this narrative has arrived [1845.]"—Dent's "Canada Since the Union," II., 20.

May 4, Louis Henry Davis, statesman, was in Charlottetown, P.E.I.

May 28, Two thousand houses were destroyed by fire in Quebec.

June 11, Rev. Dr. Medley, the first Bishop of the English Church in New Brunswick, arrived at Fredericton.

June 28, There was a greater conflagration in Quebec, 15,000 people being made homeless.

Nov. 24, Lord Metcalfe appointed six commissioners to enquire into the losses sustained by the loyal people of Lower Canada during the rebellion.

Nov. 26, Lord Metcalfe left Montreal for England, having deputed his functions to Earl Cathcart.

1846.

Jan. 5, The first number of the *Weekly Witness*, Montreal, was issued.

Feb. 9, The United States Congress passed resolutions giving advice to Great Britain that joint occupation of Oregon would cease in twelve years from notice.

March 16, Lord Cathcart was commissioned Governor of Canada.

March 20, Parliament met in Montreal.

April 18, The commissioners, appointed to enquire into the losses sustained by the loyal people of Lower Canada, gave their report: "They had recognized two thousand one hundred and seventy-six claims, amounting in the aggregate to £241,965. . . . The commissioners were of opinion that the sum of £100,000 would be sufficient to pay all real losses."

April 27, John A. Macdonald made his maiden speech in Parliament, advocating a repeal of the usury laws.

May 13, Kingston, U.C., received a City Charter.

Sir J. Harvey was made Lieut.-Governor of Nova Scotia.

At this time the popular cry in the United States was "Fifty-four-forty or fight," meaning that, unless fifty-four degrees and forty minutes be the dividing line between Oregon and British America, there would be war.

In June, Hamilton, Upper Canada, was, by Act of Parliament, incorporated into a city.

June 9, Parliament adjourned in Montreal.

June 15, Lord Pakenham, for Great Britain, and James Buchanan, for the United States, concluded a Treaty which made the 49th parallel of north latitude the boundary line between British America and the United States, from the Rocky Mountains westward "to the middle of the channel which separates the continent from Vancouver's Island; and thence southerly through the middle of the said channel, and of Fuca's Strait, to the Pacific Ocean."

July 15, The first number of the *Spectator*, Hamilton, U.C., was issued.

Aug. 17, Mr John Hillyard Cameron, having been appointed Solicitor-General, was elected by Cornwall.

Sept 5, Lord Metcalfe died in England.

1847.

Jan. 29, Lord Elgin arrived in Montreal, as Governor of Canada.

March 1, There was an election riot at Pinette, Prince Edward Island.

May 21, John A. Macdonald was appointed Receiver-General.

May 28, Mr. Sherwood was made Attorney-General for Upper Canada and Prime Minister.

June 2, Parliament was opened in Montreal.

July 28, Parliament adjourned.

In this year, 100,000 immigrants came to Canada; but, being victims of ship-fever, nearly 10,000 had hospital care; hundreds and hundreds died. Grosse Isle, the quarantine station, was the most pestilent spot in the country.

Aug. 3, The electric telegraph was introduced into Canada, connecting Quebec, Montreal, and Toronto

Normal School was opened at Fredericton, N.B.

Nov. 1, The Normal School, Toronto, was opened.
Dec. 6, Parliament of Canada was dissolved.

1848.

Jan. 24, At the general election, the Reformers swept the country.
Feb. 25, Parliament met in Montreal.
March 4, The Government of Canada resigned
March 10, " Mr. Lafontaine accepted office as Premier and Attorney-General, and for twenty four hours was sole Minister."
March 11, The second Lafontaine-Baldwin Ministry came into power. The Ministers were :—
    Hon. L. H. Lafontaine, Att.-Gen. for Lower Canada.
    " Robert Baldwin, Att.-Gen. for Upper Canada.
    " James Leslie, President of Executive Council.
    " R. B. Sullivan, Provincial Secretary.
    " R. E. Caron, Speaker of Legislative Council.
    " Francis Hincks, Inspector-General.
    " E. P. Tache, Chief Commissioner of Public Works.
    " J H. Price, Commissioner of Crown Lands.
    " T. C. Aylwin, Solicitor-General.
    " Malcolm Cameron, Assistant Commissioner of Public Works.
    " L M. Viger, Receiver-General.
March 27, Fredericton, N.B., was incorporated into a city : it is the "Celestial City."
March 29, The Niagara River nearly ran dry, the water being held back by an ice jam at Lake Erie.
    Responsible government was now assured in Canada, Nova Scotia, and New Brunswick.
July 29, "The last plank of the Suspension foot-bridge over the Niagara Falls was laid, and the engineer, Mr. Ellet, drove over and back in a buggy, and subsequently in a carriage with two horses, weighing in all over a ton and a half. 500 feet of the bridge are without railing on either side. The flooring is 220 feet high, 762 feet long, and 8 feet wide."— *American Almanac.*
    The Normal School, St. John, N.B., was opened.
Nov. 24, William Stevens Fielding, journalist and statesman, was born in Halifax, N.S.

1849.

Jan, 13, The Crown granted Vancouver Island to the Hudson's Bay Company for colonization.

Jan. 18, Parliament met in Montreal. Rebellion Losses Bill was introduced into the House.

Feb. 1, The Governor of Canada gave his assent to the Amnesty Bill. William Lyon Mackenzie quickly returned to Canada.

April 25, Lord Elgin gave his assent to the Rebellion Losses Bill. When he left the House to go to Monklands, frenzied mobs, in Montreal, pelted his carriage with every abominable missile, and strove to do him personal injury ; but, by rapid driving, he escaped them ; then, in their mad rage, they burned the House of Assembly, the public records of the Upper and Lower Canada Parliaments, and the records of the Parliament since the Union.

April 30, Lord Elgin drove into Montreal, and was soon surrounded by a hostile mob, which pelted him with stones, and drove him back to Monklands.

May 30, The College of Bytown (Ottawa) was chartered.
Parliament was prorogued.
England repealed the Navigation Laws, freeing Canada from "preferential duties."
A body of radical reformers made the "Clear Grit Departure," agitating for universal suffrage, vote by ballot, biennial parliaments, free trade, direct taxation, etc.; in Lower Canada Mr. Papineau was the recognized leader of a party still more radical, "Le Partie Rouge."
The "University of King's College," Toronto, became the University of Toronto.

Oct. 1, Wm. H. Blake was made Chancellor of Upper Canada.
In October it was decided that the two remaining sessions of the existing parliament should be held in Toronto, after which the government would be in Quebec and Toronto, alternately, every four years.
In November the government moved from Montreal to Toronto.

Dec. 14, John Sandfield Macdonald was made Solicitor-General for Upper Canada.

1850.

March 10, Gov. Blanchard arrived in Victoria, B.C.
April 19, Great Britain and the United States made the Bulwer-Clayton Treaty, "for facilitating and protecting the construction of a ship canal between the Atlantic and the Pacific Oceans."
May 14, Parliament met in Toronto. It was announced in the speech from the throne that the control of the internal post office of British North America had been vested in the provincial authorities.
June 29, The last part of Table Rock, Niagara, fell.
  Coal was discovered in Vancouver Island.
July 25, In Westminster Abbey Rev. Francis Fulford, D.D., was consecrated Bishop of Montreal.
Aug. 10, Parliament at Toronto was prorogued.
  In October the first Agricultural Exhibition in Canada was held in Montreal
Dec. 19, Mr. Brown published, in the *Globe*, a copy of Cardinal Wiseman's manifesto, and some very caustic comments thereon.

1851.

Feb. 22, Hon. James Morris was made Postmaster-General, being the first postmaster to enter the Ministry.
April 6, The Canadian Government took control of the post office of Canada.
May 20, Parliament met in Toronto.
  First postage stamp was issued by Canada.
Aug. 2, Royal assent was given to an Act which abolished the law of primogeniture in Canada.
  St. Mary's College, Montreal, was opened.
Aug 31, Parliament, Toronto, was prorogued.
Oct. 4, A violent storm swept over Prince Edward Island, doing great damage.
  In October the Lafontaine-Baldwin Ministry, "The Great Ministry," resigned.
  In October the government offices were moved from Toronto to Quebec, the Governor making Spencerwood his residence.
Oct. 15, Lady Elgin turned the first sod for the Northern Railway.

Oct. 28, The Hincks-Morin Ministry took office.
Its members were:—
Hon. Francis Hincks, Premier and Inspector-General, U.C.
" A. N. Morin, Provincial Secretary, L.C.
" W. B. Richards, Att.-Gen., West.
" L. T. Drummond, Att. Gen., East.
" Malcolm Cameron, President of Council, U.C.
" John Young, Commissioner of Public Works, L.C.
" John Rolph, Commissioner of Crown Lands, U.C.
" R. E. Caron, Speaker of Legislative Council, L.C.
James Morris, Postmaster-General, U.C.
Hon. E. P. Tache, Receiver-General, L.C.
Nov. 6, Parliament was dissolved.
Dec. 9, The Young Men's Christian Association was established in Montreal ; this was the first entrance of the Society in America.
Dec. 14, George Brown was elected to Parliament by Kent and Lambton.

1852.

Jan. 1, The Act abolishing the law of primogeniture in Canada went into effect.
Jan. 28, Bishop's University, Lennoxville, L.C., received a royal charter.
The Baptist Missionary Society of Canada was formed.
May 4, Rev. William Walsh was made the first Catholic Archbishop of Halifax, N.S.
Responsible government was now assured in Prince Edward Island.
Mrs. Moodie's "Roughing it in the Bush" was published.
July 6, McGill College, Montreal, received a new royal charter.
July 8, A large part of Montreal was destroyed by fire.
July 16, Trinity University, Toronto, received a royal charter.
A few Fathers of St. Basil began St. Michael's College, Toronto.
Aug. 19, Parliament met in Quebec.

Aug. 25, The Attorney-General of Upper Canada, at the instance of the Legislative Assembly, filed a Bill in the Court of Chancery, to test the validity of " certain letters-patent granted by Sir John Colborne, bearing date 15th January, 1836, and purporting to constitute a rectory within the township of York, to be known as the rectory of St. James, and to set apart 800 acres of the Clergy Reserve Lands as an endowment for said rectory, to be held and enjoyed forever as appurtenant thereto."

Mr. Hincks obtained for Upper Canada the Municipal Loan Fund Act.

> " It enabled municipalities to obtain money for local improvements, roads, bridges, and railway construction, which proved of great and permanent value to the country."— Withrow's " Hist. of Canada."

Oct. 18, Thos. Cooke, D.D., was made the first Catholic Bishop of Three Rivers, L.C.

Nov. 10, Parliament adjourned, cholera being in Quebec. From this date down to March 20, 1862, the Presidents of the Executive Council were *ex officio* Ministers of Agriculture.

Dec. 8, Laval University, Quebec, received a royal charter.

1853.

Feb. 14, Parliament reassembled in Quebec.

April 16, The Toronto Locomotive Works completed the "Toronto," the first locomotive built in Canada.

June 6, Father Gavazzi, an ex-monk, lectured in the Free Church, Quebec, but a mob drove him from the building.

June 9, Father Gavazzi gave a lecture in Zion Church, Montreal, which excited a riot ; Mr. Wilson, Mayor, ordered the military to fire into the rioters; five men were killed.

The Upper Canadians, before now and down to Confederation, demanded representation by population, " Rep. by Pop.," Mr. Brown being particularly insistent.

June 13, The Northern Railway was opened from Toronto to Bradford.

June 14, Parliament, Quebec, adjourned.

Dr. Alex Tache was made Archbishop of St. Boniface, Red River.

July 18 The Grand Trunk Railway was opened to Portland. In September, the College de Levis, opposite Quebec, was opened.

Nov. 1, The Great Western Railway was opened from Niagara River to Hamilton.

Dec. 31, The Great Western Railway was opened from Hamilton to London.

1854.

Jan. 27, The Great Western Railway was opened from London to Windsor.

Feb. 1, The Parliament Building, Quebec, was burned.

June 5, Lord Elgin and Wm. L. Marcy, in Washington, signed the Reciprocity Treaty.

> "The treaty provided for a free exchange of the products of the sea, the fields, the forest and the mine. It admitted Americans to the rich Canadian fisheries, and to the advantages of Canadian river and canal navigation. To Canadian farmers, lumbermen, and miners, it was beneficial; but to the Maritime Provinces it refused the only boon worth being considered in exchange for the fisheries, namely, the admission of provincial ships to the American coasting trade. On the whole the treaty was a good thing for Canada, though perhaps more advantageous to the Americans. Its provisions were to remain in force for ten years, after which either party to the agreement was left free to end it by giving one year's notice."—Roberts' "History of Canada," p. 324.

June 13, Parliament met in Quebec.

At Richmond, near Halifax, the first sod was turned for the railway from Halifax to Truro.

June 22, Parliament was dissolved.

Right Rev. Colin F. McKinnon, Bishop of Arichat, founded St. Francis Xavier's College, at Antigonish, N.S.

Aug. 11, Royal assent was given to an Act which made the Legislative Council of Canada elective.

Sept. 5, Parliament met in Quebec.

Albert College, Belleville, U.C., was established.

Sept. 8, The Hincks-Morin ministry resigned.

Sept. 11, The MacNab-Morin Government, a coalition, took office; its members were :—

Hon. Sir Allan N. MacNab, President of Council and Minister of Agriculture, U.C.
Hon. A. N. Morin, Commissioner of Crown Lands, L C.
Hon. John A. Macdonald, Att -Gen., West.
" L. T. Drummond, Att.-Gen., East.
" William Cayley, Inspector General, U.C.
" P. J. O. Chauveau, Provincial Secretary, L.C.
" Robert Spence, Postmaster-General, U.C.
" E P Tache, Receiver-General, I. C.
" Jno. Ross, Speaker of Leg slative Council, U.C.
" J. Chabot Commissioner of Public Works, L.C.
Sept. 21, London, Upper Canada, received a city charter.
Oct. 17, John A. Macdonald introduced a Bill to securalize the Clergy Reserves, providing that the proceeds of the sales of such reserves be apportioned among the municipalities of cities and counties in proportion to population.
Oct. 20, Attorney General Drummond introduced a Bill for the abolition of seignorial tenure in Lower Canada.
Oct 27, There was a collision between a passenger train and a gravel train on the Great Western Railway, between Chatham and Windsor ; 47 people were killed.
Dec. 1, P.O. Money Order offices were first opened.
Dec. 18, The Bills for the secularization of the Clergy Reserves and the abolition of seignorial tenure in Lower Canada received royal assent.
Dec. 18, Parliament, Quebec, adjourned.
Dec. 19, Sir Edmund Walker Head was sworn into office as Governor of Canada.

1855.

On the first Monday in January, Ottawa, U.C., was incorporated as a city.
Jan. 26, Hon. A. N. Morin retired from the Ministry, his health being bad.
Feb. 1, P.O. Registration system was inaugurated.
Feb. 8, Six new Legislative Councillors, Messrs. Ebenezer Perry, David M. Armstrong, Benjamin Seymour, Eusebe Cartier, Walter H. Dickson, and Joseph Legare were appointed.
Feb. 23, Parliament re-assembled in Quebec.

March 8, The first locomotive crossed the Suspension bridge at Niagara.

March 16, The Reciprocity Treaty with the United States went into effect.

The Militia Act, the beginning of our Volunteer System, was passed during this session; it made the Governor the Commander-in-Chief of the militia.

May 30, The Taché Separate School Bill for Upper Canada received Royal assent.

May 30, Parliament was prorogued.

Prosperity in Canada.

Rev. Alexander Forrester, D.D., was made Superintendent of Education in Nova Scotia.

Hon. Pierre Joseph Olivier Chauveau was made Superintendent of Education in Lower Canada.

Sir John W. Dawson published "Acadian Geology."

In October, the Government offices were moved from Quebec to Toronto.

Oct. 17, At St. Sylvester, L.C., Robert Corrigan was murdered by a mob at a cattle fair.

In November, the Normal School at Truro, N.S., was opened.

Dec. 3, The Great Western Railway was opened from Hamilton to Toronto.

1856.

Feb. 15, Parliament met in Toronto.

Feb. 26, Mr. John A. Macdonald and Mr. Geo. Brown had a bitter altercation in the Canadian Assembly.

March 7, John Hillyard Cameron, in parliament, moved for a copy of the charge delivered to the jury by Judge Duval, relating to the trial of several men at Quebec, tried for the murder of Robert Corrigan, a Protestant.

March 10, The Government was defeated on the "Corrigan murder" investigation.

April 16, Mr. John A. Macdonald and Mr. Rankin, of Essex, had a bitter dialogue in Parliament.

April 16, Mr. John Sandfield Macdonald's motion, that after 1859 Quebec should be the permanent capital of Canada, was carried.

May 11, Rev. John Farrell was made the first Catholic Bishop of Hamilton.

May 22, The MacNab-Taché Government resigned.
May 24, The Taché-Macdonald Government was formed.
July 1, Parliament adjourned.
Aug. 12, The first Legislature of Vancouver Island met at Victoria.
> The Allan Line of steamships was established ; the pioneer ships were the " Canadian," " North American," " Indian," and " Anglo-Saxon."

Oct. 27, The first passenger train went from Montreal to Toronto.
Nov. 5, A violent hurricane swept over Montreal.

1857.

Feb. 26, Parliament met in Toronto.
March 12, A passenger train went through a bridge over the Des Jardins Canal, near Hamilton ; 60 people were killed.
> Gold miners flocked to British Columbia.

April 27, Mr. Brown, in the Assembly, re-introduced a resolution " that in the opinion of this House the representation of the people in Parliament should be based on population, without regard to a separating line between Upper and Lower Canada."
> St. Hyacinthe, Lower Canada, was incorporated as a city.
>
> About this time the " Double Majority " principle was silently dropped.
>
> The Jacques Cartier Normal School in Montreal, the McGill Normal School in Montreal, and the Laval Normal School in Quebec, were established.

June 26, The steamer " Montreal " was burnt near Cap Rouge, and 250 immigrants, mostly Scotch, lost their lives.
> Financial panic : hard times.

July 9, Rev. Benjamin Cronyn, D.D., was consecrated the first Bishop of Huron.
July 23, The Grand Jury, at Quebec, reported bills for manslaughter against the owner and officers of the steamer " Montreal."
Aug. 5, The shore end of the Atlantic submarine telegraph cable was, by the Lord-Lieutenant of Ireland, taken from the U.S. war frigate " Niagara," and made fast ashore.

Aug. 11, The Atlantic Cable, being laid out by the U.S. frigate "Niagara," broke, after 335 miles had been laid on the bottom of the ocean.

Oct. 27, The British Commissioners, Captains Prevost and Richards, and the American Commissioners, Archibald Campbell, John G. Parke, and George C. Gardiner, met at Semiahmoo Bay, to confer respecting the boundary line as given in the Treaty of 1846; the conference had no result.

Nov. 25, Col. Taché retiring from the Government, John A. Macdonald became Premier.

Nov. 26, The Macdonald-Cartier Government took control of affairs.

Nov. 28, Parliament adjourned.

Dec. 30, The railway from Port Hope to Lindsay was opened.

1858.

Jan. 27, The Queen named Ottawa for the Capital of Canada.

Feb. 25, Parliament met in Toronto.

In this year, Canada first legislated for protection to home industries.

May 8, John Brown, the American abolitionist, held a convention at Chatham, Upper Canada.

May 28, The railway from Goderich to Fort Erie was opened.

July 28, The Queen having selected Ottawa for the Capital of Canada, Mr. Piche, in the House, proposed the amendment "that in the opinion of this House the City of Ottawa ought not to be the permanent seat of Government of this Province," which was carried by 64 to 50. Mr. Brown proposed an adjournment to try the strength of the Government; 50 voted for it and 61 against it.

July 29, The Macdonald Cartier Government resigned.

Sir Edmund Head called on Mr. George Brown to form a Ministry.

Aug. 1, The Brown-Dorion, or "The Short Administration," was formed; its members were:—

Hon. George Brown, Premier and Inspector-General, U.C.

" A. A. Dorion, Commissioner of Crown Lands, L.C.

" J. S. Macdonald, Att.-Gen., West.

Hon. L. T. Drummond, Att.-Gen., East.
" James Morris, Speaker of Legislative Council, U.C.
" L. H. Holton, Commissioner of Public Works, L.C.
" M. H. Foley, Postmaster General, U.C.
" F. Lemieux, Receiver-General, L.C.
" Oliver Mowat, Provincial Secretary, U.C.
" J. E. Thibaudeau, President of Council, L.C.

Aug. 3, Of 52 members in the House, 27 voted non-confidence in the new administration.

Aug. 4, Members of the Government waited on the Governor and asked for an immediate dissolution of Parliament. Sir Edmund Head gave several solid reasons for refusing to dissolve Parliament.
"The Short Administration" resigned.
During the year the 100th Regiment was recruited in Canada.

Aug 6, The Cartier-Macdonald administration was formed of the old members, not one of them holding the same portfolio that he held prior to July 29.

Aug. 7, The Ministers made a general exchange of portfolios, "The Double Shuffle." This exasperated the members of the Opposition; but competent judges afterwards decided that the Ministers had acted within the law. The members of the new Ministry were:
Hon. G. E. Cartier, Premier and Att.-Gen., East.
" J. A. Macdonald, Att.-Gen., West.
" A. T. Galt, Inspector-General, L.C.
" P. M. Vankoughnet, Commissioner of Crown Lands, U.C.
" N. F. Belleau, Speaker of Legislative Council, L.C.
" Sidney Smith, Postmaster-General, U.C.
" L. V. Sicotte, Minister of Public Works, L.C.
" John Ross, President of Council, U.C.
" Charles Alleyn, Provincial Secretary, L.C.
" George Sherwood, Receiver-General, U.C.

Aug. 16, Royal assent was given to an Act that abolished imprisonment for debt in Canada.
Parliament, in Toronto, was prorogued.

Sept. 1, The Act abolishing imprisonment for debt in Canada went into effect.
>Decimal currency, 20 cts. silver, 10 cts. silver, 5 cts. silver, and 1 cent copper, was introduced into Canada.

Dec. 9, Hon. Robert Baldwin died.

Dec. 15, The railway from Halifax to Truro was opened.

1859.

Jan. 10, The Prince of Wales, at Shorncliffe, gave the 100th Regiment its colors.

Jan. 29, Parliament met in Toronto.

Feb. 14, Queensboro, the capital of British Columbia, was laid out.

Feb. 24, In Westminster Abbey Rev. George Hills was consecrated Bishop of Columbia.

May 4, Parliament was prorogued.
>In May the Government offices were moved from Toronto to Quebec.

June 4, There was a severe frost throughout Canada.

June 30, Emile Gravelet Blondin walked a tight-rope over the Niagara River.

July 27, Captain Pickett, with American soldiers, took possession of San Juan Island.

Nov. 20, Rev. John Joseph Lynch was consecrated Catholic Bishop of Toronto.

Nov. 28, The bodies of Lount and Matthews were removed from the "potter's-field" to the Necropolis, Toronto.

Dec., John Sheridan Hogan, journalist, was murdered at River Don, Toronto.

Dec. 28, The *Nor'-Wester* appeared at Fort Garry, the first newspaper in Red River district.

1860.

Feb. 28, Parliament met in Quebec.
>The Baptists opened a college at Woodstock, U.C.
>The first oil well was sunk at Petrolea, U.C.
>The Assembly purchased the Earl of Selkirk's estates in Prince Edward Island.

May 19, Parliament was prorogued in Quebec.
>The British and the Americans nearly came to blows, on the west coast, over the San Juan boundary question.

Aug. 8, The Prince of Wales arrived at Quebec.
Aug. 13, The first number of the *Daily Witness* in Montreal, was issued.
Aug. 25, The Prince of Wales drove the last rivet of the Victoria Bridge, Montreal.
Sept, 1. The Prince of Wales laid the foundation stone of the Parliament Building, in Ottawa.
Sept. 20, The Prince of Wales entered the United States, at Detroit.
Oct. 12, The Governor of Canada went to England, leaving Sir Wm. Fenwick Williams to administer the Government.
Oct. 19, The Prince of Wales visited Bunker Hill.

1861.

Jan. 9, (The Southerners, Confederates, fired into the Federal steamer "Star of the West," beginning Civil War in the United States.)
Jan. 22, Sir Edmund Head again took the chief administration in Canada.
March 16, Parliament met in Quebec.
May 13, Queen Victoria issued a proclamation, enjoining all her subjects to maintain a strict neutrality in the civil war just beginning in the United States
May 18, Morrin College, Quebec, was chartered.
Parliament was prorogued in Quebec.
June 10, Parliament was dissolved
Gold was discovered in Nova Scotia.
The "Pioneer" was the first steamer on the Red River.
Aug. 26, Yonge Street Line, the first street railway in Canada, was opened.
Aug. 18, Wm. Lyon Mackenzie died.
Aug. 29, Dr. Joseph Morrin, founder of Morrin College, Quebec, died in Quebec.
Oct. 23, Lord Monck arrived in Quebec, as Governor of Canada.
Nov. 8. (Captain Charles Wilkes, of the U.S. warship "San Jacinto," took from the British mail ship "Trent," the Confederates John Slidell and John Y. Mason.)
Dec. 14, Death of the Prince Consort.
Three thousand imperial troops came to Canada.

1862.

Jan. 1, (The United States released John Slidell and John Y. Mason.)

Mar. 20, Parliament met in Quebec. Heretofore, the Crown had appointed the Speaker from the Council, but now the first election of the Speaker took place, Sir Allan MacNab being chosen.

March 25, In Kingston, Rev. John Travers Lewis, D.D., was consecrated Bishop of Ontario ; this was the first Episcopal consecration, of English Church, in Canada.

April 25, John A. Macdonald presented a Bill to Parliament to promote a more efficient organization of the Canadian Militia.

During the Civil War in the United States, the Canadian farmer had a good market for his produce and stock, especially horses ; many young Canadians were also attracted across the border by the heavy bounties paid for "substitutes."

May 20, The Government was defeated on Mr. Macdonald's Militia Bill.

May 21, The Cartier-Macdonald Ministry resigned.

May 24, Messrs. John Sandfield Macdonald and L. V. Sicotte formed a Ministry ; its members were :—

Hon. John S. Macdonald, Premier and Att.-Gen., West.
" L. V. Sicotte, Att.-Gen., East.
" M. H. Foley, Postmaster-General, U.C.
" A. A. Dorion, Provincial Secretary, L.C.
" W. P. Howland, Minister of Finance, U.C.
" T. D. McGee, President of the Council, L.C.
" W. McDougall, Commissioner of Crown Lands, U.C.
" U. J. Tessier, Commissioner of Public Works, L.C.
" James Morris, Receiver-General, U.C.
" François Evanturel, Minister of Agriculture, L.C.
" Adam Wilson, Solicitor-General, West
" J. J. C. Abbott, Solicitor-General, East.

May 31, The Bank of British Columbia received a royal charter.

June 9, Parliament was prorogued.
Aug. 2, Victoria, B.C., was incorporated into a city.
Aug. 8, Sir Allan MacNab died.
Oct. 6, Hon. William McDougall, at Manitowaning, made the Manitoulin Island Treaty, with Ottawas, Chippewas, etc.

1863.

Jan 31, Death of Sir John Beverley Robinson.
Feb. 12, Parliament met in Quebec.
About this time Mr. Brown's "Rep. by Pop." cry was at its height.
March 10, The Prince of Wales and Princess Alexandra of Denmark were married.
May 5, Royal assent was given to Mr. R. W. Scott's Separate School Bill.
In the general election in June, the Government just held its own.
Aug. 12, The Ministry was readjusted as follows :—
    Hon. John S. Macdonald, Premier and Att.-Gen., West.
    " A. A. Dorion, Att.-Gen., East.
    " Wm. McDougall, Commissioner of Crown Lands, U.C.
    " L. H. Holton, Minister of Finance, L.C.
    " W. P. Howland, Receiver-General, U.C.
    " Isidore Thibaudeau, President of Council, L.C.
    " A. J. Ferguson-Blair, Provincial Secretary, U.C.
    " L. Letellier, de St. Just, Minister of Agriculture, L.C.
    " Oliver Mowat, Postmaster-General, U.C.
    " L. S. Huntingdon, Solicitor-General, East.
    " Maurice Laframboise, Commissioner of Public Works.
Aug. 13, Parliament met in Quebec.
Sept. 5, Hon. L. V. Sicotte was made Judge of the Superior Court of Lower Canada.
Milton and Cheadle crossed the continent.
Sept. 18, The *Gleaner*, Huntingdon, L.C., first appeared.
Oct. 15, Parliament was prorogued.
Oct. 28, The first number of the *Advertiser*, London, Ont was issued.

1864.

Jan. 21, The first Legislative Council of British Columbia met at New Westminster, nine members being present.
Feb. 19, Parliament met in Quebec.
Feb. 26, Mr. La Fontaine died in Montreal.
March 21, The Government resigned.
March 30, The Taché Macdonald Administration took office. Its members were : —
  Hon. Sir E. P. Taché, Premier and Receiver-General, L. C.
  " J. A. Macdonald, Att -Gen., West.
  " G. E. Cartier, Att.-Gen., East.
  " Alex. Campbell, Commissioner of Crown Lands, U. C.
  " A. T. Galt, Minister of Finance, L.C.
  " M. H. Foley, Postmaster-General, U.C.
  " J. C. Chapais, Commissioner of Public Works, L.C.
  " Isaac Buchanan, President of Council, U.C.
  " T. D. McGee, Minister of Agriculture, L C.
  " John Simpson, Provincial Secretary, U.C.
  " H. L. Langevin, Solicitor-General, East.
  " James Cockburn, Solicitor-General, West.
March 31, Parliament adjourned.
  Dr. Tupper improved the School System in Nova Scotia.
  The land question was settled in Prince Edward Island.
May 3, Parliament reassembled.
June 14, The Ministry was defeated on a very unimportant matter. There was a " Dead-Lock."
June 17, Messrs. John A. Macdonald and Galt waited upon Mr. George Brown in the St. Louis Hotel, Quebec, to confer with him respecting the constitutional difficulties between the two sections of the province, the result being that Mr Brown joined hands with the Government to assist in effecting some improvement.
June 29, An emigrant train fell into the Richelieu River, near Belœil, L.C., 86 people being killed.
June 30, The Dunkin Act was passed.

Mr. George Brown was made President of the Council, Mr. Mowat, Postmaster-General, and Mr. McDougall, Provincial Secretary.

In September, Messrs. John A. Macdonald, George Brown, G. E. Cartier, A. T. Galt, T. D. McGee, H. L. Langevin, Wm. McDougall, and Alex Campbell, went to Charlottetown, P.E.I., to point out to the Unionists of N.S., N.B. and P.E.I. (who were then in Charlottetown consulting about a union of the three Maritime Provinces) the greater and more complete scheme of a union of all the provinces.

Oct. 10, The Quebec Conference met in Quebec. The representatives of Lower Canada that attended were Messrs. E. P. Tache, G. E. Cartier, A. T. Galt, J. C. Chapais, T. D. McGee, and H. L. Langevin ; of Upper Canada, Messrs. John A. Macdonald, George Brown, Alex. Campbell, Oliver Mowat, Wm. McDougall, and James Cockburn ; of Nova Scotia, Messrs. Chas. Tupper, Wm. Alex. Henry, Jonathan McCully, Robert B. Dickey, and Adams Geo. Archibald ; of New Brunswick, Messrs. Samuel Leonard Tilley, John M. Johnson, Wm. H. Steeves, Edward Barron Chandler, Peter Mitchell, John Hamilton Gray, and Charles Fisher ; of Prince Edward Island, Messrs. John Hamilton Gray, Edward Palmer, William H. Pope, A. A. Macdonald, Edward Whelan, George Coles, and T. H. Haviland ; and of Newfoundland, Messrs. F. B. Carter and John Ambrose Shea. The object of the conference was to effect a Confederation of the British American provinces.

Oct. 19, About forty Southerners, living in Canada, headed by Bennett H. Young, made a raid into Vermont as far as St. Alban's, where they killed one man, robbed the banks, and returned to Canada.

Oct. 28, The Quebec Conference closed ; all agreed to recommend confederation to the provincial legislatures.

1865.

Jan. 19, Parliament met in Quebec.

March 10, The Parliament of Canada passed an address to the Imperial Parliament, praying that the Imperial Parliament grant a measure to unite the Colonies of

Canada, Nova Scotia, New Brunswick, Prince Edward Island, and Newfoundland in one Government.
March 18, Parliament was prorogued.
March 23, The Imperial Parliament granted £50,000 for the defence of Canada.
March 30, The St. Alban's raiders were discharged.
 In April Messrs. John A. Macdonald, Brown, Cartier, and Galt went to England, to advance the scheme of Confederation.
April 9, Gen. Lee surrendered to Gen. Grant, virtually ending the civil war in the United States.
 Gen. Sir Fenwick Williams was made Lieut.-Gov. of Nova Scotia.
April 14, Wilkes Booth, an actor, shot President Lincoln in Ford's Theatre, Washington.
May 1, Trinity College School was opened at Weston, U.C.
June 23, There was a very destructive fire in Quebec.
July 30, Sir E. P. Taché died.
Aug. 8, Parliament met in Quebec, to consider the report of the four delegates that had returned from England.
Sept. 18, Parliament was closed in Quebec.
Dec. 21, Hon. George Brown withdrew from the Ministry.

1866.

Feb. 10, The Governor of Canada informed the Americans that their fishing privileges had ceased.
March 17, Reciprocity with the United States ended.
 The volunteers were under arms all day, expecting a Fenian invasion of the country.
May 31, "General" O'Neil led a horde of Fenians into Canada, crossing from Buffalo to Fort Erie.
June 2, There was a skirmish at Ridgeway, U.C., the Canadian volunteers being greatly outnumbered.
June 8, "General" Spear, with 2,000 Fenians, crossed the boundary near St. Alban's, and occupied Pigeon Hill, but the Hochelaga Voltigeurs soon drove him across the border.
June 8, The last session of the Provincial Parliament met in Ottawa ; this was the first Parliament in Ottawa.
 Gold was discovered in Hastings County, Upper Canada.

July 29, The Atlantic cable having been successfully laid, the first message passed through it.
Aug. 1, The Civil Code of Lower Canada went into effect.
Aug. 15, The College of Ottawa, by royal charter, became the University of Ottawa.
Aug. 15, The last session of the Provincial Parliament closed.
Nov. 17, British Columbia and Vancouver Island were united.
Dec. 4, Messrs John A. Macdonald, Galt, Cartier, Howland, McDougall, and Langevin, from Canada; Messrs. Tupper, Archibald, McCully, and Ritchie, from Nova Scotia; and Messrs. Tilley, Fisher, Mitchell, Johnston, and R. D. Wilmot, from New Brunswick, "The Fathers of Confederation," met at Westminster Hall to frame an act to unite the provinces they represented.
Dec. 24, The Conference at Westminster Hall ended.

1867.

Feb. 7th, The Earl of Carnarvon introduced the Confederation Bill in the House of Lords.
March 8, The Imperial Parliament passed the Confederation Bill.
March 29, The Confederation Bill received royal assent.
April 12, The Imperial Government passed an Act authorizing the commissioners of the treasury to guarantee interest on a loan not exceeding £3,000,000 for the construction of an intercolonial railway from Halifax to the St. Lawrence.
May 22, Her Majesty, by proclamation, issued at Windsor Castle, declared that the Confederation Act should go into effect the first day of the next July; she also gave the names of seventy-two Senators, thirty-six Conservatives and thirty-six Reformers.
June 27, Reform Convention in Toronto.
June 28, The first yearly meeting (of Quakers) in Canada was constituted.
July 1, DOMINION DAY. Lord Monck announced his appointment as Governor-General of the Dominion of Canada, and, by Her Majesty's authority, conferred the Order of Knighthood on Hon. John A. Macdonald, and the honor of Companionship of the

Bath on Messrs. Tilley, Tupper, Cartier, Galt, McDougall, and Howland.

July 2, LORD MONCK was sworn in as Governor-General of Canada, by Chief Justice Draper.
Sir John A. Macdonald, at the request of the Governor-General, formed a Coalition Ministry; its members were:—
Right Hon. Sir John A. Macdonald, Premier and Minister of Justice.
Hon. Alexander Campbell, Postmaster-General.
" A. J. Fergusson-Blair, President of Privy Council.
" W. P. Howland, Minister of Inland Revenue.
" Wm. McDougall, Minister of Public Works.
" G. E. Cartier, Minister of Militia and Defence.
" A. T. Galt, Minister of Finance.
" J. C. Chapais, Minister of Agriculture.
" H. L. Langevin, Secretary of State of Canada.
" S. L. Tilley, Minister of Customs.
" Peter Mitchell, Minister of Marine and Fisheries.
" A. G. Archibald, Secretary of State for the Provinces.
" Edward Kenny, Receiver-General.

Aug., Champlain's astrolabe was found in Ross Tp., County of Renfrew; it had "Paris," "1603" on it.
In September, there was a Dominion election, the Conservatives winning.
Nov. 1, Bishop Strachan died in Toronto.
Nov. 7, The First Session of the First Parliament of the Dominion met at Ottawa, Mr Cauchon being made Speaker of the Senate, and Mr. Cockburn being elected Speaker of the Commons.
Nov. 8, Hon. John Rose was made Minister of Finance.
Dec. 4, Hon. Wm. McDougall proposed a series of resolutions, praying that Rupert's Land and the North-West Territories be added to the Dominion.
Dec. 21, A Bill was passed empowering the Government to raise money for the construction of the Intercolonial Railway.
Dec. 21, Parliament adjourned.

Dec. 29, Hon. A. J. Fergusson-Blair, President of the Privy Council, died in Ottawa.

1868.

Feb. 28, The Canada Southern Railway was chartered.
March, Canada issued a three-cent letter stamp.
> The Legislature of Nova Scotia passed an address to the Queen, praying for a repeal of "so much of the Act for the Union of Canada, Nova Scotia, and New Brunswick, as relates to Nova Scotia."

April 1, Post-Office Savings Banks were first opened.
April 7, Patrick James Whalen shot Hon. D'Arcy McGee in Ottawa. Parliament adjourned.
April 13, Hon. D'Arcy McGee's funeral was in Montreal.
April 14, Parliament reassembled.
May 22, Lord Monck assented to a Bill passed in the House, that empowers the Senate to examine witnesses on oath at its Bar.
> The Militia Act was passed.

May 22, The First Session of the First Dominion Parliament was prorogued.
May 26, The Great Seal of Canada was prescribed by Royal Warrant.
June 4, The Duke of Buckingham informed the Governor-General that the Home Government would not allow Nova Scotia to withdraw from Confederation.
> Trinity College School was moved from Weston to Port Hope.

Oct 1, Sir Patrick L. McDougall was made Commander of the Militia.
Nov. 13, Lord Monck relinquished the Governor-Generalship of Canada.
Dec. 29, Lord Lisgar was appointed Governor-General of Canada.

1869.

Jan. 16, The first number of the *Star*, Montreal, was issued.
Jan. 25, By an Order in Council, "better terms" were granted to Nova Scotia, the provincial debt assumed by the Dominion being increased from the original $8,000,000 to $9,186,756 and an annual subsidy of $82,698, granted to the Province for ten years, being computed from July 1, 1867.

Jan. 30, Hon. Joseph Howe was made President of the Privy Council.
Feb. 2, LORD LISGAR took office as Governor-General of Canada.
Feb. 11, Patrick James Whalen was hung in Ottawa, the last public execution in Canada.
April 15, The Second Session of the First Dominion Parliament was opened.
May 5, Lieut.-Col. P. Robertson Ross was made Commander of the Militia.
June 23, The Second Session of the First Dominion Parliament was prorogued.
  Lieut.-Col. Dennis was sent to the Red River country, to begin public surveys.
Aug. 7, Royal assent was given to an Act which fixed the salary of the Governor-General at £10,000, or $48,666.63, to be paid out of the consolidated revenue of Canada.
Sept. 28, Hon. Wm. McDougall was made Lieut.-Gov. of the North-West Territories.
Oct. 9, Hon. Sir Francis Hincks was made Minister of Finance.
Oct. 11, Half-breeds, under Louis Riel, compelled Mr. Webb, surveyor, to stop surveying in Manitoba.
Oct. 31, Hon. Wm. McDougall was stopped at Pembina, by a half-breed, who forbade him to enter Manitoba.
Nov. 16, Hon. Christopher Dunkin was made Minister of Agriculture.
  Hon Joseph Howe was made Secretary of State for the Provinces.
  " Alexander Morris was made Minister of Inland Revenue.
  " J. C. Chapais was made Receiver-General.
  " Edward Kenny was made President of Council.
Nov. 24, Louis Riel, "President of Provisional Government at Red River," took Fort Garry, and appropriated its contents.
Dec. 1, Canada, by paying Hudson's Bay Company £300,000, the transaction being made by the Imperial Government, received the North-West Territories and Rupert's Land.
Dec. 7, Louis Riel made Dr. Schultz a prisoner.

Dec. 8, Hon. Hector L. Langevin was made Minister of Public Works.
" James Cox Aikins was made Secretary of State of Canada.

1870.

Jan. 28, The "City of Boston" left Halifax, but was never again heard of.
Feb. 15, The Third Session of the First Dominion Parliament was opened.
Feb. 17, Louis Riel captured Major Bolton and 47 men.
March 4, Louis Riel enforced the brutal murder of Thomas Scott at Fort Garry.
March 20, John Joseph Lynch, D.D., was made the first Catholic Archbishop of Toronto.
May 11, £300,000 was paid to Hudson's Bay Company.
May 12, The Third Session of the First Dominion Parliament was prorogued.
May 25 "General" O'Neil made another "Fenian invasion" into the Eastern townships.
June 21, Sir Charles Tupper was made President of Council.
June 23, An order of the Queen-in-Council transferred Rupert's Land and the North-West Territory to Canada.
The Dominion Line of Steamships was established.
July 15, Manitoba and the North-West Territories were admitted to the Dominion.
Aug. 9, Canada Defences Loan Act was passed.
Aug. 24, Colonel Wolseley, who had led 1,300 men through a wilderness route, arrived at Fort Garry.
Oct. 20, An earthquake shook the country.

1871.

Feb. 15, The Fourth Session of the First Dominion Parliament met.
Feb. 27, The Joint High Commission met in Washington
March 19, Archbishop Lynch, of Toronto, consecrated Rev. Elzear Alexandre Taschereau Archbishop of Quebec.
Professors Bryce and Hart established Manitoba College.
The Minister of Inland Revenue introduced a measure " to render permissive the use of the met-

ric, or decimal, system of weights and measures," which became law.

April 14, The Fourth Session of the First Dominion Parliament closed.

May 8, The Joint High Commission concluded the Treaty of Washington, which provided for the settlement of the Alabama claims by a Board of Arbitration, to be held at Geneva, Switzerland; the San Juan boundary was to be settled by the Emperor of Germany; the fisheries were to be open for ten years, fish and fish oil to be admitted free into Canada and the United States; and it was agreed that a Commission should settle the money compensation to Canada by the United States; the Americans were accorded the free navigation of the St. Lawrence and the Canadian canals, and the Canadians were to have free navigation in Lake Michigan.

Ontario School Act was improved.

New Brunswick adopted a School System similar to Ontario.

May 16, An Imperial Order-in-Council was passed, authorizing the admission of British Columbia into the Dominion.

May 17, The New Brunswick School Bill, introduced into the New Brunswick Legislature by Hon. Geo. E. King, Premier of the Province, was passed. The Catholics complained of its terms. After much discussion in the Dominion Parliament, the case was sent to England for settlement; but the Imperial Government refused to interfere.

June 29, The Imperial Parliament passed " the British North America Act, 1871," empowering the Parliament of Canada to create new provinces.

July 1, Dominion currency was made uniform.

Parliament Library, Ottawa, was founded.

July 20, British Columbia was admitted to the Dominion.

Oct. 5, Messrs. W. M. Simpson, S. J. Dawson, and W. J. Pether made the " North-West Angle Treaty," with the Ojibbeways.

O'Neil and O'Donohue led Fenians into Manitoba, but U.S. troops followed them and captured them.

Oct. 25, Hon. John Henry Pope was made Minister of Agriculture.
Nov. 28. The Post Office Department of Canada first issued Post Cards.

1872.

April 11, The Fifth Session of the First Dominion Parliament was opened.
May 22, The Earl of Dufferin was appointed Governor-General of Canada.
June 14, The Fifth Session of the First Dominion Parliament was prorogued.
The *Mail*, Toronto, first appeared.
June 22, There was a railroad disaster near Belleville, Ontario; 30 killed.
June 25, The EARL OF DUFFERIN took office as Governor-General of Canada.
July 2, Hon. Charles Tupper was made Minister of Inland Revenue.
Hon. John O'Connor was made President of Council.
July 8, Parliament was dissolved.
July 29, Dominion election; Conservatives won.

"The elections came off through the summer and early autumn, and the Government found itself confronted by staunch opposition. The ghost of poor Scott, murdered in the Northwest, rose against it; the Washington Treaty 'was shaken in the face of the country'; the gigantic railway building, a duty to which the country had been pledged, was declared by the Opposition to be a mad and impossible scheme; and the Reform party in Ontario was made sturdy by the strength of Mr. Blake and the Provincial Ministry. The Government came shattered, though not defeated, out of the contest."—Collin's " Life of Sir John A. Macdonald," p. 383.

Sept. 14, The Tribunal of Arbitration, Switzerland, decided that Great Britain pay to the United States $15,500,000 for losses by Confederate cruisers.
Oct. 21, William, Emperor of Germany, decided that, according to the Treaty of June 15, 1846, the boundary line should pass through the Haro Channel; this gave San Juan Island to the United States.
Oct. 25, Hon. Oliver Mowat was made Premier of Ontario.
Dec. 24, The Quebec Legislature decided that the Lieutenant-

Governor has power to nominate Queen's Counsel from the Provincial Bar.

1873.

Jan. 30, Hon. Theodore Robitaille was made Receiver-General.

Feb. 19, A railroad company, the Canadian Pacific Railway Company, Sir Hugh Allan, President, obtained a charter.

Feb. 22, Hon. Sir Chas. Tupper was made Minister of Customs.

Feb. 24, Hon. Sir S. L. Tilley was made Minister of Finance.

March 4, Hon. John O'Connor was made Minister of Inland Revenue.

March 15, The First Session of the Second Dominion Parliament was opened.

March 29, The Ontario Legislature passed an Act which declared that the Lieutenant-Governor, under the great seal of the province, can lawfully select Queen's Counsel from the Ontario Bar.

The Northwest Police was organized.

April 1, The White Star steamer "Atlantic" struck on Meagher rock, west of Sambro ; 560 people were lost.

April 2, Mr. Huntingdon declared in the Commons that the Government had chartered Sir Hugh Allan's Company on the understanding that Sir Hugh advance money to defray expenses of electing Ministers and their supporters. This began the "Pacific Scandal."

April 8, Sir John A. Macdonald's motion, that a select committee of five members be appointed by the House to examine the charges made by Mr. Huntingdon, was passed. The House named Hon. Mr. Blanchet, Macdonald and Cameron, supporters of the Government, and Hon. Edward Blake and Hon. M. Dorion, members of the Opposition.

April 18, Hon. John Hillyard Cameron introduced an Oaths Bill into the House, so that the Select Committee could examine witnesses on oath.

May 3, Office of Minister of Interior was created.

The Oaths Bill received royal assent.

May 18, St. Vincent de Paul Penitentiary, near Montreal, Quebec, was opened.

May 20, Sir George Cartier died in London.

May 23, Parliament adjourned.
May 24, Mr. J. W. Bengough began the *Grip*, Toronto.
June 1, Hon. Joseph Howe died in Halifax.
June 14, Hon. Hugh McDonald was made President of Council.
Hon. T. N. Gibbs was made Secretary of State for the Provinces.
June 27, At Quebec the Governor-General received a telegram from the Earl of Kimberley, "Oaths Bill is disallowed."
July 1, Hon. Hugh McDonald was made Minister of Militia and Defence.
" John O'Connor was made Postmaster-General.
" Thos. N. Gibbs was made Minister of Inland Revenue.
" Alexander Campbell was made the first Minister of Interior.
July 18, McMullen, an American contractor, published letters in Canadian papers, which, if true, told hard against members of the Government.
Aug. 13, Parliament reassembled; but the committee appointed to investigate the charges against the Administration not having completed their report, the Gov.-Gen., at the request of the Ministerialists, and against the appeals of the Opposition, prorogued Parliament.
Sept. 20, Wesleyan Theological College, Montreal, was opened.
Oct. 23, The Second Session of the Second Dominion Parliament met.
Oct. 31, The International Bridge across the Niagara river near Lake Erie, was opened.
Nov. 5, The Government resigned.
Nov. 7, Hon. Alexander Mackenzie formed a Liberal Ministry; its members were:—
Hon. Alex. Mackenzie, Premier and Minister of Public Works.
" David Laird, Minister of Interior.
" Isaac Burpee, Minister of Customs.
" R. J. Cartwright, Minister of Finance.
" Luc Letellier de St. Just, Minister of Agriculture.

Hon. David Christie, Secretary of State of Canada.
" Sir A. J. Smith, Minister of Marine and Fisheries.
" William Ross, Minister of Militia and Defence.
" A. A. Dorion, Minister of Justice.
" Telesphore Fournier, Minister of Inland Revenue.
" Donald A. Macdonald, Postmaster-General.
" Thomas Coffin, Receiver-General.
" Edward Blake, no portfolio.
" R. W. Scott, no portfolio.

Nov. 15, The Canada Southern Railway was opened.

1876.

Jan. 3, The Second Session of the Second Dominion Parliament was dissolved.
Jan. 9, Hon. R. W. Scott was made Secretary of State.
Jan. 20, Hon. L. S. Huntingdon was made President of the Council.
Jan. 22, Dominion election; Liberals won.
March 26, The First Session of the Third Dominion Parliament was opened.
March 30, Louis Riel, elected for Provencher, Manitoba, appeared at Ottawa.
April 15, Hon. Mackenzie Bowell moved Riel's expulsion from Parliament.
April 16, Parliament expelled Riel from the House.
An Agricultural College and Experimental Farm was established at Guelph, Ont.
Hansard was begun.
May 26, An Act was passed that introduced vote by ballot, simultaneous elections, the abolition of property qualifications for members of the Commons, and stringent enactments against "corrupt practices" at elections.
The First Session of the Third Dominion Parliament was prorogued.
June 2, Dominion Grange was formed in London, Ont.
July 6, The first number of the *Daily Free Press*, Winnipeg, was issued.
July 8, Hon. Telesphore Fournier was made Minister of Justice and Attorney-General.

THE CARDINAL FACTS OF CANADIAN HISTORY 169

    Hon. Felix Geoffrion was made Minister of Inland Revenue.
Sept. 11, Maj.-Gen. Edward Selby Smith was made Commander of the Militia.
Sept. 15, Hon. Alex. Morris, Hon. David Laird, and Hon. W. J. Christie made the Qu'Appelle Treaty with the Crees and Chippewas at Fort Qu'Appelle.
Sept. 30, Hon W. B. Vail was made Minister of Militia and Defence.
Oct. 15, The Court of Queen's Bench of Manitoba issued a warrant of outlawry against Louis Riel.
Nov. 17, Lord Carnarvon gave his final judgment, "Carnarvon Terms," respecting the complaints of British Columbia against the Dominion.
Dec. 18, An Order-in-Council was sent to England, expressing satisfaction with Earl Carnarvon's terms respecting the treatment of British Columbia by the Dominion.

          1875.

Jan. 14, The first number of the *Halifax Herald*, Halifax, N. S., was issued
Feb. 4, The Second Session of the Third Dominion Parliament was opened.
    Winnipeg, Manitoba, was made a city.
    Sir John W. Dawson published "The Dawn of Life."
April 25, Hon. Alex. Mackenzie secured a general amnesty for all the participants in the Red River trouble, except Riel, Lepine, and O'Donoghue.
    Icelanders settled in Manitoba.
May 19, Hon. Edward Blake was made Minister of Justice. Hon. Telesphore Fournier was made Postmaster-General.
June 15, In Montreal, the Presbyterian Church of Canada in connection with the Church of Scotland, the Canada Presbyterian Church, the Presbyterian Church of the Lower Provinces, and the Presbyterian Church of the Maritime Provinces in connection with the Church of Scotland, united, and became the General Assembly of the Presbyterian Church in Canada.
July 19, The Imperial Parliament repealed section eighteen of the British North America Act, 1867, and substituted another section.

Sept. 18, The Supreme Court of Canada was organized.
Sept., Hon. James McKay and Lieut.-Gov. Morris made the Winnipeg Treaty with the Indians
Sept. 26, A Catholic procession was mobbed in Toronto.
The Normal School, Ottawa, was opened.
Oct. 3, A Catholic procession in Toronto, escorted by a strong body of police, was again mobbed.
Oct. 9, Hon. L. S. Huntingdon was made Postmaster General.
Dec. 7, Hon. Joseph Cauchon was made President of Council.
Dec. 24, Sherbrooke, Quebec, received a city charter.
Dominion debt, $116,008,378.

1876.

Jan. 26, Hon. Gideon Ouimet was made Superintendent of Education for Quebec.
Feb. 10, The Third Session of the Third Dominion Parliament was opened.
Feb. 19, Hon. Adam Crooks was made Minister of Education for Ontario.
April 12, The Third Session of the Third Dominion Parliament was prorogued.
April 27, Queen Victoria was proclaimed Empress of India.
May 1, St. Catharines, Ontario, was incorporated into a city.
May 10, President Grant opened the Centennial Exhibition in Philadelphia.
May 19, British Columbia passed an Act to support Public Schools, requiring every male resident of the Province to pay $3 a year for educational purposes.
June 1, The Royal Military College, Kingston, was opened.
June 5, Manitoba abolished its Legislative Council.
Keewatin was separated from the other North-West Territories and put under the government of Manitoba.
July 1, The Intercolonial Railway was opened.
July 31, The Earl and the Countess of Dufferin took a car at Ottawa for a trip to British Columbia.
Sept. 3, Fire destroyed 500 houses at St. Hyacinthe, Quebec; loss $2,000,000.
Oct. 24, Hon. David Mills was made Minister of Interior.
Nov. 9, Hon. Rodolphe Laflamme was made Minister of Inland Revenue.
Nov. 14, John Hillyard Cameron died in Toronto.

1877.

A strike of the G. T. R. engine drivers interrupted business, checked the mails, and finally called for the intervention of the militia.

Jan. 26, Hon. Charles Alphonse P. Pelletier was made Minister of Agriculture.
Feb. 8, The Fourth Session of the Third Dominion Parliament was opened.
April 28, The Fourth Session of the Third Dominion Parliament was prorogued.
May 20, Rev. Dr. Hannan was consecrated Catholic Archbishop of Halifax, N.S.
May 31, Brantford, Ontario, was made a city.

In June, the Halifax Fishery Commission met at Halifax, N.S.: Sir A. T. Galt for Great Britain; Hon. E. H. Kellogg for the United States, and M. Delfosse, Belgian Minister at Washington. Canada claimed $14,880,000.

June 8, Hon. Rodolphe Laflamme was made Minister of Justice.

Hon. Edward Blake was made President of Council.
Hon. Joseph Edouard Cauchon was made Minister of Inland Revenue.

June 20, St. John, New Brunswick, was almost destroyed by fire.

The first business telephone in Canada was established at Hamilton, Ont.

The University of Manitoba was established.

Sept. 22, Hon. David Laird and Col. McLeod, on Bow River, made "Treaty Number Seven," or the Blackfeet Treaty.
Oct. 8, Hon Wilfrid Laurier was made Minister of Inland Revenue.
Nov. 3, Hon. William H. Draper died in Yorkville, Ont.
Nov. 27, The Halifax Fishery Commission ended its labors, and concluded that the United States pay $5,500,000 for fishing privileges for twelve years.

1878.

Jan. 1, Belleville, Ontario, received a city charter.
Jan. 21, Hon. A. G. Jones was made Minister of Militia and Defence.

Feb. 7, The Fifth Session of the Third Dominion Parliament was opened.
Feb. 11, The first Branch of the Catholic Mutual Benefit Association in Canada was organized at Windsor, Ont.
March 12, Sir John A. Macdonald, in Parliament, expressed his opinion that Canada to be prosperous must adopt a "National Policy," a protection of home industries.
March 24, Luc Letellier de St. Just, Lieutenant-Governor of Quebec, being at variance with the provincial premier, Hon. M. de Boucherville, and members of the Administration, dismissed the Provincial Cabinet.
May 10, The Homestead Exemption Act was passed.
The Scott Act was passed.
May 10, The Fifth Session of the Third Dominion Parliament was prorogued.
June 26, Harvard University conferred LL.D. on Earl of Dufferin.
July 12, Riot in Montreal, Hackett being killed.
Aug. 17, Parliament was dissolved.
Aug. 28, The first number of the *Examiner*, Sherbrooke, Quebec, was issued.
Sept. 28, Dominion Election, the Conservatives won, the result being 146 Conservatives and 60 Liberals.
Oct. 5, Marquis of Lorne was appointed Governor-General of Canada.
Oct. 16, The Mackenzie Ministry resigned.
Oct. 17, Sir John A. Macdonald formed a Ministry; the members were:—
Hon. Sir John A. Macdonald, Premier and Minister of Interior.
Hon. Sir S. L. Tilley, Minister of Finance.
" Sir Charles Tupper, Minister of Public Works.
" J. H. Pope, Minister of Agriculture.
" John O'Connor, President of Council.
" James Macdonald, Minister of Justice.
" Sir Hector L. Langevin, Postmaster-General.
" F. R. Masson, Minister of Militia and Defence, (Oct. 19.)
" James C. Aikens, Secretary of State, (Oct. 19.)
" Mackenzie Bowell, Minister of Customs, (Oct. 19.)

Hon. J. C. Pope, Minister of Marine and Fisheries, (Oct. 19.)
" L. F. G. Baby, Minister of Inland Revenue, (Oct. 26.)
" A. Campbell, Receiver-General, (Nov. 8.)
" R. D. Wilmot, President of Senate.
Oct. 19, Earl of Dufferin left Canada, Gen. Sir P. L. Macdougall assuming the reins of Government.
Nov. 21, The United States paid the Halifax Award.
Nov. 25, MARQUIS OF LORNE took office as Governor General of Canada.

1879.

Jan. 25, Rev. William B. Bond was consecrated Bishop of Montreal
Feb. 9, The North Shore R.R., north of River St. Lawrence, from Montreal to Quebec, was completed.
Feb. 13, The First Session of the Fourth Dominion Parliament was opened.
Feb. 23, The first number of *La Patrie*, Montreal, was issued.
March 14, Sir S. L. Tilley laid a new tariff before Parliament.
March 15, The National Policy went into effect.
April 23, Guelph, Ontario, was incorporated into a city.
May 1, Rev. Arthur Sweatman was consecrated Bishop of Toronto
May 15, The First Session of the Fourth Dominion Parliament was prorogued.
May 20, Sir H. L. Langevin was made Minister of Public Works.
Sir Charles Tupper was made Minister of Railways and Canals.
Hon. Sir A. Campbell was made Postmaster-General.
May 24, Authorized by Her Majesty, the Governor-General held an investiture of "the most distinguished order of St. Michael and St. George," at Montreal, when six Canadian gentlemen were created Knights Commanders of the order.
July 25, The Dominion Government deposed Luc Letellier de St. Just from the office of Lieut.-Gov. of Quebec.
July 26, Hon. Theodore Robitaille was made Lieutenant-Governor of Quebec.

Aug. 5, A devastating cyclone swept through New Brunswick.
Aug. 14, Sir John A. Macdonald was sworn in as a member of Her Majesty's Privy Council.
In the City of Quebec, the Irish and French sections of the Ship-Labourers' Union had several severe conflicts.
Nov. 4, The Supreme Court of the Dominion decided that the Queen or her representative, the Governor-General, has the sole right to appoint Queen's Counsel.

1880.

Jan. 15, Hon. Sir Alex. Campbell was made Minister of Militia and Defence.
Hon. John O'Connor was made Postmaster-General.
Hon. L. F. R. Masson was made President of Council.
Feb. 12, The Second Session of the Fourth Dominion Parliament was opened.
Feb. 25, The Parliament Buildings at Fredericton, New Brunswick, were destroyed by fire.
March 25, George Bennett, a discharged employee, shot Hon. George Brown, in the *Globe* office, Toronto.
March 26, Maj.-Gen. R. G. A. Luard was made Commander of the Militia.
April 27, Hon. Alex. Mackenzie ceased to be Leader of the Opposition.
May 7, The Second Session of the Fourth Dominion Parliament was prorogued.
May 9, Hon. George Brown died.
May 11, Sir Alexander T. Galt was appointed the first High Commissioner for Canada, to reside in England.
July 31, An Imperial Order in Council declared that "from and after the 1st of September, 1880, all British territories and possessions in North America, not already included within the Dominion of Canada, and all islands adjacent to any of such territories or possessions shall (with the exception of the colony of Newfoundland and its dependencies) become and be annexed to and form part of the said Dominion of Canada ; and become and be subject to the laws, for the time being in force in the said Dominion, in so far as such laws may be applicable thereto."

Aug. 19, The first number of the *World*, Toronto, was issued.
Oct. 21, The contract was signed for the construction of the C.P.R.
Nov. 8, Hon. John O'Connor was made Secretary of State of Canada.
" Joseph A. Mousseau was made President of Council.
" Sir A. P. Caron was made Minister of Militia and Defence.
" Sir A. Campbell was made Postmaster-General.
" James Cox Aikins was made Minister of Inland Revenue.
Nov. 12, An explosion in the "Foord" pit, at Stellarton, Nova Scotia, killed 50 miners.
Nov. 21, Rev. James Vincent Cleary was consecrated Bishop of Kingston, Ontario.
Dec. 9, The Third Session of the Fourth Dominion Parliament was opened.
Dec. 10, At midnight, the contract for building the C.P.R. was laid before the House.
Dec. 23, The Dominion Parliament adjourned.

1881.

Jan. 4, The Dominion Parliament reassembled.
Jan. 17, Sir Charles Tupper submitted to Parliament the offer of a new syndicate, which would build the C.P R. for $22,000,000 and 22,000,000 acres of land; the Government declined the offer.
Feb. 16, Letters patent were issued to the Canadian Pacific Railway Company; and, for building the C.P.R., the Government gave $25,000,000, and 25,000,000 acres of land.
March 4, St. Thomas, Ontario, received a city charter.
March 21, The Third Session of the Fourth Dominion Parliament was prorogued.
May 2, The C.P.R. Co. broke ground for the great trans-continental railway.
May 20, Hon. John O'Connor was made Postmaster-General.
" Joseph Alfred Mousseau was made Secretary of State of Canada.
" A. W. McLelan was made President of Council.

Hon. Sir Alex. Campbell was made Minister of Justice.

May 21, The Gov.-Gen. in Council disallowed the "Streams Bill," which the Legislature of Ontario had passed.

May 24, The steamer "Victoria," on the Thames, London, Ontario, collapsed, over 200 people being lost.

June 8, The suburb of St. John, Quebec, was nearly destroyed by fire.

Population of the Dominion 4,324,810.

1882.

Feb. 9, The Fourth Session of the Fourth Dominion Parliament was opened.

Feb. 19, Dr. Ryerson died in Toronto.

During the session, Mr. Costigan introduced a motion in the Commons that a petition be sent to the Queen, favoring Home Rule for Ireland and a release of the suspects. Both Houses passed it without a dissenting voice. The Government received a very curt acknowledgment of it from Lord Kimberly, the Colonial Secretary.

Feb. 23, Sir Hector L. Langevin introduced a Bill to reorganize the Civil Service.

March 5, A violent blizzard swept over Manitoba.

May 2, The Government passed the Civil Service Bill.

May 8, Four new districts—Alberta, Assiniboia, Athabasca, and Saskatchewan—were formed in the Northwest.

May 17, The Fourth Session of the Fourth Dominion Parliament was prorogued, It has been called the "Long Session."

May 18, Parliament was dissolved.

May 23, Hon. John Costigan was made Minister of Inland Revenue.

Hon. John Carling was made Postmaster-General.

May 25, The Royal Society was formed, and met, Sir John W. Dawson being its first President.

June 14, The Redistribution Bill was framed; it altered the forms of the constituencies for the Commons; the Opposition called it "Gerrymandering."

June 20, Dominion election; Conservatives won.

July 10, Hon. A. W. McLelan was made Minister of Marine.

July 29, Hon. Joseph Adolphe Chapleau was made Secretary of State of Canada.
Hon. Sir Frank Smith entered the Ministry, without portifolio.
Aug. 12, The Grand Trunk Railroad and the Great Western Railroad amalgamated, under the title of Grand Trunk Railway Co.
Aug. 23, Regina was made the capital of the Northwest Territories.
Sept. 20, The Gov.-Gen. in Council again disallowed the "Streams Bill," which the Ontario Legislature had reaffirmed.
Sept. 21, Rev. Jean François Jamot was made the first Catholic Bishop of Peterboro, Ontario.
Dec. 12, The Michigan Central R.R. agreed to operate the Canada Southern R.R. and its leased and controlled lines for 21 years, beginning on Jan. 1, 1883.

1883.

Feb 8, The First Session of the Fifth Dominion Parliament was opened.
March 16, The Gov.-Gen. in Council once more disallowed the "Streams Bill," which the Ontario Legislature had reaffirmed.
April 19, Parliament Buildings, Quebec, were burned.
5,000 settlers entered the North-West.
May 25, The First Session of the Fifth Dominion Parliament was prorogued.
May 30, Sir Charles Tupper was appointed High Commissioner to England.
July 18, The Privy Council of Great Britain and Ireland decided Escheats in Real Property in favor of Ontario.
Aug. 18, The Marquis of Lansdowne was appointed Governor-General of Canada.
Aug. 29, The Methodist Church of Canada, the Methodist Episcopal Church in Canada, the Primitive Methodist Church in Canada, and the Bible Christian Church of Canada, at Belleville, Ontario, united, and became the Methodist Church of Canada.
The Salvation Army began to work in Canada.

Oct. 17, Hon. Sir David L. Macpherson was made Minister of Interior.
Rt. Hon. Sir John A. Macdonald was made President of Council.
Oct. 23, MARQUIS OF LANSDOWNE took office as Governor General of Canada.
Nov. Hon. George W. Ross was made Minister of Education for Ontario.

1884.

Jan. 2, There was a collision on the G.T.R. near Toronto; 25 people killed.
Jan. 17, The Second Session of the Fifth Dominion Parliament was opened.
April 7, The Imperial Privy Council overruled the disallowance re "Streams Bill," made by the Gov.-Gen in Council, sustaining the Legislature of Ontario. "Escheats in Real Property" and the "Streams Bill" were marked triumphs for Hon. Oliver Mowat, Premier of Ontario.
April 19, The Second Session of the Fifth Dominion Parliament was prorogued.
May 23, Maj.-Gen. F. D. Middleton was made Commander of the Militia.
June 16, Centennial of the settlement of the U.E.L.'s in Upper Canada was held at Adolphustown.
July 8, Louis Riel arrived at Duck Lake, and began to inflame the discontent of the half-breeds and Indians, who feared dispossession of their lands by the incoming of settlers.
Oct. 1, The International prime-meridian conference opened in Washington, D.C., at which Sir Sandford Fleming represented the Dominion of Canada.
Oct. 20, The first number of *La Presse*, Montreal, was issued.
Nov. 18, Imperial Federation League was established in London.
Dec. 17, A great Conservative Convention was held in the Grand Opera House, Toronto; ten thousand delegates were present.

1885.

Jan. 12, A great Conservative Convention was held in Montreal.
Jan. 29, Statue of Sir George E. Cartier was unveiled at Ottawa.

Jan. 29, The Third Session of the Fifth Dominion Parliament was opened.
March 18, The half-breeds imprisoned the Indian agent at Duck Lake, and some teamsters.
March 24, Maj.-Gen. Middleton left Ottawa for the North-West.
March 25, The half-breeds seized the public stores at Duck Lake.
March 26, The half-breeds, under Gabriel Dumont, defeated Major L. N. F. Crosier, Superintendent of the North-West Police, two miles from Duck Lake, killing fourteen of his men and forcing him to retire.
March 29, Indians murdered farm-instructor Payne.
April 3, Big Bear's Indians, at Frog Lake, murdered Fathers Marchand and Fafard, Indian agent Finn, and six others; and imprisoned Mrs. Gowanlock and Mrs. Delaney.
April 24, Gen. Middleton engaged the rebels at Fish Creek, losing 11 killed and 48 wounded.
May 1, Col. Otter, to bring Poundmaker to an engagement, left Battleford for Cut-Knife Hill, Poundmaker's reserve.
May 2, Col. Otter fought Poundmaker's Indians at Cut-Knife Creek, losing 8 killed and 13 wounded.
Maj.-Gen. T. B. Strange relieved Edmonton.
May 9, Gen. Middleton attacked the rebels, entrenched in rifle-pits, in front of Batoche.
May 13, Gen. Middleton, by a daring charge, drove the rebels out of Batoche, when the prisoners were rescued.
May 16, Louis Riel surrendered.
May 26, Poundmaker and his principal men were arrested.
June 30, Gen. Middleton massed his forces at Battleford, having stamped out the rebellion.
The fishery clauses of the Washington Treaty expired. During this Parliament, the "Electoral Franchise Act" was passed, making voters' qualifications in the Dominion uniform, and granting the franchise to Indians; it was stoutly opposed by the Opposition.
July 2, Big Bear was captured
July 20, The Third Session of the Fifth Dominion Parliament was prorogued.

Aug. 5, Hon. Thomas White was made Minister of Interior.
Aug. 18, Sir Francis Hincks died in Montreal.
Sept. 25, Hon. John Carling was made Minister of Agriculture.
" John Henry Pope was made Minister of Railways and Canals.
" Sir A. Campbell was made Postmaster-General.
" Sir J. S. D. Thompson was made Minister of Justice.
Nov. 7, The last spike of the C.P.R. was driven in Eagle Pass.
Nov. 16, Louis Riel was hung at Regina.
Dec. 10, Hon. A. W. McLelan was made Minister of Finance.
" Geo. E. Foster was made Minister of Marine.
Dominion Debt, $196,407,692.

1886.

Feb. 18, Archbishop Taché baptized Poundmaker and 28 of his braves in Stony Mountain Penitentiary.
Feb. 25, The Fourth Session of the Fifth Dominion Parliament was opened.
March 20, Canada warned American fishermen not to transgress the treaty of 1818.
June 2, The Fourth Session of the Fifth Dominion Parliament was adjourned.
June 13, The town of Vancouver was destroyed by fire.
July 14, A new Extradition Treaty was signed by Great Britain and the United States.
July 21, In the Basilica, Quebec, Archbishop Lynch, of Toronto, invested Cardinal Taschereau with the *beretta*.
July 29, Most Rev. Joseph Thomas Duhamel was made the first Archbishop of Ottawa.
Oct. 13, Monument to Joseph Brant was unveiled at Brantford, Ontario.

1887.

Jan. 15, Parliament was dissolved.
Jan. 17, Hon. A. W. McLelan was made Postmaster-General.
Jan. 27, Hon. Sir Charles Tupper was made Minister of Finance
" Honore Mercier was made Premier of Quebec.
Feb. 22, Dominion election ; Conservatives won.
April 13, The First Session of the Sixth Dominion Parliament was opened.

April 23, McMaster University (Baptist), Toronto, was chartered.
May 12, The Quebec Government incorporated the Society of Jesus.
May 26, The main line of the C.P.R. was opened throughout, 2.904.8 miles.
The Imperial Government empowered the Dominion to negotiate its own commercial treaties with foreign countries.
June 14, The first C.P.R. steamer from Yokohama, Japan, reached Victoria.
June 23, The First Session of the Sixth Dominion Parliament was prorogued.
July 15, Railway collision at St. Thomas, Ontario; 13 killed.
July 30, The railroad bridge across the St. Lawrence, at Lachine, was completed.
Oct. 17, Samuel S. Nelles, D.D, President of Victoria College, Cobourg, died.
In October, delegates from Quebec, Ontario, Nova Scotia, New Brunswick, and Manitoba, met in Quebec, to consider propositions for the amendment of the B.N.A. Act, of 1867.

1888.

Jan. 21, The Grand Trunk Railway Company united with the Northern Railway Company and its leased line, the Hamilton and Northwestern Railway.
Feb. 23, The Second Session of the Sixth Dominion Parliament was opened.
May 1, Lord Stanley was appointed Governor-General of Canada.
May 22, The Second Session of the Sixth Dominion Parliament was prorogued.
May 23, Sir Charles Tupper was appointed High Commissioner to England.
May 24, Queen Victoria Park, Niagara, was opened.
May 29, Hon. George E. Foster was made Minister of Finance.
May 31, Hon. C. H. Tupper was made Minister of Marine.
June 11, LORD STANLEY took office as Governor-General of Canada.
The Equal Rights Party appeared.

July 12, The Quebec Government passed the Jesuit Estates Bill, partially compensating the Jesuits for their spoliation by the Crown.
Aug. 3, Hon. Edgar Dewdney was made Minister of Interior. Hon. John Haggart was made Postmaster-General.

1889.

Jan. 31, The Third Session of the Sixth Dominion Parliament was opened.
Feb. 27, Railway disaster near St. George, Ontario; 10 killed.
March 3, The Commons sustained " An Act respecting the settlement of the Jesuits' Estates," by a vote of 188 to 13.
March 20, By Act of Parliament the Baptist Convention was organized.
March 21, Sorel, Quebec, obtained a city charter.
May 2, The Third Session of the Sixth Dominion Parliament was prorogued.
Sept. 19, In Quebec, 45 people were killed by a land-slide from the Citadel Rock.
Nov. 5, The Province of Quebec paid the Society of Jesus $400 000, $60,000 being turned over to the Protestant Board of Education.
Nov. 28, Rt. Hon. Sir John A. Macdonald was made Minister of Railways and Canals.
Nov. 28, Hon. C. C. Colby was made President of Council.

1890.

Jan. 16, The Fourth Session of the Sixth Dominion Parliament was opened.
Feb. 1, The Canada Atlantic Railway opened its bridge over the St. Lawrence, at Coteau.
Feb. 14, Toronto University was damaged by fire; loss $500,000.
March 31, The Manitoba Legislature passed Hon. Joseph Martin's Act to suppress Separate Schools in Manitoba.
May 6, Lunatic Asylum at Longue Point was destroyed by fire; 70 lives lost.
May 16, Royal assent was given to the Dominion Bank Act; this regulates the management of banks, and forbids them to issue notes of a lower denomination than $5, and compels all their notes to be multiples of $5.

Hon. Clarke Wallace's Bill to incorporate the Grand Orange Lodge of British America was passed.

May 16, The Fourth Session of the Sixth Dominion Parliament was prorogued.

Aug. 15, Delegates from the Anglican Synods of British North America met at Winnipeg to establish a General Synod for the government of the Anglican Church in Canada.

Sept. 14, Petroleum was discovered along the Athabasca River.

Sept. 27, Major-Gen. I. J. C. Herbert was made Commander of the Militia.

La Grippe became epidemic, and laid up a good part of the people.

Oct. 6, The McKinley Tariff went into effect.

1891.

Jan. 12, Canada brought suit before the U. S. Supreme Court concerning seizures of vessels in Behring Sea.

Feb. 3, Parliament was dissolved.

March 5, Dominion elections; Conservatives won.

March 8, The people of Quebec, a Provincial election being held, overthrew the Mercier party and put the Conservatives in power.

April 29, The First Session of the Seventh Dominion Parliament was opened.

June 6, Sir John A. Macdonald died in Ottawa.

June 10, The body of Sir John A. Macdonald was conveyed from Ottawa to Kingston, and deposited in the Cataraqui cemetery.

June 16, Hon. J. J. C. Abbott became Premier of Canada, and President of Council.

Hon. C. H. Tupper was made Minister of Marine.

July 1, The Dominion Bank Act went into effect.

July 14, Annual Convention of the National Education Association of the United States met in Toronto.

Aug. 14, Hon. Sir Frank Smith was made Minister of Public Works.

Sept. 19, St. Clair Tunnel was opened.

Sept. 30, The First Session of the Seventh Dominion Parliament was prorogued.

Dec. 16, Lieut.-Gov. Angers, of Quebec, dismissed the Mercier Ministry for alleged bribery and corruption, Pacaud's name being freely used.
Population of the Dominion, 4,832,679.

1892.

Jan. 11, Hon. John G. Haggart was made Minister of Railways and Canals.
Hon. Joseph A. Ouimet was made Minister of Public Works.
Jan. 25, Hon. Joseph A. Chapleau was made Minister of Customs.
Hon. James C. Patterson was made Secretary of State for Canada.
Hon. Sir A. P. Caron was made Postmaster General.
Hon Sir Mackenzie Bowell was made Minister of Militia and Defence.
Hon. W. B. Ives was made President of Council.
Feb. 25, The Second Session of the Seventh Dominion Parliament was opened.
March 14, A Royal Commission was appointed, Sir Joseph Hickson, Chairman, to investigate the liquor traffic.
April 14, Windsor, Ontario, got a city charter.
April 17, Hon. Alexander Mackenzie died.
May 3, Newfoundland renewed a tariff, discriminating against Canada.
May 7, Behring Sea Arbitration agreement was ratified by Great Britain and the United States.
July 9, The Second Session of the Seventh Dominion Parliament was prorogued.
Aug. 15, The Government terminated the canal tolls system.
Sept. 28, New Brunswick abolished its Legislative Council.
Sept. 30, Close of the Pan-Presbyterian Council in Toronto.
Oct. 17, Hon. Thomas M. Daly was made Minister of Interior.
Nov. 25, Sir John S. D. Thompson became Premier of Canada, Sir J. J. C. Abbott having resigned on account of failing health.
Dec. 3, The Minister of Inland Revenue became Controller of Inland Revenue.
Dec. 5, Hon. N. Clark Wallace was made Comptroller of Customs.

Hon. Sir John Carling entered the Ministry, without a portfolio.
" Auguste R. Angers was made Minister of Agriculture.
" John Costigan was made Secretary of State of Canada.
" Sir C. H. Tupper was made Minister of Marine.
" John F. Wood was made Controller of Inland Revenue.
Dec. 7, " J. C. Patterson was made Minister of Militia and Defence.
" Sir Mackenzie Bowell was made Minister of Trade and Commerce.

1893.

Jan. 26, The Third Session of the Seventh Dominion Parliament was opened.
March 23, Behring Sea Tribunal of Arbitration met in Paris.
April 1, The Third Session of the Seventh Dominion Parliament was prorogued.
May 1, (The World's Columbian Exposition was opened in Chicago.)
May 22, Earl of Aberdeen was appointed Governor-General of Canada.
June 1, The Baie Des Chaleurs Railway was opened.
June 21, A Liberal convention was held in Ottawa.
July 15, Lord Stanley left for England, and Lieut.-General Montgomery-Moore took the administration of the Government.
Aug. 15, The Behring Sea Tribunal of Arbitration gave the decision that Behring Sea be kept open and that seals be protected
Sept. 13, The Montreal Presbytery found Professor Campbell guilty of heresy.
Sept. 18, The EARL OF ABERDEEN took office as Governor General of Canada.
Oct. 30, Sir J. J. C. Abbott died.
Nov. 1, Statue to Sir John A. Macdonald was unveiled in Hamilton ; Sir John Thompson gave the speech of the occasion.

In this year Canada raised 50,000,000 bushels of wheat, of which 39,800,000 were for home consumption.

1894.

Feb. 6, Prohibition Plebiscite was carried in Ontario.

March 15, The Fourth Session of the Seventh Dominion Parliament was opened.

June 28, The Colonial Trade Conference opened at Ottawa, to effect commercial interchange between the British colonies.

July 23, The Fourth Session of the Seventh Dominion Parliament was prorogued.

Oct. 23, Hon. Honore Mercier died in Montreal.

Dec. 12, Sir John S. D Thompson, Premier of Canada, died at Windsor, England.

Dec. 21, Sir Mackenzie Bowell became Premier of Canada.

    Hon. Arthur R. Dickey was made Secretary of State of Canada.

    " John Costigan was made Minister of Marine.

    " Sir C. H. Tupper was made Minister of Justice.

    " W. B. Ives was made Minister of Trade and Commerce.

    " W. H. Montague entered the Ministry, without a portfolio.

    " D. Ferguson entered the Ministry, without a portfolio.

1895.

Jan. 2, Sir John S. D. Thompson's funeral was celebrated in the Cathedral of St. Mary, Halifax.

The Privy Council reversed the decision of the Canadian Supreme Court, in the Manitoba school case, and decided that the Dominion Government has power to legislate in the matter.

March 18, The Fifth Session of the Seventh Dominion Parliament was opened.

March 26, Hon. Walter H. Montague was made Secretary of State of Canada.

March 29, The royal commission, appointed in 1832 to investigate the liquor traffic, presented its report, a very voluminous one. One of its conclusions was

that prohibitory laws do not lessen the sale of intoxicating beverages.
April 1, Hon. R. B. Dickey was made Minister of Militia and Defence.
April 10, Hon. Pierre Boucher de la Bruere was made Superintendent of Education for Quebec.
April 16, Chatham, Ontario, was incorporated into a city.
June 5, Mr. Davin introduced a motion in the House, favouring woman suffrage; it was defeated by a majority of 54.
June 6, Sir John A. Macdonald's Memorial, Montreal, was unveiled.
June 13, The Sault Ste. Marie Canal was opened.
Manitoba refused to obey the Remedial Order.
July 11, Hon. J. A. Ouimet became acting Minister of Agriculture.
July 22, The Fifth Session of the Seventh Dominion Parliament was prorogued.
Oct. 2, Maj.-Gen. W. J. Gascoigne was made Commander of the Militia.
Oct. 14, Treaty with France went into operation: it allows 21 Canadian articles to enter France at a minimum duty and French wines to enter Canada at low rates.
Nov. 25, Successful close of Copyright Conference in Ottawa.
Dec. 19, Hon. John F. Wood was made Controller of Customs.
Dec. 24, Hon. G. E. Prior was made Controller of Inland Revenue.
Dominion Debt, $253,074,927.

1896.

Jan. 2, The Sixth Session of the Seventh Dominion Parliament was opened.
Jan. 6, Sir Mackenzie Bowell was made Minister of Militia and Defence.
Jan. 7, Sir Adolphe Caron announced the resignation of seven Cabinet Members.
Jan. 11, Canada agreed to arbitration of Behring Sea seizure claims.
Jan. 15, Hon. W. B. Ives was made Minister of Trade and Commerce.

Hon. A. R. Dickey was made Minister of Justice.
" W. H. Montague was made Minister of Agriculture.
Sir Charles Tupper was made Secretary of State of Canada.

Jan. 16, Hon. L. G. Desjardins was made Minister of Militia and Defence.

Feb. 11, The Remedial Bill was introduced into the Commons, to restore Separate Schools to Manitoba.

Feb. 27, The Legislature of Manitoba protested against the interference of the Dominion in Manitoba School affairs.

March 3, Sir Charles Tupper moved a second reading of the Remedial Bill; Hon. Wilfrid Laurier moved a six-months' hoist.

March 20, Death of Alexander McLaughlin, poet.

April 14, There was a dead-lock in the Commons on the Remedial Bill.

April 15, The Government withdrew the Remedial Bill.

April 23, The Sixth Session of the Seventh Dominion Parliament was prorogued

April 24, Lord Strathcona and Mount Royal was appointed High Commissioner to England.
Parliament was dissolved.

April 27, Sir Mackenzie Bowell, Premier of Canada, tendered his resignation.

April 27, Hon. John Costigan was made Minister of Marine.
" A. R. Angers was made President of Council.
" L. O. Taillon was made Postmaster-General.

May 1, Sir Charles Tupper became Premier of Canada.
Hon. D. Tisdale was made Minister of Militia and Defence.
" Alphonse Desjardins was made Minister of Public Works.
" Hugh John Macdonald was made Minister of Interior.

May 10, The Imperial Privy Council announced that "the province of Ontario had the right to enact local pro hibition under the Federal Constitution, but that the province can neither stop the manufacture of liquor for sale outside of its boundaries, nor trench on the

right of the Federal Government to govern the importation of liquor into the several provinces of the Dominion."
May 26, The Point Ellice Bridge disaster, B.C., took place; several lives were lost.
June 23, Dominion election; the Liberals won a great victory.
June 25, Death of Sir Leonard Tilley.
July 8, Sir Charles Tupper, Premier of Canada, resigned.
The Governor General refused to endorse the Orders-in Council, made by the Ministry before retiring.
July 13, Hon. Wilfrid Laurier, Premier of Canada, formed a Ministry; its members were: —
Hon. Wilfrid Laurier, Premier and President of Privy Council.
" W. S. Fielding, Minister of Finance (July 20.)
" A. G. Blair, Minister of Railways and Canals (July 20.)
" Sir Oliver Mowat, Minister of Justice.
" Sir L. H. Dav s, Minister of Marine.
" S. A. Fisher. Minister of Agriculture.
" J. Israel Tarte, Minister of Public Works.
" Sir Richard Cartwright, Minister of Trade and Commerce.
" W. S. Borden, Minister of Militia and Defence.
" William Mulock, Postmaster-General.
" William Paterson, Controller of Customs.
" Richard W. Scott, Secretary of State of Canada.
" Joly de Lotbiniere, Controller of Inland revenue (July 14.)
Aug. 16. Death of Sir David L. Macpherson.
Aug. 19, The First Session of the Eighth Dominion Parliament was opened.
Aug. 24, 25, 26, the "Canada," of Toronto, beat the "Vencedor," of Chicago, at Toledo.
About this time, the Government axe made cruel havoc among the placemen for alleged interference in electioneering work. The Opposition called it "Spoils System."
Sept. 21, The Central Exposition was opened in Ottawa.
Sept. 29, Telegraph operators and despatchers of the C.P.R. went on strike.

Oct. 5, The First Session of the Eighth Dominion Parliament was prorogued
Nov. 17, Hon. Clifford Sifton was made Minister of Interior.

1897.

Feb. 11, A wing of the Parliament Building, Ottawa, was burned.
March 25, The Second Session of the Eighth Dominion Parliament was opened.
March 31, The U.S. Congress passed the Dingley Tariff Bill.
April 22, Hon. W. S. Fielding, in a budget speech, introduced a new tariff.
June 16, The Behring Sea Commission met in Montreal.
June 20, First day of Queen Victoria's Jubilee; it was joyously celebrated throughout the Dominion.
June 29, Hon. Wm. Paterson was made Minister of Customs.
July 28, A royalty was imposed on the gold taken from the Klondike mines.
July 29, The G.T.R. steel arch bridge, Niagara, was completed.
Aug. 1, One half of the reduction of the Tariff Act went into effect : it provided that goods entering Canada from Great Britain or her Colonies should have a tariff rate 25 per cent. less than that collected on goods from other countries.
Aug. 6, The Government took steps to enforce the Alien Labor law against the United States.
Aug. 8, Mgr. Bruchesi was consecrated Archbishop of Montreal. Monseigneur Merry del Val, papal legate, made a general enquiry into the School question.
Aug. 12, British naval authorities permitted the United States to dry dock the battle ship "Indiana," at Halifax.
Aug. 31, First meeting of the British Medical Association was held in Canada at Montreal.
Oct. 21, The World's W.C.T.U. met in Toronto.
Nov. 11, In Washington, Sir Wilfred Laurier, Premier of Canada, and Secretary Sherman had a conference respecting the differences between Canada and the United States.
Nov. 18, Hon. David Mills was made Minister of Justice.

Dec. 22, The Behring Sea Arbitrators, in Ottawa, decided that the United States pay $464,000 to Canadian sealers.

1898.

Feb. 3, The Third Session of the Eighth Dominion Parliament was opened.
April 12, Death of Cardinal Taschereau.
June 13, The Third Session of the Eighth Dominion Parliament was prorogued.
July 25, The Earl of Minto was appointed Governor-General of Canada.
July 31, Death of Archbishop Walsh, Toronto.
Aug. 1, The other half of the reduction made by the Tariff Act went into effect.
Aug. 18, Maj.-Gen. E. T. H. Hutton was made Commander of the Militia.
Aug. 23, The Anglo-American Commission met in Quebec.

> The questions for discussion were: "Reciprocity of trade; fur seals in Bering Sea and the North Pacific Ocean; Atlantic and Pacific coast fisheries and fisheries in inland waters contiguous to the frontier; mining rights of citizens of one country within the territory of another; alien labor laws; war vessels on the lakes; delimitation of the Alaska-Canadian boundary; transportation of merchandise in bond through the United States and Canada; the conveyance of persons in custody of officers of one country through the territory of the other."—"Appleton's Annual."

Sept. 11, New Westminster was destroyed by fire.
Sept. 21, Champlain's Monument, Quebec, was unveiled.
Sept. 29, Prohibition plebiscite was carried in Canada.
Oct. 10, The Anglo-American Commission finished its sitting in Quebec.
Nov. 12, The EARL OF MINTO took office as Governor-General of Canada.
Lord and Lady Aberdeen left Canada.
Dec. 29, Two-cent letter postage was announced.

1899.

Jan. 1, Letter postage was reduced from 3 to 2 cents.
Jan. 20, 2,300 Doukhobors from the south of Russia landed at Halifax, on their way to settle in the North-West.

March 16, The Fourth Session of the Eighth Dominion Parliament was opened.
Aug. 11, The Fourth Session of the Eighth Dominion Parliament was prorogued.
Oct. 1, Mgr. Falconio, apostolic delegate, arrived at Quebec.
Oct. 21, Hon. Geo. W. Ross was made Premier of Ontario.
Hon. Richard Harcourt was made Minister of Education for Ontario.
Oct. 30, The Second Battalion, Royal Canadian Regiment of Infantry, Colonel Otter in command, left Quebec, on the "Sardinian," to serve in the Boer War, South Africa.

THE
BRITISH NORTH AMERICA ACT,
1867.

An Act for the Union of Canada, Nova Scotia, and New Brunswick, and the Government thereof; and for purposes connected therewith.

[29*th March*, 1867.]

WHEREAS the Provinces of Canada, Nova Scotia, and New Brunswick have expressed their Desire to be federally united into One Dominion under the Crown of the United Kingdom of Great Britain and Ireland, with a Constitution similar in Principle to that of the United Kingdom:

And whereas such a Union would conduce to the Welfare of the Provinces and promote the Interests of the British Empire:

And whereas on the Establishment of the Union by Authority of Parliament it is expedient, not only that the Constitution of the Legislative Authority in the Dominion be provided for, but also that the Nature of the Executive Government therein be declared:

And whereas it is expedient that Provision be made for the eventual Admission into the Union of other Parts of British North America:

Be it therefore enacted and declared by the Queen's Most Excellent Majesty, by and with the Advice and Consent of the Lords Spiritual and Temporal, and Commons, in this present Parliament assembled, and by the Authority of the same, as follows:

I.—Preliminary.

1. This Act may be cited as The British North America Act, 1867.

2. The Provisions of this Act referring to Her Majesty the Queen extend also to the Heirs and Successors of Her Majesty, Kings and Queens of the United Kingdom of Great Britain and Ireland.

II.—UNION.

3. It shall be lawful for the Queen, by and with the Advice of Her Most Honorable Privy Council, to declare by Proclamation that, on and after a Day therein appointed, not being more than Six Months after the passing of this Act, the Provinces of Canada, Nova Scotia, and New Brunswick shall form and be One Dominion under the Name of Canada; and on and after that Day those Three Provinces shall form and be One Dominion under that name accordingly.

4. The subsequent Provisions of this Act shall, unless it is otherwise expressed or implied, commence and have effect on and after the Union, that is to say, on and after the Day appointed for the Union taking effect in the Queen's Proclamation; and in the same Provisions, unless it is otherwise expressed or implied, the Name Canada shall be taken to mean Canada as constituted under this Act.

5. Canada shall be divided into four Provinces, named Ontario, Quebec, Nova Scotia, and New Brunswick.

6. The Parts of the Province of Canada (as it exists at the passing of this Act) which formerly constituted respectively the Provinces of Upper Canada and Lower Canada shall be deemed to be severed, and shall form Two separate Provinces. The Part which formerly constituted the Province of Upper Canada shall constitute the Province of Ontario; and the Part which formerly constituted the Province of Lower Canada shall constitute the Province of Quebec.

7. The Provinces of Nova Scotia and New Brunswick shall have the same Limits as at the passing of this Act.

8. In the General Census of the Population of Canada which is hereby required to be taken in the Year One thousand eight hundred and seventy-one, and in every Tenth Year thereafter, the respective Populations of the Four Provinces shall be distinguished.

III.—EXECUTIVE POWER.

9. The Executive Government and Authority of and over Canada is hereby declared to continue and be vested in the Queen.

10. The Provisions of this Act referring to the Governor General extend and apply to the Governor General for the Time being of Canada, or other the Chief Executive Officer or Administrator for the Time being carrying on the Government of Canada on behalf and in the Name of the Queen, by whatever Title he is designated.

11. There shall be a Council to aid and advise in the Government of Canada, to be styled the Queen's Privy Council for Canada ; and the Persons who are to be Members of that Council shall be from Time to Time chosen and summoned by the Governor General and sworn in as Privy Councillors, and Members thereof may be from Time to Time removed by the Governor General

12. All Powers, Authorities, and Functions which under any Act of the Parliament of Great Britain, or of the Parliament of the United Kingdom of Great Britain and Ireland, or of the Legislature of Upper Canada, Lower Canada, Canada, Nova Scotia, or New Brunswick, are at the Union vested in or exerciseable by the respective Governors or Lieutenant Governors of those Provinces, with the Advice, or with the Advice and Consent, of the respective Executive Councils thereof, or in conjunction with those Councils, or with any Number of Members thereof, or by those Governors or Lieutenant Governors individually, shall, as far as the same continue in existence and capable of being exercised after the Union in relation to the Government of Canada, be vested in and exerciseable by the Governor General, with the Advice or with the Advice and Consent of or in conjunction with the Queen's Privy Council for Canada, or any Members thereof, or by the Governor General individually, as the Case requires, subject nevertheless (except with respect to such as exist under Acts of the Parliament of Great Britain or of the Parliament of the United Kingdom of Great Britain and Ireland) to be abolished or altered by the Parliament of Canada.

13. The Provisions of this Act referring to the Governor General in Council shall be construed as referring to the Governor General acting by and with the Advice of the Queen's Privy Council for Canada.

14. It shall be lawful for the Queen, if Her Majesty thinks fit, to authorize the Governor General from Time to Time to appoint any Person or any Persons jointly or severally to be his Deputy or Deputies within any Part or Parts of Canada, and in that Capacity to exercise during the Pleasure of the Governor General such of the Powers, Authorities, and Functions of the Governor General as the Governor General deems it necessary or expedient to assign to him or them, subject to any Limitations or Directions expressed or given by the Queen : but the Appointment of such a Deputy or Deputies shall not affect the Exercise by the Governor General himself of any Power, Authority, or Function.

15. The Command-in-Chief of the Land and Naval Militia, and of all Naval and Military Forces, of and in Canada, is hereby declared to continue and be vested in the Queen

16. Until the Queen otherwise directs, the Seat of Government of Canada shall be Ottawa.

IV.—LEGISLATIVE POWER.

17. There shall be one Parliament for Canada, consisting of the Queen, and Upper House styled the Senate, and the House of Commons.

18. The Privileges, Immunities, and Powers to be held, enjoyed, and exercised by the Senate and by the House of Commons, and by the Members thereof, respectively, shall be such as are from Time to Time defined by Act of the Parliament of Canada, but so that the same shall never exceed those at the passing of this Act held, enjoyed, and exercised by the Commons House of Parliament of the United Kingdom of Great Britain and Ireland and by the Members thereof.

19. The Parliament of Canada shall be called together not later than Six Months after the Union.

20. There shall be a Session of the Parliament of Canada once at least in every Year, so that Twelve Months shall not intervene between the last Sitting of the Parliament in one Session and its first Sitting in the next Session.

The Senate.

21. The Senate shall, subject to the Provisions of this Act, consist of Seventy-two Members, who shall be styled Senators.

22. In relation to the Constitution of the Senate, Canada shall be deemed to consist of Three Divisions—

1. Ontario;
2. Quebec;
3. The Maritime Provinces, Nova Scotia and New Brunswick; which Three Divisions shall (subject to the Provisions of this Act) be equally represented in the Senate as follows: Ontario by Twenty-four Senators; Quebec by Twenty-four Senators; and the Maritime Provinces by Twenty-four Senators, Twelve thereof representing Nova Scotia, and Twelve thereof representing New Brunswick.

In the Case of Quebec each of the Twenty-four Senators representing that Province shall be appointed for One of the Twenty-four Electoral Divisions of Lower Canada specified in Schedule A. to Chapter One of the Consolidated Statutes of Canada.

23. The Qualifications of a Senator shall be as follows:—

(1.) He shall be of the full Age of Thirty Years:

(2.) He shall be either a Natural-born Subject of the Queen, or a Subject of the Queen naturalized by an Act of the Parliament of Great Britain, or of the Parliament of the United Kingdom of Great Britain and Ireland, or of the Legislature of One of the Provinces of Upper Canada, Lower Canada, Canada, Nova Scotia, or New Brunswick, before the Union, or of the Parliament of Canada after the Union:

(3.) He shall be legally or equitably seised as of Freehold for his own Use and Benefit of Lands or Tenements held in free and common Socage, or seised or possessed for his own Use and Benefit of Lands or Tenements held in Franc-alleu or in Roture, within the Province for which he is appointed, of the Value of Four thousand Dollars, over and above all Rents, Dues, Debts, Charges, Mortgages, and Incumbrances due or payable out of or charged on or affecting the same:

(4.) His Real and Personal Property shall be together worth Four thousand Dollars over and above his Debts and Liabilities:

(5.) He shall be resident in the Province for which he is appointed:

(6.) In the Case of Quebec he shall have his Real Property Qualification in the Electoral Division for which he is appointed, or shall be resident in that Division:

24. The Governor General shall from Time to Time, in the Queen's Name, by Instrument under the Great Seal of Canada, summon qualified Persons to the Senate; and, subject to the Provisions of this Act, every Person so summoned shall become and be a Member of the Senate and a Senator.

25. Such Persons shall be first summoned to the Senate as the Queen by Warrant under Her Majesty's Royal Sign Manual thinks fit to approve, and their Names shall be inserted in the Queen's Proclamation of Union.

26. If at any Time on the Recommendation of the Governor General the Queen thinks fit to direct that Three or Six Members be added to the Senate, the Governor General may by Summons to Three or Six qualified Persons (as the Case may be), representing equally the Three Divisions of Canada, add to the Senate accordingly.

27. In case of such Addition being at any Time made the Governor General shall not summon any Person to the Senate, except on a further like Direction by the Queen on the like Recommendation, until each of the Three Divisions of Canada is represented by Twenty-four Senators and no more.

28. The Number of Senators shall not at any Time exceed Seventy-eight.

29. A Senator shall, subject to the Provisions of this Act, hold his Place in the Senate for Life.

30. A Senator may by Writing under his Hand addressed to the Governor General resign his Place in the Senate, and thereupon the same shall be vacant.

31. The Place of a Senator shall become vacant in any of the following Cases:—

(1.) If for Two consecutive Sessions of the Parliament he fails to give his Attendance in the Senate:

(2.) If he takes an Oath or makes a Declaration or Acknowledgment of Allegiance, Obedience, or Adherence to a Foreign Power, or does an Act whereby he becomes a Subject or Citizen, or entitled to the Rights or Privileges of a Subject or Citizen, of a Foreign Power:

(3.) If he is adjudged Bankrupt or Insolvent, or applies for the Benefit of any Law relating to Insolvent Debtors, or becomes a public Defaulter:

(4.) If he is attainted of Treason or convicted of Felony or of any infamous Crime:

(5.) If he ceases to be qualified in respect of Property or of Residence; provided, that a Senator shall not be deemed to have ceased to be qualified in respect of Residence by reason only of his residing at the Seat of the Government of Canada while holding an Office under that Government requiring his Presence there.

32. When a Vacancy happens in the Senate by Resignation, Death, or otherwise, the Governor General shall by Summons to a fit and qualified Person fill the Vacancy.

33. If any Question arises respecting the Qualification of a Senator or a Vacancy in the Senate the same shall be heard and determined by the Senate.

34. The Governor General may from Time to Time, by Instrument under the Great Seal of Canada, appoint a Senator to be Speaker of the Senate, and may remove him and appoint another in his Stead.

35 Until the Parliament of Canada otherwise provides, the Presence of at least Fifteen Senators, including the Speaker, shall be necessary to constitute a Meeting of the Senate for the Exercise of its Powers.

36. Questions arising in the Senate shall be decided by a Majority of Voices, and the Speaker shall in all Cases have a Vote, and when the Voices are equal the Decision shall be deemed to be in the Negative.

The House of Commons.

37. The House of Commons shall, subject to the Provisions of this Act, consist of One hundred and eighty-one Members, of whom Eighty-two shall be elected for Ontario, Sixty-five for Quebec, Nineteen for Nova Scotia, and Fifteen for New Brunswick.

38. The Governor General shall from Time to Time, in the Queen's Name, by Instrument under the Great Seal of Canada, summon and call together the House of Commons.

39. A Senator shall not be capable of being elected or of sitting or voting as a Member of the House of Commons.

40. Until the Parliament of Canada otherwise provides, Ontario, Quebec, Nova Scotia, and New Brunswick shall, for the Purposes of the Election of Members to serve in the House of Commons, be divided into Electoral Districts as follows :—

1.—ONTARIO.

Ontario shall be divided into the Counties, Ridings of Counties, Cities, Parts of Cities, and Towns enumerated in the First Schedule of this Act, each whereof shall be an Electoral District, each such District as numbered in that Schedule being entitled to return One Member.

2.—QUEBEC.

Quebec shall be divided into Sixty-five Electoral Districts, composed of the Sixty-five Electoral Divisions into which Lower Canada is at the passing of this Act divided under Chapter Two of the Consolidated Statutes of Canada, Chapter Seventy-five of the Consolidated Statutes for Lower Canada, and the Act of the Province of Canada of the Twenty-third Year of the Queen, Chapter One, or any other Act amending the same in force at the Union, so that each such Electoral Division shall be for the Purposes of this Act an Electoral District entitled to return One Member.

3.—*NOVA SCOTIA*.

Each of the Eighteen Counties of Nova Scotia shall be an Electoral District. The County of Halifax shall be entitled to return Two Members, and each of the other Counties One Member.

4.—*NEW BRUNSWICK*.

Each of the Fourteen Counties into which New Brunswick is divided, including the City and County of St. John, shall be an Electoral District. The City of St. John shall also be a separate Electoral District. Each of those Fifteen Electoral Districts shall be entitled to return One Member.

41. Until the Parliament of Canada otherwise provides, all Laws in force in the several Provinces at the Union relative to the following Matters or any of them, namely,—the Qualifications and Disqualifications of Persons to be elected or to sit or vote as Members of the House of Assembly or Legislative Assembly in the several Provinces, the Voters at Elections of such Members, the Oaths to be taken by Voters, the Returning Officers, their Powers and Duties, the Proceedings at Elections, the Periods during which Elections may be continued, the Trial of controverted Elections, and Proceedings incident thereto, the vacating of Seats of Members, and the Execution of new Writs in case of Seats vacated otherwise than by Dissolution,—shall respectively apply to Elections of Members to serve in the House of Commons for the same several Provinces.

Provided that, until the Parliament of Canada otherwise provides, at any Election for a Member of the House of Commons for the District of Algoma, in addition to Persons qualified by the Law of the Province of Canada to vote, every male British Subject, aged Twenty-one Years or upwards, being a Householder, shall have a Vote.

42. For the First Election of Members to serve in the House of Commons the Governor General shall cause Writs to be issued by such Person, in such Form, and addressed to such Returning Officers as he thinks fit.

The Person issuing Writs under this Section shall have the like Powers as are possessed at the Union by the Officers charged with the issuing of Writs for the Election of Members to serve in the respective House of Assembly or Legislative Assembly of the Province of Canada, Nova Scotia, or New Brunswick ; and the Returning Officers to whom Writs are directed under this Section shall have the like Powers as are possessed at the Union by the Officers charged with the returning of

Writs for the Election of Members to serve in the same respective House of Assembly or Legislative Assembly.

43. In case a Vacancy in the Representation in the House of Commons of any Electoral District happens before the Meeting of the Parliament, or after the Meeting of the Parliament before Provision is made by the Parliament in this Behalf, the Provisions of the last foregoing Section of this Act shall extend and apply to the issuing and returning of a Writ in respect of such vacant District.

44. The House of Commons on its first assembling after a General Election shall proceed with all practicable Speed to elect One of its Members to be Speaker.

45. In case of a Vacancy happening in the Office of Speaker by Death, Resignation, or otherwise, the House of Commons shall with all practicable Speed proceed to elect another of its Members to be Speaker.

46. The Speaker shall preside at all Meetings of the House of Commons.

47. Until the Parliament of Canada otherwise provides, in case of the Absence for any Reason of the Speaker from the Chair of the House of Commons for a Period of Forty-eight consecutive Hours, the House may elect another of its Members to act as Speaker, and the Member so elected shall during the Continuance of such Absence of the Speaker have and execute all the Powers, Privileges, and Duties of Speaker.

48. The Presence of at least Twenty Members of the House of Commons shall be necessary to constitute a Meeting of the House for the Exercise of its Powers; and for that Purpose the Speaker shall be reckoned as a Member.

49. Questions arising in the House of Commons shall be decided by a Majority of Voices other than that of the Speaker, and when the Voices are equal, but not otherwise, the Speaker shall have a Vote.

50 Every House of Commons shall continue for Five Years from the Day of the Return of the Writs for choosing the House (subject to be sooner dissolved by the Governor General), and no longer.

51. On the Completion of the Census in the Year One thousand eight hundred and seventy-one, and of each subsequent decennial Census, the Representation of the Four Provinces shall be readjusted by such Authority, in such Manner, and from such Time, as the Parliament of Canada from Time to Time provides, subject and according to the following Rules:—

(1) Quebec shall have the fixed Number of Sixty five Members:

(2.) There shall be assigned to each of the other Provinces such a Number of Members as will bear the same Proportion to the Number of its Population (ascertained at such Census) as the Number Sixty-five bears to the Number of the Population of Quebec (so ascertained) :

(3.) In the Computation of the Number of Members for a Province a fractional Part not exceeding One Half of the whole Number requisite for entitling the Province to a Member shall be disregarded ; but a fractional Part exceeding One Half of that Number shall be equivalent to the whole Number :

(4.) On any such Re-adjustment the Number of Members for a Province shall not be reduced unless the Proportion which the Number of the Population of the Province bore to the Number of the aggregate Population of Canada at the then last preceding Re-adjustment of the Number of Members for the Province is ascertained at the then latest Census to be diminished by One Twentieth Part or upwards :

(5.) Such Re-adjustment shall not take effect until the Termination of the then existing Parliament.

52. The Number of Members of the House of Commons may be from Time to Time increased by the Parliament of Canada, provided the proportionate Representation of the Provinces prescribed by this Act is not thereby disturbed.

Money Votes; Royal Assent.

53. Bills for appropriating any Part of the Public Revenue, or for imposing any Tax or Impost, shall originate in the House of Commons.

54. It shall not be lawful for the House of Commons to adopt or pass any Vote, Resolution, Address, or Bill for the Appropriation of any Part of the Public Revenue, or of any Tax or Impost, to any Purpose that has not been first recommended to that House by Message of the Governor General in the Session in which such Vote, Resolution, Address, or Bill is proposed.

55. Where a Bill passed by the Houses of the Parliament is presented to the Governor General for the Queen's Assent, he shall declare, according to his Discretion, but subject to the Provisions of this Act and to Her Majesty's Instructions, either that he assents thereto in the Queen's Name, or that he withholds the Queen's Assent, or that he reserves the Bill for the Signification of the Queen's Pleasure.

56 Where the Governor General assents to a Bill in the Queen's Name, he shall by the first convenient Opportunity send an authentic Copy of the Act to One of Her Majesty's Principal Secretaries of State, and if the Queen in Council within Two Years after Receipt thereof by the Secretary of State thinks fit to disallow the Act, such Disallowance (with a Certificate of the Secretary of State of the Day on which the Act was received by him) being signified by the Governor General, by Speech or Message to each of the Houses of the Parliament or by Proclamation, shall annul the Act from and after the Day of such Signification.

57. A bill reserved for the Signification of the Queen's Pleasure shall not have any Force unless and until within Two Years from the Day on which it was presented to the Governor General for the Queen's Assent, the Governor General signifies, by Speech or Message to each of the Houses of the Parliament or by Proclamation, that it has received the Assent of the Queen in Council.

An Entry of every such Speech, Message, or Proclamation shall be made in the Journal of each House, and a Duplicate thereof duly attested shall be delivered to the proper Officer to be kept among the Records of Canada.

V.—PROVINCIAL CONSTITUTIONS.

Executive Power.

58. For each Province there shall be an Officer, styled the Lieutenant Governor, appointed by the Governor General in Council by Instrument under the Great Seal of Canada.

59. A Lieutenant Governor shall hold Office during the Pleasure of the Governor General; but any Lieutenant Governor appointed after the Commencement of the First Session of the Parliament of Canada shall not be removable within Five Years from his Appointment, except for Cause assigned, which shall be communicated to him in Writing within One Month after the Order for his Removal is made, and shall be communicated by Message to the Senate and to the House of Commons within One Week thereafter if the Parliament is then sitting, and if not then within One Week after the Commencement of the next Session of the Parliament.

60. The Salaries of the Lieutenant Governors shall be fixed and provided by the Parliament of Canada.

61. Every Lieutenant Governor shall, before assuming the Duties of his Office, make and subscribe before the Governor General or some Person authorized by him, Oaths of Allegiance and Office similar to those taken by the Governor General.

62. The Provisions of this Act referring to the Lieutenant Governor extend and apply to the Lieutenant Governor for the Time being of each Province or other the Chief Executive Officer or Administrator for the Time being carrying on the Government of the Province, by whatever Title he is designated.

63. The Executive Council of Ontario and of Quebec shall be composed of such Persons as the Lieutenant Governor from Time to Time thinks fit, and in the first instance of the following Officers, namely,— the Attorney General, the Secretary and Registrar of the Province, the Treasurer of the Province, the Commissioner of Crown Lands, and the Commissioner of Agriculture and Public Works, with in Quebec, the Speaker of the Legislative Council and the Solicitor General.

64. The Constitution of the Executive Authority in each of the Provinces of Nova Scotia and New Brunswick shall, subject to the Provisions of this Act, continue as it exists at the Union until altered under the Authority of this Act.

65. All Powers, Authorities, and functions which under any Act of the Parliament of Great Britain, or of the Parliament of the United Kingdom of Great Britain and Ireland, or of the Legislature of Upper Canada, Lower Canada, or Canada, were or are before or at the Union vested in or exerciseable by the respective Governors or Lieutenant Governors of those Provinces, with the Advice, or with the Advice and Consent, of the respective Executive Councils thereof, or in conjunction with those Councils, or with any Number of Members thereof, or by those Governors or Lieutenant Governors individually, shall, as far as the same are capable of being exercised after the Union in relation to the Government of Ontario and Quebec respectively, be vested in and shall or may be exercised by the Lieutenant Governor of Ontario and Quebec respectively, with the Advice or with the Advice and Consent of or in conjunction with the respective Executive Councils, or any Members thereof, or by the Lieutenant Governor individually, as the Case requires, subject nevertheless (except with respect to such as exist under Acts of the Parliament of Great Britain, or of the Parliament of the United Kingdom of Great Britain and Ireland,) to be abolished or altered by the respective Legislatures of Ontario and Quebec.

66. The Provisions of this Act referring to the Lieutenant Governor in Council shall be construed as referring to the Lieutenant Governor of the Province acting by and with the Advice of the Executive Council thereof.

67. The Governor General in Council may from Time to Time appoint an Administrator to execute the office and Functions of Lieutenant Governor during his Absence, Illness, or other Inability.

68. Unless and until the Executive Government of any Province otherwise directs with respect to that Province, the Seats of Government of the Provinces shall be as follows, namely, - of Ontario, the City of Toronto ; of Quebec, the City of Quebec ; of Nova Scotia, the City of Halifax ; and of New Brunswick, the City of Fredericton.

Legislative Power.

1.—*ONTARIO.*

69. There shall be a Legislature for Ontario consisting of the Lieutenant Governor and of One House, styled the Legislative Assembly of Ontario.

70. The Legislative Assembly of Ontario shall be composed of Eighty two Members, to be elected to represent the Eighty-two Electoral Districts set forth in the First Schedule to this Act.

2.—*QUEBEC.*

71. There shall be a Legislature for Quebec consisting of the Lieutenant Governor and of Two Houses, styled the Legislative Council of Quebec and the Legislative Assembly of Quebec.

72. The Legislative Council of Quebec shall be composed of Twenty-four Members, to be appointed by the Lieutenant Governor in the Queen's name, by Instrument under the Great Seal of Quebec, one being appointed to represent each of the Twenty-four Electoral Divisions of Lower Canada in this Act referred to, and each holding Office for the Term of his Life, unless the Legislature of Quebec otherwise provides under the Provisions of this Act.

73. The Qualifications of the Legislative Councillors of Quebec shall be the same as those of the Senators for Quebec.

74. The Place of a Legislative Councillor of Quebec shall become vacant in the Cases, *mutatis mutandis*, in which the Place of Senator becomes vacant.

75. When a Vacancy happens in the Legislative Council of Quebec by Resignation, Death, or otherwise, the Lieutenant Governor, in the Queen's Name, by Instrument under the Great Seal of Quebec, shall appoint a fit and qualified Person to fill the Vacancy.

76. If any Question arises respecting the Qualification of a Legislative Councillor of Quebec, or a Vacancy in the Legislative Council of Quebec, the same shall be heard and determined by the Legislative Council.

77. The Lieutenant Governor may from Time to Time, by Instrument under the Great Seal of Quebec, appoint a Member of the Legislative Council of Quebec to be Speaker thereof, and may remove him and appoint another in his Stead.

78. Until the Legislature of Quebec otherwise provides, the Presence of at least Ten Members of the Legislative Council, including the Speaker, shall be necessary to constitute a Meeting for the Exercise of its Powers.

79. Questions arising in the Legislative Council of Quebec shall be decided by a Majority of Voices, and the Speaker shall in all Cases have a Vote, and when the Voices are equal the Decision shall be deemed to be in the negative.

80. The Legislative Assembly of Quebec shall be composed of Sixty-five Members, to be elected to represent the Sixty-five Electoral Divisions or Districts of Lower Canada in this Act referred to, subject to Alteration thereof by the Legislature of Quebec : Provided that it shall not be lawful to present to the Lieutenant Governor of Quebec for Assent any Bill for altering the Limits of any of the Electoral Divisions or Districts mentioned in the Second Schedule in this Act, unless the Second and Third Readings of such Bill have been passed in the Legislative Assembly with the Concurrence of the Majority of the Members representing all those Electoral Divisions or Districts, and the Assent shall not be given to such Bill unless an Address has been presented by the Legislative Assembly to the Lieutenant Governor stating that it has been so passed.

3.—*ONTARIO AND QUEBEC.*

81. The Legislatures of Ontario and Quebec respectively shall be called together not later than Six Months after the Union.

82. The Lieutenant Governor of Ontario and of Quebec shall from Time to Time, in the Queen's Name, by Instrument under the Great Seal of the Province, summon and call together the Legislative Assembly of the Province.

83. Until the Legislature of Ontario or of Quebec otherwise provides, a Person accepting or holding in Ontario or in Quebec any Office, Commission, or Employment permanent or temporary, at the Nomination of the Lieutenant Governor, to which an annual Salary, or any Fee, Allowance, Emolument, or profit of any Kind or Amount whatever from the Province is attached, shall not be eligible as a Member of the Legislative Assembly of the respective Province, nor shall he sit or vote as such ; but nothing in this Section shall make ineligible any Person being a Member of the Executive Council of the respective Province, or holding any of the following Offices, that is to say, the Offices of Attorney General, Secretary and Registrar of the Province, Treasurer of the Province, Commissioner of Crown Lands, and Commissioner of Agriculture and Public Works, and in Quebec Solicitor General, or shall disqualify him to sit or vote in the House for which he is elected, provided he is elected while holding such Office.

84. Until the Legislatures of Ontario and Quebec respectively otherwise provide, all Laws which at the Union are in force in those Provinces respectively, relative to the following Matters, or any of them, namely,—the Qualifications and Disqualifications of Persons to be elected or to sit or vote as Members of the Assembly of Canada, the Qualifications or Disqualifications of Voters, the Oaths to be taken by Voters, the Returning Officers, their Powers and Duties, the Proceedings at Elections, the Periods during which such Elections may be continued, and the Trial of controverted Elections and the Proceedings incident thereto, the vacating of the Seats of Members and the issuing and Execution of new Writs in case of Seats vacated otherwise than by Dissolution, shall respectively apply to Elections of Members to serve in the respective Legislative Assemblies of Ontario and Quebec.

Provided that until the Legislature of Ontario otherwise provides, at any Election for a Member of the Legislative Assembly of Ontario for the District of Algoma, in addition to Persons qualified by the Law of the Province of Canada to vote, every British Subject, aged Twenty-one Years or upwards, being a Householder, shall have a Vote.

85. Every Legislative Assembly of Ontario and every Legislative Assembly of Quebec shall continue for Four Years from the Day of the

Return of the Writs for choosing the same (subject nevertheless to either the Legislative Assembly of Ontario or the Legislative Assembly of Quebec being sooner dissolved by the Lieutenant Governor of the Province), and no longer.

86. There shall be a session of the Legislature of Ontario and of that of Quebec once at least in every Year, so that Twelve Months shall not intervene between the last Sitting of the Legislature in each Province in one Session and its first Sitting in the next Session.

87. The following Provisions of this Act respecting the House of Commons of Canada shall extend and apply to the Legislative Assemblies of Ontario and Quebec, that is to say,—the Provisions relating to the Election of a Speaker originally and on Vacancies, the Duties of the Speaker, the absence of the Speaker, the Quorum, and the Mode of voting, as if those Provisions were here re-enacted and made applicable in Terms to each such Legislative Assembly.

4.—NOVA SCOTIA AND NEW BRUNSWICK.

88. The Constitution of the Legislature of each of the Provinces of Nova Scotia and New Brunswick shall, subject to the Provisions of this Act, continue as it exists at the Union until altered under the Authority of this Act; and the House of Assembly of New Brunswick existing at the passing of this Act shall, unless sooner dissolved, continue for the Period for which it was elected.

5.—ONTARIO, QUEBEC, AND NOVA SCOTIA.

89. Each of the Lieutenant Governors of Ontario, Quebec and Nova Scotia shall cause Writs to be issued for the First Election of Members of the Legislative Assembly thereof in such Form and by such Person as he thinks fit, and at such Time and addressed to such Returning Officer as the Governor General directs, and so that the First Election of Member of Assembly for any Electoral District or any Subdivision thereof shall be held at the same Time and at the same Places as the Election for a Member to serve in the House of Commons of Canada for that Electoral District.

6.—THE FOUR PROVINCES.

90. The following Provisions of this Act respecting the Parliament of Canada, namely,—the Provisions relating to Appropriation and Tax Bills, the Recommendation of Money Votes, the Assent to Bills, the Disallowance of Acts, and the Signification of Pleasure on Bills reserved,

—shall extend and apply to the Legislatures of the several Provinces as if those Provisions were here re-enacted and made applicable in Terms to the respective Provinces and the Legislatures thereof, with the Substitution of the Lieutenant Governor of the Province for the Governor General, of the Governor General for the Queen and for a Secretary of State, of One Year for Two Years, and of the Province for Canada.

VI.—DISTRIBUTION OF LEGISLATIVE POWERS.

Powers of the Parliament.

91. It shall be lawful for the Queen, by and with the Advice and Consent of the Senate and House of Commons, to make Laws for the Peace, Order, and good Government of Canada, in relation to all Matters not coming within the Classes of Subjects by this Act assigned exclusively to the Legislatures of the Provinces; and for greater Certainty, but not so as to restrict the Generality of the foregoing Terms of this Section, it is hereby declared that (notwithstanding anything in this Act) the exclusive Legislative Authority of the Parliament of Canada extends to all Matters coming within the Classes of Subjects next hereinafter enumerated; that is to say :—

1. The Public Debt and Property.
2. The Regulation of Trade and Commerce.
3. The raising of Money by any Mode or System of Taxation.
4. The borrowing of Money on the Public Credit.
5. Postal Service.
6. The Census and Statistics.
7. Militia, Military and Naval Service, and Defence.
8. The fixing of and providing for the Salaries and Allowances of Civil and other Officers of the Government of Canada.
9. Beacons, Buoys, Lighthouses, and Sable Island.
10. Navigation and Shipping.
11. Quarantine and the Establishment and Maintenance of Marine Hospitals.
12. Sea Coast and Inland Fisheries.
13. Ferries between a Province and any British or Foreign Country or between Two Provinces.
14. Currency and Coinage.
15. Banking, Incorporation of Banks, and the Issue of Paper Money.
16. Savings Banks.
17. Weights and Measures.
18. Bills of Exchange and Promissory Notes.

19. Interest.
20. Legal Tender.
21. Bankruptcy and Insolvency.
22. Patents of Invention and Discovery.
23. Copyrights.
24. Indians, and Lands reserved for the Indians.
25. Naturalization and Aliens.
26. Marriage and Divorce.
27. The Criminal Law, except the Constitution of Courts of Criminal Jurisdiction, but including the Procedure in Criminal Matters.
28. The Establishment, Maintenance, and Management of Penitentiaries.
29. Such Classes of Subjects as are expressly excepted in the Enumeration of the Classes of Subjects by this Act assigned exclusively to the Legislatures of the Provinces.

And any Matter coming within any of the Classes of Subjects enumerated in this Section shall not be deemed to come within the Class of Matters of a local or private Nature comprised in the Enumeration of the Classes of Subjects by this Act assigned exclusively to the Legislatures of the Provinces.

Exclusive Powers of Provincial Legislatures.

92. In each Province the Legislature may exclusively make Laws in relation to Matters coming within the Classes of Subjects next hereinafter enumerated, that is to say,—

1. The Amendment from Time to Time, notwithstanding anything in this Act, of the Constitution of the Province, except as regards the Office of Lieutenant Governor.
2. Direct Taxation within the Province in order to the raising of a Revenue for Provincial Purposes.
3. The borrowing of Money on the sole Credit of the Province.
4. The Establishment and Tenure of Provincial Offices and the Appointment and Payment of Provincial Officers.
5. The Management and Sale of the Public Lands belonging to the Province and of the Timber and Wood thereon.
6. The Establishment, Maintenance, and Management of Public and Reformatory Prisons in and for the Province.
7. The Establishment, Maintenance, and Management of Hospitals, Asylums, Charities, and Eleemosynary Institutions in and for the Province, other than Marine Hospitals.
8. Municipal Institutions in the Province.

9. Shop, Saloon, Tavern, Auctioneer, and other Licenses in order to the raising of a Revenue for Provincial, Local, or Municipal Purposes.
10. Local Works and Undertakings other than such as are of the following Classes,—
   a. Lines of Steam or other Ships, Railways, Canals, Telegraphs, and other Works and Undertakings connecting the Province with any other or others of the Provinces, or extending beyond the Limits of the Province :
   b. Lines of Steam Ships between the Province and any British or Foreign Country :
   c. Such Works as, although wholly situate within the Province, are before or after their Execution declared by the Parliament of Canada to be for the general Advantage of Canada or for the Advantage of Two or more of the Provinces.
11. The Incorporation of Companies with Provincial Objects.
12. The Solemnization of Marriage in the Province.
13. Property and Civil Rights in the Province.
14. The Administration of Justice in the Province, including the Constitution, Maintenance, and Organization of Provincial Courts, both of Civil and of Criminal Jurisdiction, and including Procedure in Civil Matters in those Courts.
15. The Imposition of Punishment by Fine, Penalty, or Imprisonment for enforcing any Law of the Province made in relation to any Matter coming within any of the Classes of Subjects enumerated in this section.
16. Generally all matters of a merely local or private Nature in the Province.

Education.

93. In and for each Province the Legislature may exclusively make Laws in relation to Education, subject and according to the following Provisions :—

(1.) Nothing in any such Law shall prejudicially affect any Right or Privilege with respect to denominational Schools which any Class of Persons have by Law in the Province at the Union :

(2.) All the Powers, Privileges, and Duties at the Union by Law conferred and imposed in Upper Canada on the Separate Schools and School Trustees of the Queen's Roman Catholic Subjects shall be and the same are hereby extended to the Dissentient Schools of the Queen's Protestant and Roman Catholic Subjects in Quebec:

(3) Where in any Province a System of Separate or Dissentient Schools exists by Law at the Union or is thereafter established by the Legislature of the Province, an Appeal shall lie to the Governor General in Council from any Act or Decision of any Provincial Authority affecting any Right or Privilege of the Protestant or Roman Catholic Minority of the Queen's Subjects in relation to Education:

(4.) In case any such Provincial Law as from Time to Time seems to the Governor General in Council requisite for the due Execution of the Provisions of this Section is not made, or in case any Decision of the Governor General in Council on any Appeal under this Section is not duly executed by the proper Provincial Authority in that Behalf, then and in every such Case, and as far only as the Circumstances of each Case require, the Parliament of Canada may make remedial Laws for the due Execution of the Provisions of this Section and of any Decision of the Governor General in Council under this Section.

Uniformity of Laws in Ontario, Nova Scotia, and New Brunswick.

94. Notwithstanding anything in this Act, the Parliament of Canada may make Provision for the Uniformity of all or any of the Laws relative to Property and Civil Rights in Ontario, Nova Scotia and New Brunswick, and of the Procedure of all or any of the Courts in those Three Provinces, and from and after the passing of any Act in that Behalf the Power of the Parliament of Canada to make Laws in relation to any Matter comprised in any such Act shall, notwithstanding anything in this Act, be unrestricted ; but any Act of the Parliament of Canada making Provision for such Uniformity shall not have effect in any Province unless and until it is adopted and enacted as Law by the Legislature thereof.

Agriculture and Immigration.

95. In each Province the Legislature may make Laws in relation to Agriculture in the Province, and to Immigration into the Province ; and it is hereby declared that the Parliament of Canada may from Time to Time make Laws in relation to Agriculture in all or any of the Provinces, and to Immigration into all or any of the Provinces ; and any Law of the Legislature of a Province relative to Agriculture or to Immigration shall have effect in and for the Province as long and as far only as it is not repugnant to any Act of the Parliament of Canada.

VII.—JUDICATURE.

96. The Governor General shall appoint the Judges of the Superior, District, and County Courts in each Province, except those of the Courts of Probate in Nova Scotia and New Brunswick.

97. Until the Laws relative to Property and Civil Rights in Ontario, Nova Scotia, and New Brunswick, and the Procedure of the Courts in those Provinces, are made uniform, the Judges of the Courts of those Provinces appointed by the Governor General shall be selected from the respective Bars of those Provinces.

98. The Judges of the Courts of Quebec, shall be selected from the Bar of that Province.

99. The Judges of the Superior Courts shall hold office during good Behaviour, but shall be removable by the Governor General on Address of the Senate and House of Commons.

100. The Salaries, Allowances, and Pensions of the Judges of the Superior, District and County Courts (except the Courts of Probate in Nova Scotia and New Brunswick,) and of the Admiralty Courts in Cases where the Judges thereof are for the Time being paid by Salary, shall be fixed and provided by the Parliament of Canada.

101. The Parliament of Canada may, notwithstanding anything in this Act, from Time to Time, provide for the Constitution, Maintenance, and Organization of a General Court of Appeal for Canada, and for the Establishment of any additional Courts for the better Administration of the Laws of Canada.

VIII.—REVENUES; DEBTS; ASSETS; TAXATION.

102. All Duties and Revenues over which the respective Legislatures of Canada, Nova Scotia, and New Brunswick before and at the Union had and have Power of Appropriation, except such Portions thereof as are by this Act reserved to the respective Legislatures of the Provinces, or are raised by them in accordance with the special Powers conferred on them by this Act, shall form One Consolidated Revenue Fund, to be appropriated for the Public Service of Canada in the Manner and subject to the Charges in this Act provided.

103. The Consolidated Revenue Fund of Canada shall be permanently charged with the Costs, Charges, and Expenses incident to the Collection, Management, and Receipt thereof, and the same shall form the First Charge thereon, subject to be reviewed and audited in such

Manner as shall be ordered by the Governor General in Council until the Parliament otherwise provides.

104. The annual Interest of the Public Debts of the several Provinces of Canada, Nova Scotia, and New Brunswick at the Union shall form the Second Charge on the Consolidated Revenue Fund of Canada.

105. Unless altered by the Parliament of Canada, the Salary of the Governor General shall be Ten thousand Pounds Sterling Money of the United Kingdom of Great Britain and Ireland, payable out of the Consolidated Revenue Fund of Canada, and the same shall form the Third Charge thereon.

106. Subject to the several Payments by this Act charged on the Consolidated Revenue Fund of Canada, the same shall be appropriated by the Parliament of Canada for the Public Service.

107. All Stocks, Cash, Banker's Balances, and Securities for Money belonging to each Province at the Time of the Union, except as in this Act mentioned, shall be the Property of Canada, and shall be taken in Reduction of the amount of the respective Debts of the Provinces at the Union.

108. The Public Works and Property of each Province, enumerated in the Third Schedule to this Act, shall be the Property of Canada.

109. All Lands, Mines, Minerals, and Royalties belonging to the several Provinces of Canada, Nova Scotia, and New Brunswick at the Union, and all Sums then due or payable for such Lands, Mines, Minerals, or Royalties, shall belong to the several Provinces of Ontario, Quebec, Nova Scotia, and New Brunswick in which the same are situate or arise, subject to any Trusts existing in respect thereof, and to any Interest other than that of the Province in the same.

110. All Assets connected with such Portions of the Public Debt of each Province as are assumed by that Province shall belong to that Province.

111. Canada shall be liable for the Debts and Liabilities of each Province existing at the Union.

112. Ontario and Quebec conjointly shall be liable to Canada for the Amount (if any) by which the Debt of the Province of Canada exceeds at the Union Sixty-two million five hundred thousand Dollars, and shall be charged with Interest at the Rate of Five per Centum per Annum thereon.

113. The Assets enumerated in the Fourth Schedule to this Act belonging at the Union to the Province of Canada shall be the Property of Ontario and Quebec conjointly.

114. Nova Scotia shall be liable to Canada for the Amount (if any) by which its Public Debt exceeds at the Union Eight million Dollars, and shall be charged with Interest at the Rate of Five per Centum per Annum thereon.

115. New Brunswick shall be liable to Canada for the Amount (if any) by which its Public Debt exceeds at the Union Seven million Dollars, and shall be charged with Interest at the Rate of Five per Centum per Annum thereon.

116. In case the Public Debts of Nova Scotia and New Brunswick do not at the Union amount to Eight million and Seven million Dollars respectively, they shall respectively receive by half-yearly Payments in advance from the Government of Canada Interest at Five per Centum per Annum on the Difference between the actual Amounts of their respective Debts and such stipulated Amounts.

117. The several Provinces shall retain all their respective Public Property not otherwise disposed of in this Act, subject to the Right of Canada to assume any Lands or Public Property required for Fortifications or for the Defence of the Country.

118. The following Sums shall be paid yearly by Canada to the several Provinces for the Support of their Governments and Legislatures :

	Dollars.
Ontario	Eighty thousand.
Quebec	Seventy thousand.
Nova Scotia	Sixty thousand.
New Brunswick	Fifty thousand.

Two hundred and sixty thousand ; and an annual Grant in aid of each Province shall be made, equal to Eighty Cents per Head of the Population as ascertained by the Census of One thousand eight hundred and sixty-one, and in the Case of Nova Scotia and New Brunswick, by each subsequent Decennial Census until the Population of each of those two Provinces amounts to Four hundred thousand Souls, at which Rate such Grant shall thereafter remain. Such Grants shall be in full Settlement of all future Demands on Canada, and shall be paid half-yearly in advance to each Province ; but the

Government of Canada shall deduct from such Grants, as against any Province, all Sums chargeable as Interest on the Public Debt of that Province in excess of the several Amounts stipulated in this Act.

119. New Brunswick shall receive by half-yearly payments in advance from Canada for the Period of Ten Years from the Union an additional Allowance of Sixty-three thousand Dollars per Annum ; but as long as the Public Debt of that Province remains under Seven million Dollars, a Deduction equal to the Interest at Five per Centum per Annum on such Deficiency shall be made from that Allowance of Sixty-three thousand Dollars.

120. All Payments to be made under this Act, or in discharge of Liabilities created under any Act of the Provinces of Canada, Nova Scotia, and New Brunswick respectively, and assumed by Canada, shall, until the Parliament of Canada otherwise directs, be made in such Form and Manner as may from Time to Time be ordered by the Governor General in Council.

121. All Articles of the Growth, Produce, or Manufacture of any one of the Provinces shall, from and after the Union, be admitted free into each of the other Provinces.

122. The Customs and Excise Laws of each Province shall, subject to the Provisions of this Act, continue in force until altered by the Parliament of Canada.

123. Where Customs Duties are, at the Union, leviable on any Goods, Wares, or Merchandises in any Two Provinces, those Goods, Wares, and Merchandises may, from and after the Union, be imported from one of those Provinces into the other of them on Proof of Payment of the Customs Duty leviable thereon in the Province of Exportation, and on Payment of such further Amount (if any) of Customs Duty as is leviable thereon in the Province of Importation.

124. Nothing in this Act shall affect the Right of New Brunswick to levy the Lumber Dues provided in Chapter Fifteen of Title Three of the Revised Statutes of New Brunswick, or in any Act amending that Act before or after the Union, and not increasing the Amount of such Dues ; but the Lumber of any of the Provinces other than New Brunswick shall not be subject to such Dues.

125. No Lands or Property belonging to Canada or any Province shall be liable to Taxation.

126. Such Portions of the Duties and Revenues over which the respective Legislatures of Canada, Nova Scotia, and New Brunswick had before the Union Power of Appropriation as are by this Act reserved to the respective Governments or Legislatures of the Provinces, and all Duties and Revenues raised by them in accordance with the special Powers conferred upon them by this Act, shall in each Province form One Consolidated Revenue Fund to be appropriated for the Public Service of the Province.

IX.—MISCELLANEOUS PROVISIONS.

General.

127. If any Person being at the passing of this Act a Member of the Legislative Council of Canada, Nova Scotia, or New Brunswick, to whom a Place in the Senate is offered, does not within Thirty Days thereafter, by Writing under his Hand addressed to the Governor General of the Province of Canada or to the Lieutenant Governor of Nova Scotia or New Brunswick (as the Case may be), accept the same, he shall be deemed to have declined the same ; and any Person who, being at the passing of this Act a Member of the Legislative Council of Nova Scotia or New Brunswick, accepts a Place in the Senate shall thereby vacate his Seat in such Legislative Council.

128. Every Member of the Senate or House of Commons of Canada shall before taking his Seat therein take and subscribe before the Governor General or some Person authorized by him, and every Member of a Legislative Council or Legislative Assembly of any Province shall before taking his Seat therein take and subscribe before the Lieutenant Governor of the Province or some Person authorized by him, the Oath of Allegiance contained in the Fifth Schedule to this Act ; and every Member of the Senate of Canada and every Member of the Legislative Council of Quebec shall also, before taking his Seat therein, take and subscribe before the Governor General, or some Person authorized by him, the Declaration of Qualification contained in the same Schedule.

129. Except as otherwise provided by this Act, all Laws in force in Canada, Nova Scotia, or New Brunswick at the Union, and all Courts of Civil and Criminal Jurisdiction, and all legal Commissions, Powers, and Authorities, and all Officers, Judicial, Administrative, and Ministerial, existing therein at the Union, shall continue in Ontario, Quebec, Nova Scotia, and New Brunswick respectively, as if the Union had not been made ; subject nevertheless (except with respect to such as are enacted by or exist under Acts of the Parliament of Great Britain or of the Parliament of the United Kingdom of Great Britain and Ireland), to be repealed, abolished or altered by the Parliament of Canada, or by the Legislature of the respective Province, according to the Authority of the Parliament or of that Legislature under this Act.

130. Until the Parliament of Canada otherwise provides, all Officers of the several Provinces having Duties to discharge in relation to Matters other than those coming within the Classes of Subjects by this Act assigned exclusively to the Legislatures of the Provinces shall be Officers of Canada, and shall continue to discharge the Duties of their respective Offices under the same Liabilities, Responsibilities, and Penalties as if the Union had not been made.

131. Until the Parliament of Canada otherwise provides, the Governor General in Council may from Time to Time appoint such Officers as the Governor General in Council deems necessary or proper for the effectual Execution of this Act.

132. The Parliament and Government of Canada shall have all Powers necessary or proper for performing the Obligations of Canada or of any Province thereof, as Part of the British Empire, towards Foreign Countries, arising under Treaties between the Empire and such Foreign Countries.

133. Either the English or the French Language may be used by any Person in the Debates of the Houses of the Parliament of Canada and of the Houses of the Legislature of Quebec; and both those Languages shall be used in the respective Records and Journals of those Houses; and either of those Languages may be used by any Person or in any Pleading or Process in or issuing from any Court of Canada established under this Act, and in or from all or any of the Courts of Quebec.

The Acts of the Parliament of Canada and of the Legislature of Quebec shall be printed and published in both those Languages.

Ontario and Quebec.

134. Until the Legislature of Ontario or of Quebec otherwise provides, the Lieutenant Governors of Ontario and Quebec may each appoint under the Great Seal of the Province the following Officers, to hold Office during Pleasure, that is to say,—the Attorney General, the Secretary and Registrar of the Province, the Treasurer of the Province, the Commissioner of Crown Lands, and the Commissioner of Agriculture and Public Works, and in the Case of Quebec the Solicitor General; and may, by Order of the Lieutenant Governor in Council, from Time to Time prescribe the Duties of those Officers and of the several Departments over which they shall preside or to which they shall belong, and of the Officers and Clerks thereof ; and may also appoint other and additional Officers to hold Office during Pleasure, and may from Time to Time prescribe the Duties of those Officers, and of the several Departments over which they shall preside or to which they shall belong, and of the Officers and Clerks thereof.

135. Until the Legislature of Ontario or Quebec otherwise provides, all Rights, Powers, Duties, Functions, Responsibilities, or Authorities at the passing of this Act vested in or imposed on the Attorney General, Solicitor General, Secretary and Registrar of the Province of Canada, Minister of Finance, Commissioner of Crown Lands, Commissioner of Public Works, and Minister of Agriculture and Receiver General, by any Law, Statute or Ordinance of Upper Canada, Lower Canada, or Canada, and not repugnant to this Act, shall be vested in or imposed on any Officer to be appointed by the Lieutenant Governor for the Discharge of the same or any of them ; and the Commissioner of Agriculture and Public Works shall perform the Duties and Functions of the Office of Minister of Agriculture at the passing of this Act imposed by the Law of the Province of Canada, as well as those of the Commissioner of Public Works.

136. Until altered by the Lieutenant Governor in Council, the Great Seals of Ontario and Quebec respectively shall be the same, or of the same Design, as those used in the Provinces of Upper Canada and Lower Canada respectively before their Union as the Province of Canada.

137. The Words " and from thence to the End of the then next ensuing Session of the Legislature," or Words to the same Effect, used in any temporary Act of the Province of Canada not expired before the Union, shall be construed to extend and apply to the next Session of the Parliament of Canada, if the Subject Matter of the Act is within the Powers of the same, as defined by this Act, or to the next Sessions of the Legislatures of Ontario and Quebec respectively, if the Subject Matter of the Act is within the Powers of the same as defined by this Act.

138. From and after the Union the Use of the Words " Upper Canada " instead of " Ontario," or " Lower Canada " instead of " Quebec," in any Deed, Writ, Process, Pleading, Document, Matter, or Thing, shall not invalidate the same.

139. Any Proclamation under the Great Seal of the Province of Canada issued before the Union to take effect at a Time which is subsequent to the Union, whether relating to that Province, or to Upper Canada, or to Lower Canada, and the several Matters and Things therein proclaimed shall be and continue of like Force and Effect as if the Union had not been made.

140. Any Proclamation which is authorized by any Act of the Legislature of the Province of Canada to be issued under the Great Seal of the Province of Canada, whether relating to that Province, or to Upper Canada, or to Lower Canada, and which is not issued before the Union, may be issued by the Lieutenant Governor of Ontario or of Quebec, as its Subject Matter requires, under the Great Seal thereof; and from and after the Issue of such Proclamation the same and the several Matters and Things therein proclaimed shall be and continue of the like Force and Effect in Ontario or Quebec as if the Union had not been made.

141. The Penitentiary of the Province of Canada shall, until the Parliament of Canada otherwise provides, be and continue the Penitentiary of Ontario and of Quebec.

142. The Division and Adjustment of the Debts, Credits, Liabilities, Properties, and Assets of Upper Canada and Lower Canada shall be referred to the Arbitrament of Three Arbitrators, One chosen by the Government of Ontario, One by the Government of Quebec, and One by the Government of Canada; and the Selection of the Arbitrators shall not be made until the Parliament of Canada and the Legislatures of Ontario and Quebec have met; and the Arbitrator chosen by the Government of Canada shall not be a resident either in Ontario or in Quebec.

143. The Governor General in Council may from Time to Time order that such and so many of the Records, Books, and Documents of the Province of Canada as he thinks fit shall be appropriated and delivered either to Ontario or to Quebec, and the same shall thenceforth be the Property of that Province; and any Copy thereof or Extract therefrom, duly certified by the Officer having charge of the Original thereof, shall be admitted as Evidence.

144. The Lieutenant Governor of Quebec may from Time to Time, by Proclamation under the Great Seal of the Province, to take effect from a day to be appointed therein, constitute Townships in those Parts of the Province of Quebec in which Townships are not then already constituted, and fix the Metes and Bounds thereof.

X.—INTERCOLONIAL RAILWAY.

145. Inasmuch as the Provinces of Canada, Nova Scotia, and New Brunswick have joined in a Declaration that the Construction of the Intercolonial Railway is essential to the Consolidation of the Union of British North America, and to the Assent thereto of Nova Scotia and New Brunswick, and have consequently agreed that Provision should be made for its immediate Construction by the Government of Canada: Therefore, in order to give effect to that Agreement, it shall be the Duty of the Government and Parliament of Canada to provide for the Commencement within Six Months after the Union, of a Railway connecting the River St. Lawrence with City of Halifax in Nova Scotia, and for the Construction thereof without Intermission, and the Completion thereof with all practicable Speed.

XI.—ADMISSION OF OTHER COLONIES.

146. It shall be lawful for the Queen, by and with the Advice of Her Majesty's Most Honourable Privy Council, on Addresses from the Houses of the Parliament of Canada, and from the Houses of the respective Legislatures of the Colonies or Provinces of Newfoundland, Prince Edward Island, and British Columbia, to admit those Colonies or Provinces, or any of them, into the Union, and on Address from the Houses of the Parliament of Canada to admit Rupert's Land and the Northwestern Territory, or either of them, into the Union, on such Terms and Conditions in each Case as are in the Addresses expressed and as the Queen thinks fit to approve, subject to the Provisions of this Act; and the Provisions of any Order in Council in that Behalf shall have effect as if they had been enacted by the Parliament of the United Kingdom of Great Britain and Ireland.

147. In case of the Admission of Newfoundland and Prince Edward Island, or either of them, each shall be entitled to a Representation in the Senate of Canada of Four Members, and (notwithstanding anything in this Act) in case of the Admission of Newfoundland the normal Number of Senators shall be Seventy-six and their maximum Number shall be Eighty-two; but Prince Edward Island when admitted shall be deemed to be comprised in the Third of the Three Divisions into which Canada is, in relation to the Constitution of the Senate, divided by this Act, and accordingly, after the Admission of Prince Edward Island, whether Newfoundland is admitted or not, the Representation of Nova Scotia and New Brunswick in the Senate shall, as Vacancies occur, be reduced from Twelve to Ten Members respectively, and the Representation of each of Those Provinces shall not be increased at any Time beyond Ten, except under the Provisions of this Act for the Appointment of Three or Six additional Senators under the Direction of the Queen.

INDEX.

Abercrombie, def., 1758.
Aberdeen, 1893.
Acadia became N.S., 1621.
Acadians, 1755.
Act of Union, 1840.
Adam Daulac, 1660.
"Advocate" wrecked, 1826.
Alberta, 1882.
Algonquin bravery, 1645.
Amnesty Bill, 1849.
Andastes, 1647.
Argall, 1613.
Argenson, 1658.
Articles of Confederation, 1781.
Army Bills, 1812, 1820.
" Aroostook War," 1839.
Assiniboia, 1882.
Athabasca, 1882.
" Atlantic," 1873.
Atlantic Cable, 1866.
Avaugour, 1661.
Aylmer, 1830.

Bagot, 1842.
Ballot Act, 1874.
Bank Act, 1890.
Bank of Montreal, 1817.
Bank of Kingston, 1819.
Baptists, 1794, 1800, 1819, 1852, 1860, 1887.
Baronets of N.S., 1625.
Battles: Beaver Dam, 1813; Bloody Run, 1763; Bushy Run, 1763; Chateauguay, 1813; Chippewa, 1814; Chrystler's Farm, 1813; Frenchtown, 1813; Lake Champlain, 1814; Lake Erie, 1813; Lake Ontario 1813; Lundy's Lane, 1814; Moravian Tn., 1813; Plains of Abraham, 1759; Queenston, 1812; Ste. Foye, 1760; Stony Creek, 1813; Three Rivers, 1776; Ticonderoga, 1758.

Beauharnois, 1726.
Behring Sea Arbitration, 1893.
Behring Strait, 1728.
Berlin Decree, 1806.
Better Terms to N.S., 1869.
Bishopp, 1813.
Bonne St. Anne, 1658.
Braddock def., 1755.
British Columbia, 1871.
British N. A. Act, 1867, 1875.
Brock, 1806, 1812.
Brock's Monument, 1824, 1840.
Brown, Geo., 1843-1880.

Caldwell, 1823.
Callieres, 1699.
Can. Alliance Soc., 1834.
Can. Company, 1826.
Can. P.R.R., 1881, 1885.
Can S.R.R., 1868, 1873.
Can. Trade Act, 1822.
Canals: Lachine, 1821, 1825; Rideau, 1832; Sault Ste. Marie, 1895; Shubenacadie, 1827; Welland, 1829.
Canal tolls, 1892.
Card money, 1685.
Carignan Regt., 1665.
Carleton, 1766.
"Carnarvon Terms," 1874.
" Caroline," 1837.
" Carrick," 1832.
Cartier-Macdonald Ad., 1858.
Census, 1867.
Champlain married, 1610; died, 1635.
Chapter, Cath., 1684.
Charlevoix, 1720.
Chateau St. Louis, 1834.
Cholera, 1832, 1852.
Christian Bros., 1737.
Civil Code of L.C., 1866.
Civil Service, 1882.
Civil War in U.S., 1861-1865.

223

"Clear Grit," 1849.
Clergy Reserves, 1791, 1840, 1854.
Colborne, 1839.
Colonial Conf., 1894.
Common Sch Act, 1824.
Congregational, 1801.
Congress, 1774, 1775, 1776.
Constitutional Act, 1791.
Constitution of U.S., 1787.
Copyright Conf., 1895.
Corrigan murder, 1855.
Courcelles, 1665.
Coureurs de Bois, 1664.
Coutume de Paris, 1663.
Covington, 1813.
Craig, 1807.

D'Ailleboust, 1647.
Dalhousie, 1820.
Danforth Road, 1799.
Dark Afternoon, 1785.
Dark Day, 1780.
"Dead Lock," 1864.
De Celeron, 1749.
Decimal Currency, 1858.
Dec. of Independence, 1776.
Deerfield, 1704.
De Mesy, 1663.
Denonville, 1685.
"De Salaberry," 1823.
Des Jardins Canal, 1857.
Detroit, 1701.
Devil's Hole, 1763.
Dieskau, 1755.
Dobbs, 1814.
Dom. Grange, 1874.
Dorchester, 1786.
Double Majority, 1845.
Double Shuffle, 1858.
Duc d'Anville, 1746.
Duchess d'Aiguillon, 1637.
Duels, 1800, 1806, 1817.
Dufferin, 1872.
Dunkin Act, 1864.
Dupuys, 1656.
DuQuesne, 1754, 1758.
Durham boat, 1816.

Earthquakes, 1663, 1870.
Elections, Dom., 1867, 1872, 1874, 1878, 1882, 1887, 1891, 1896.

Elgin, 1847.
English Ch., 1787, 1789, 1804, 1805, 1820, 1836, 1839, 1843, 1890, 1895.
Equal Rights Party, 1888.
Eries, 1655.
Escheats in Real Property, 1883.
Extradition, 1842, 1886.

Fabrique Act, 1824.
Family Compact, 1820.
"Fathers of Confederation," 1866.
Fenians, 1866, 1870.
"Fifty-four-forty or Fight," 1846.
First things: Agric. Exhib., 1850, Agric. Soc., 1818, Ball. 1667; Bank, 1817, Birth, 1587. Bishop, 1674, Book, 1765, Brewery, 1667, Church, 1615, 1786, C.M.B.A., 1878, Coinage, 1823, Copyright, 1841, Daily Newspaper. 1840 Dominion Day, 1867, Farmer, 1617, Forge, 1733, Governor, 1632, High Comm., 1880, Horse, 1647, Locomotive, 1853, Hospital, 1643, Marriage, 1617, Masonic Lodge, 1738, Mass, 1615, Mill, 1629. Negro, 1630, Newspaper, 1752, 1764, 1793, Orange Lodge, 1830, Patent, 1824, Ploughing, 1628, Post, 1721, Postage Cards, 1871, Postage Stamps, 1851, P.O. Money Orders, 1824, P O. Registration, 1855, Rabbi, 1778, Railway, 1836, Rep. Gov't., 1758, Road, 1665, School, 1637, 1785, Seignior, 1634, Settlement, 1605, Steamboat, 1809, 1816, Steam Engine, 1827, Steamship, 1826, Stone House, 1599, Street Railroad, 1861, Submarine Tel., 1866, Telegraph, 1847, Telephone, 1877, Temperance Meeting, 1648, Tobacco Export, 1739, Wheat, 1644, Y.M.C.A., 1851,
Fitzgibbons, 1813.
Fort Beausejour, 1755.
Fort Edward, 1755.
Fort Erie, 1814.
Fort Frontenac, 1673, 1689, 1695, 1758.

INDEX. 225

Fort George, 1813.
Fort Massachusetts, 1746.
Fort Necessity, 1754.
Fort Pitt, 1758, 1763.
Franchise Act, 1885.
"Frontenac," 1816.
Frontenac, 1672, 1689.
Galissonniere, 1747.
Gavazzi Riot, 1853.
Geneva Arbitration, 1872.
Geusing, 1716.
Gosford, 1835.
Gourlay, 1817, 1818.
Grand River Reserve, 1784.
Grand Trunk, 1853.
"Great Comet," 1680.
"Great Ministry," 1851.
Great Seal of Can., 1858.
Great Western R.R., 1853.
"Griffin," 1679.
Guibord, 1875.

Hackett, 1878.
Haldimand, 1778.
Halifax Award, 1878.
Halifax Commission, 1877.
Halifax Founded, 1749.
Hansard, 1874.
Head, 1835.
Henry, John, 1808, 1812.
Hincks-Morin Ad., 1851.
Historical Soc., 1824.
Homestead Act, 1878.
Hôtel Dieu, 1639.
Hudson's Bay, 1611, 1697, 1686.
Hudson's Bay Co., 1670, 1821, 1835, 1869.
Hull, 1812.
Hundred Associates, 1627, 1645, 1663.
Hundredth Regt., 1858, 1859.
"Hungry Year," 1788.
Hunter's Lodges, 1838.
Hurons dispersed, 1649.

Iberville in Nfld., 1696, entered Mississippi, 1699.
Icelanders, 1875.
Imperial Fed. League, 1884.
Imprisonment for debt abol., 1858.
Intendants, 1665, 1668, 1670, 1675,
1682, 1686, 1702, 1705, 1710, 1726, 1729, 1748.
Intercolonial R.R., 1867, 1876.
Iroquois, 1641.

Jamestown, 1607.
Jefferson's Embargo, 1807.
Jesuits, 1611, 1625, 1678, 1800, 1842, 1887, 1889.
Joint High Com., 1871.
Jonquiere, 1749.
Judge Willis, 1828.
Jumonville, 1754.

Keewatin, 1876.
Kempt, 1828.
Kirke, 1628, 1629.

La Barre, 1682.
Lachine Massacre, 1689.
La Compagnie des Forges, 1737.
Lafontaine-Baldwin Ad., 1848.
La France, Joseph, 1742.
La Grippe, 1890.
Land Grants, 1763.
Lansdowne, 1883.
La Presentation, 1748.
La Salle, 1666, 1669, 1673, 1674, 1678, 1679, 1680, 1681, 1682, 1685, 1687.
Laurier, 1896,
Lauson, 1651.
Laval, 1659, 1663.
Law Soc., 1822.
Law of Primogeniture, 1851, 1852.
"Le Canadien," suppressed 1810.
Legislative Council, Elective, 1854.
Letellier, 1879.
Letters of Agricola, 1818.
Library, Parliament, 1871.
Lincoln shot, 1865.
Lisgar, 1868.
London Company, 1608.
Lord Durham's Report, 1839.
Lorne, 1878.
Louisbourg fortified, 1720; taken 1745, 1758.

Macdonald, John A., 1844-1891.
Macdonald-Cartier Ad., 1857.
Macdonald-Sicotte Ad. 1862.

16

Mackenzie, Alex., 1793.
MacNab-Morin Ad., 1854.
Madame de la Peltrie, 1639, 1646, 1671.
Madame La Tour, 1645.
Mademoiselle de Mance, 1641.
Maine Boundary, 1831, 1842.
Man. entered Dom. 1870.
Margaret Bourgeois, 1653, 1659, 1700.
Marie de l'Incarnation, 1639, 1672
Marquette, 1668, 1673, 1675.
Maroons, 1796, 1800.
Marquis de Tracy, 1665.
Martyrs: Brebeuf, 1649; Buteux, 1652; Chabanal, 1649; Daniel, 1648; Garnier, 1649; Garreau, 1656; Goupil, 1642; Jogues, 1646; Lalande, 1646; Lalemant, 1649; Rasles, 1724.
McGee, 1868.
McGill Coll., 1823.
Mennonites, 1874.
Medcalf, Lieut., 1813.
Merchants' Exchange, 1717.
Metcalfe, 1843.
Methodism, 1780, 1782, 1790, 1791, 1792, 1801, 1808, 1811, 1818, 1828, 1836, 1841, 1854, 1873, 1883.
Metric System, 1871.
Military Rule, 1760, 1764.
Militia Act, 1855, 1868.
Miramichi Fire, 1825.
Mission of La Prairie, 1669.
Mission of Mountain, 1676.
Mississippi found, 1673.
Monck, 1861.
Montcalm, 1756, 1757, 1758, 1759.
Montgomery, 1776.
Montmagny, 1636.
Montreal, 1640, 1642, 1775, 1760, 1849.
"Montreal," 1857.
Municipal Act, 1841.
Municipal Loan Fund Act, 1852.

National Policy, 1878.
Navigation Laws, 1849.
N. B. School Bill, 1871.
Neutral Nation, 1626.

Ninety-two Resolutions, 1834.
Non-Intercourse Act, 1809.
Northern R.R., 1851.
North Shore R.R., 1879.
North-West Co., 1805, 1821.
North-West Police, 1873.
N. W. Territories entered Dominion, 1870.
Notre Dame Church, 1829, 1824.

Oaths Bill, 1873.
Ohio Co., 1749.
Olier, 1640.
"Ontario" lost, 1780.
Orangeism, 1890.
Orders in Council, 1806, 1812.
Osgoode, 1792, 1794.
Oswego, 1725, 1757.
Ottawa, 1858, 1867.

"Pacific Scandal," 1873.
Parrtown, 1873.
P. E. I. entered Dominion, 1873.
Phips, 1690.
Pictou colony, 1767.
Pike, Gen., 1813.
Pilgrims, 1620.
Plymouth Co., 1606.
Pontiac's conspiracy, 1763.
Port Royal, 1605, 1690.
Post Office, 1851.
Premiers of Dominion, 1867, 1873, 1878, 1891, 1892, 1896.
Presbyterianism, 1765, 1770, 1787, 1792, 1796, 1810, 1817, 1819, 1827, 1842, 1844, 1875, 1892.
Prescott, 1796.
Prevost, 1811.
Prince Consort, 1861.
Prince of Wales, 1841, 1860.
Prohibition, 1894, 1896, 1898.

Quakers, 1867.
Quarantine, 1832.
Quebec, 1608, 1629, 1690, 1759, 1760, 1775.
Quebec Act, 1774.
Quebec Bank, 1818.
Quebec Conference, 1864.
Queen's Counsel, 1872, 1873, 1879.
Queen Victoria, 1837, 1840, 1897.

INDEX. 227

Quit Rents, 1834.
"Rat," 1688.
Rebellion in Canada, 1837.
Rebellion in North-West, 1885.
Rebellion Losses Bill, 1849.
Reciprocity, 1650, 1854, 1866.
Recollets, 1615.
Redistribution Bill, 1882.
Red River, 1811, 1812.
"Relations of Jesuits," 1632.
Remedial Bill, 1896.
Representation by population. 1853.
Responsible Government, 1848.
Richmond, 1818.
Riot in Montreal, 1849.
Royal Military College, 1876.
Royal Rule, 1663.
Royal Society, 1882.
"Royal William," 1831, 1833.

Salvation Army, 1883.
"Sam Slick," 1835.
San Juan Boundary, 1871, 1872.
Saskatchewan, 1882.
Scott Act, 1878.
Scott, Thos., 1870.
Secord, Mrs., 1813.
Sedition Act, 1804.
Seignorial Tenure, 1854.
Selkirk, 1811, 1816, 1818.
Separate Schools, 1841, 1843, 1855.
"Seven Oaks," 1816.
"Shamrock," 1842.
Sherbrooke, 1816.
Ship Fever, 1847.
"Short Administration," 1858.
Sieur St. Lusson, 1671.
"Sir Robert Peel," 1838.
Six Nations, 1713.
Slavery, 1689, 1793, 1802, 1803.
Society of Notre Dame of Montreal, 1640.
Sovereign Council, 1655, 1684, 1703.
"Speedy" lost, 1804.
Stamp Act, 1765, 1766.
St. Alban's Raid, 1864.
"St. Lawrence," 1814.
"St. Paul's Bay Disease," 1775, 1787.

Stanley, 1888.
Steamships, 1840, 1856.
Streams Bill, 1881, 1884.
"Strikes," 1877, 1896.
Submarine Telegraph, 1857, 1866.
Sulpicians, 1657.
Supreme Court of Canada, 1875.
Swift, Gen., 1814.
Sydenham, 1839.

Tache-Macdonald Ad., 1856, 1864
Talbot, 1803.
Tallow Company, 1832.
Talon, 1667.
Tariff Act, 1897.
Tariff, McKinley, 1890.
Tariff, Dingley, 1897.
Tax for Education, 1663.
Tecumseh, 1812, 1813.
Ten Resolutions, 1837.
Thompson, David, 1800.
"Three Estates," 1672.
Tobacco, 1739.
Tobacco Nation, 1639.
Toronto, 1749.
Tracy, 1665, 1666.
Transit of Venus, 1761.
Treaties: Aix-la-Chapelle, 1748; Ashburton, 1842; Breda, 1667; Bulwer-Clayton, 1850; Convention of, 1817; "Famine Cove," 1684; French, 1895; Ghent, 1814; "Jay's Treaty," 1794; "London Convention," 1818; Manitoulin Island, 1862; North-west Angle, 1871; Oregon Boundary, 1846; Pacific Ocean, 1825; Paris, 1763, 1783; Qu'-Appelle, 1874; Ryswick, 1697; St. Germain-en-Laye, 1632; "Treaty Number Seven," 1877; Utrecht, 1713; Washington, 1871.

U. C. divided into four parts, 1788.
United Empire Loyalists, 1783, 1789.
Ursuline Convent, 1639.
Vaudreuil, 1703.
Vaudreuil, 1755.

Vercheres, 1692.
Verendrye, 1731, 1735.
"Victoria," 1881.
Vincennes, 1778, 1779.
Virginia settled, 1607.

Walker, Sir Hovenden, 1711.
Wars: American Revolution, 1775-1783; King George's, 1744; King William's, 1689; Queen Anne's, 1702; War with U.S., 1812-1814.

Weir, Lieut., 1837.
West India Company, 1664-1674.
Wives for Colonists, 1667.
Wolfe, 1758, 1759.
Woman Suffrage, 1893.

X. Y. Z. Co., 1796, 1805.

Y.M.C.A., 1851.
York taken, 1813.

www.ingramcontent.com/pod-product-compliance
Lightning Source LLC
Chambersburg PA
CBHW021838230426
43669CB00008B/1009